Translation and Multilingual Natural Language Processing

Editors: Oliver Czulo (Universität Leipzig), Silvia Hansen-Schirra (Johannes Gutenberg-Universität Mainz), Reinhard Rapp (Johannes Gutenberg-Universität Mainz)

In this series:

1. Fantinuoli, Claudio & Federico Zanettin (eds.). New directions in corpus-based translation studies.

2. Hansen-Schirra, Silvia & Sambor Grucza (eds.). Eyetracking and Applied Linguistics.

3. Neumann, Stella, Oliver Čulo & Silvia Hansen-Schirra (eds.). Annotation, exploitation and evaluation of parallel corpora: TC3 I.

4. Czulo, Oliver & Silvia Hansen-Schirra (eds.). Crossroads between Contrastive Linguistics, Translation Studies and Machine Translation: TC3 II.

5. Rehm, Georg, Felix Sasaki, Daniel Stein & Andreas Witt (eds.). Language technologies for a multilingual Europe: TC3 III.

6. Menzel, Katrin, Ekaterina Lapshinova-Koltunski & Kerstin Anna Kunz (eds.). New perspectives on cohesion and coherence: Implications for translation.

7. Hansen-Schirra, Silvia, Oliver Czulo & Sascha Hofmann (eds). Empirical modelling of translation and interpreting.

8. Svoboda, Tomáš, Łucja Biel & Krzysztof Łoboda (eds.). Quality aspects in institutional translation.

9. Fox, Wendy. Can integrated titles improve the viewing experience? Investigating the impact of subtitling on the reception and enjoyment of film using eye tracking and questionnaire data.

10. Moran, Steven & Michael Cysouw. The Unicode cookbook for linguists: Managing writing systems using orthography profiles.

ISSN: 2364-8899

Language technologies for a multilingual Europe

TC3 III

Edited by

Georg Rehm

Felix Sasaki

Daniel Stein

Andreas Witt

Georg Rehm, Felix Sasaki, Daniel Stein & Andreas Witt (eds.). 2018. *Language technologies for a multilingual Europe: TC3 III* (Translation and Multilingual Natural Language Processing 5). Berlin: Language Science Press.

This title can be downloaded at:
http://langsci-press.org/catalog/book/106
ISBN: 978-3-946234-73-9 (Digital)
        978-3-946234-77-7 (Hardcover)

ISSN: 2364-8899
DOI:10.5281/zenodo.1291947
Source code available from www.github.com/langsci/106
Collaborative reading: paperhive.org/documents/remote?type=langsci&id=106

Cover and concept of design: Ulrike Harbort
Typesetting: Felix Kopecky, Florian Stuhlmann, Iana Stefanova, Sebastian Nordhoff, Stefanie Hegele
Proofreading: Ahmet Bilal Özdemir, Alessia Battisti, Alexis Michaud, Amr Zawawy, Anne Kilgus, Brett Reynolds, Benedikt Singpiel, David Lukeš, Eleni Koutso, Eran Asoulin, Ikmi Nur Oktavianti, Jeroen van de Weijer, Matthew Weber, Lea Schäfer, Rosetta Berger, Stathis Selimis
Fonts: Linux Libertine, Libertinus Math, Arimo, DejaVu Sans Mono
Typesetting software: XƎLATEX

Language Science Press
Unter den Linden 6
10099 Berlin, Germany
langsci-press.org

Storage and cataloguing done by FU Berlin

Freie Universität Berlin

Contents

Contents

Preface

This book, Language Technologies for a Multilingual Europe, is a reissue of the Special Issue on Technologies for a Multilingual Europe, which was originally published as Vol. 3, No. 1 of the Open Access online journal Translation: Computation, Corpora, Cognition (TC3). After the editors of TC3 had decided to transition the journal into a different format – into the Open Access book series Translation and Multilingual Natural Language Processing – they invited us to prepare a reissue of our compilation, originally published in 2013. While several smaller typos in the original manuscripts have been fixed, the papers in this collection have not been substantially modified with regard to the original publication, which is still, for archival reasons, available at http://www.blogs.uni-mainz.de/fb06-tc3/vol-3-no-1-2013/.

Since the original publication, Multilingual Europe has made several important steps forward. A new set of EU projects on multilingual technologies and machine translation was funded in 2015, e.g., QT21, HimL and CRACKER. The Cracking the Language Barrier federation (http://www.cracking-the-language-barrier.eu) was established as an umbrella organisation for all projects and organisations working on technologies for a multilingual Europe. At the time of writing META-NET is organising the next META-FORUM conference, which is to take place in Brussels on 13/14 November 2017. One of the key topics of this conference is the Human Language Project – a large, coordinated funding programme spanning from education to research to innovation, which aims at bringing about the much needed boost in research and a paradigm shift in processing language automatically. First steps towards the Human Language Project were discussed at a workshop in the European Parliament in early 2017. Moreover, the Common Language Resources and Technology Infrastructure (CLARIN), founded in 2012 by ten European countries, doubled its number of members since then.

The editors of this special issue would like to thank the series editors, especially Oliver Culo, for the opportunity to publish a reissue of our original compilation.

Georg Rehm, Felix Sasaki, Daniel Stein, Andreas Witt   August 28, 2017

Chapter 1

Editorial

Georg Rehm

Felix Sasaki

Daniel Stein

Andreas Witt

The roots of this special issue of *Translation: Computation, Corpora, Cognition* go all the way back to 2011. At the end of September of that year, the guest editors organised a workshop at the Conference of the German Society for Computational Linguistics and Language Technology (GSCL), which took place in Hamburg. The topic of the GSCL 2011 conference – "Multilingual Resources and Multilingual Applications" – had already set the stage for our pre-conference workshop on September 27, 2011, which put special emphasis on "Language Technology for a Multilingual Europe".

Our intention behind this workshop was to bring together various groups concerned with the umbrella topics of multilingualism and language technology, especially multilingual technologies. This encompassed, on the one hand, representatives from research and development in the field of language technologies, and on the other hand users from diverse areas such as, among others, industry, administration and funding agencies. Two examples of language technologies that we mentioned in the call for contributions were Machine Translation and processing of texts from the humanities with methods drawn from language technology, such as automatic topic indexing, and text mining, as well as integrating numerous texts and additional information across languages.

What these kinds of application areas and research and development in language technology have in common is that they either rely – critically – on language resources (lexicons, corpora, grammars, language models etc.) or produce

Georg Rehm, Felix Sasaki, Daniel Stein & Andreas Witt. Editorial. In Georg Rehm, Felix Sasaki, Daniel Stein & Andreas Witt (eds.), *Language technologies for a multilingual Europe: TC3 III*, 1–4. Berlin: Language Science Press. DOI:10.5281/zenodo.1291922

these resources. A multilingual Europe supported by language technology is only possible if an adequate and interoperable infrastructure of resources (including the related tooling) is available for all European and other important languages. It is necessary that the aforementioned groups and other communities of developers and users of language technology stand as a single homogenous community. Only if all members of our (quite heterogeneous and hitherto mostly fragmented) community stand together and speak with one voice, it will be possible to assure the long-term political acceptance of the "Language Technology" topic in Europe.

The Workshop "Language Technology for a Multilingual Europe" was co-organised by two GSCL working groups (*Text Technology* and *Machine Translation*) and META-NET (http://www.meta-net.eu). META-NET, an EU-funded Network of Excellence, is dedicated to building the technological foundations of a multilingual European information society. To this end, META-NET is forging META, the Multilingual Europe Technology Alliance.

This special issue of *Translation: Corpora, Computation, Cognition* includes the majority of the papers presented at the GSCL 2011 Workshop "Language Technology for a Multilingual Europe", held at the University of Hamburg on September 27, 2011, along with several additional contributions.

The first article, "Machine Translation – Past, Present and Future", provides an overview of what must be considered the essential core of multilingual technologies. Setting the stage, Daniel Stein looks at the history of MT and discusses current approaches and future perspectives. The backgrounds of the next two articles are two interlinked EU-funded initiatives. Georg Rehm describes the Network of Excellence META-NET, which consists of 60 research centres in 34 European countries, and its goal to build the technological foundations of a multilingual Europe. He provides a summary of one of the key outcomes of the initiative, "The META-NET Strategic Research Agenda for Language Technology in Europe". In his article "Metadata for the Multilingual Web", Felix Sasaki provides an overview of the Internationalization Tag Set (ITS) which will become a W3C recommendation later in 2013. ITS 2.0 is one of the key results from the European Union-funded Multilingual Web project.

The second part of this special issue contains six full research papers. First is Uwe Reinke with a paper on the "State of the Art in Translation Memory Technology", that focused upon technologies applied by human translators. He takes a detailed look at major concepts and recent trends in research and also in commercial Translation Memory (TM) systems, with an emphasis on integrating MT into TM, data exchange formats, and approaches of improving the information retrieval performance of TM systems. As a complement to the technologies used by translators, Melanie Siegel examines "Authoring Support for Controlled Language and Machine Translation", i. e., language technologies that help and assist authors to produce high quality documents. She concludes that it is necessary to combine methods from authoring support and MT and to make them integrated tools in the production and translation process. The paper "Integration of Machine Translation in On-line Multilingual Applications" by Mirela-Stefania Duma and Cristina Vertan takes a look at a difficult and challenging problem that MT, especially statistical MT, is confronted with domain adaptation. The method employed by the authors for this task is language model interpolation, which produces good results even when only sparse domain-specific training data is available. This, in turn, is an advantage for less-resourced languages. The next article concentrates on a specialised application that provides help for users of monolingual or crosslingual search. In "Disambiguate Yourself – Supporting Users in Searching Documents with Query Disambiguation Suggestions", Ernesto William De Luca and Christian Scheel describe a semantic approach and a corresponding architecture and prototype for making more sense of queries as they are typed in by the user. The penultimate article, "Multilingual Knowledge in Aligned Wiktionary and OmegaWiki for Translation Applications", goes back to the topic of MT. Michael Matuschek, Christian M. Meyer, and Iryna Gurevych take a look at multilingual lexical-semantic resources and their role in translingual technologies. They focus on two crowd-sourced resources and present methods for aligning these resources in order to combine them on the level of word senses, this way providing increased coverage and improved interoperability. In the final article, Igor Leturia and colleagues present "The BerbaTek project for Basque: Promoting a less-resourced language via language technology for translation, content management and learning". In this joint project between companies and research centres, the partners developed several technologies for the Basque language which is, as the META-NET study "Europe's Languages in the Digital Age" pointed out, among the 21 European languages in danger of digital extinction.

Since we held the workshop, there have been quite a few very positive developments in the area of multilingual language technologies *from* Europe *for* Europe. Among those developments are a new series of projects funded by the European Commission such as, for example, QTLaunchPad, or additional projects around the open source machine translation system Moses. In addition, META-NET organised its third META-FORUM conference in June 2012, which was attended by more than 250 participants from the domains of research, industry, administration, and politics. Important milestones for the work of META-NET were the publica-

Georg Rehm, Felix Sasaki, Daniel Stein & Andreas Witt

tion of the META-NET *Language White Papers* (September 2012) and the META-NET *Strategic Research Agenda for Multilingual Europe 2020* (January 2013). While the first funded phase of the initiative came to an end on January 31, 2013, there will be a fourth META-FORUM conference later this year (http://www.meta-forum.eu). Among the topics of META-FORUM 2013 are upcoming opportunities for multilingual technologies in the frameworks of Connecting Europe Facility (CEF) and Horizon 2020. On February 29, 2012, the Common Language Resources and Technology Infrastructure (CLARIN) received EU-ERIC legal status, as the second European Research Infrastructure overall. These initiatives clearly demonstrate the emphasis the European Commission lays on the further development of language resources and language technology.

This special issue would not have been possible without the help of several colleagues. First of all, the guest editors would like to thank all authors who contributed articles to this special issue and those who presented papers at the workshop back in September 2011. We would like to thank the reviewers who provided valuable and helpful feedback to all authors. Many thanks are also due to our colleague Sarah Weichert (DFKI) who supported us in a critical phase during the preparation of this special issue. Finally, we would like to express our gratitude towards the editors of *Translation: Computation, Corpora, Cognition*, especially Oliver Čulo, who not only made it possible that we could publish the results of our workshop in this journal but also constantly supported us whenever necessary.

Georg Rehm, Felix Sasaki, Daniel Stein, Andreas Witt   June 21, 2013

Chapter 2

Machine translation: Past, present and future

Daniel Stein

Universität Hamburg, Hamburger Zentrum für Sprachkorpora

The attempt to translate meaning from one language to another by formal means traces back to the philosophical schools of secret and universal languages as they were originated by Ramon Llull (13th c.) or Johann Joachim Becher (17th c.). Today, machine translation (MT) is known as the crowning discipline of natural language processing. Due to current MT approaches, the time needed to develop new systems with similar power to older ones has decreased enormously. In this article, the history of MT, the difference with computer aided translation, current approaches and future perspectives are discussed.

1 History of machine translation

Although the first systems of MT were built on the first computers in the years right after World War II, the history of MT does not begin, as often stated, in the 1940s, but some hundred years ago. In order to judge current developments in MT properly, it is important to understand its historical development.

1.1 Universal and secret languages

Most likely the first thoughts on MT emerged out of two philosophical schools that dealt with the nature of language and resulted in similar insights, although stemming from different directions. The first was directed at creating secret languages and codes in order to communicate in secrecy. The second evolved from the ideal of a universal language which would allow communication without borders in the times after Babylonian language confusion.

Daniel Stein. Machine translation: Past, present and future. In Georg Rehm, Felix Sasaki, Daniel Stein & Andreas Witt (eds.), *Language technologies for a multilingual Europe: TC3 III*, 5–17. Berlin: Language Science Press. DOI:10.5281/zenodo.1291924

Daniel Stein

Noteworthy proponents of the movement of universal languages were the Catalan philosopher Ramon Llull (1243 to ca. 1316, often referred to by the latinized version of his name, Raimundus Lullus) and the German philosopher and mathematician Gottfried Wilhelm Leibnitz (1646–1716). Llull developed a theory of logic that allowed objectifying the reasoning on God and the world by means of a formal language. His ideas were later used by Leibnitz in his theory of monades (first use of this term in 1696), in which he tries to develop a set of the smallest units of meaning ("termini primi") to compose all thinkable thoughts. Other attempts were started by a precise determination of the inventory of the world in the form of a taxonomy in order to find all sayable things (Gardt 1999).

In the long history of secret languages and hidden codes, the German physician and alchemist Johann Joachim Becher developed a system in 1661 that is especially interesting in the context of MT, as it appears to be very similar to the first technical approaches in the late 1940s. It is called "Character pro notitia linguarum universal" and offers "Eine geheimschriftliche Erfindung, bisher unerhört, womit jeder beim Lesen in seiner eigenen Sprache verschiedene, ja sogar alle Sprachen, durch eintägiges Einarbeiten erklären und verstehen kann" (Becher 1962) ("A secret and currently unknown language invention that enables everyone to explain and understand different and even all languages after a one-day orientation by reading in their own language."). The approach is based on dictionaries that are related to each other by number codes, which is more or less identical to what was then called "mechanical translation". But despite the obvious relationship to Becher, the influence of the school of universal languages on MT was small. In contrast, with the development of the science of secret languages, cryptology continuously gained in importance.

In World War II, the decipherment of the German ENIGMA code was regarded as a crucial point. The British team around Alan Turing, located in Bletchley Park, was responsible for this urgent project and achieved the breaking of the code by means of statistical methods that were processed on computing machines. Without their knowledge, these scientists laid the foundations for practical MT.

Considering the experiences of Bletchley Park, the exchange of letters by Warren Weaver and Andrew Booth is regarded as the birth of MT. Weaver wrote:

> [...] it is very tempting to say that a book written in Chinese is simply a book written in English which was coded into the 'Chinese Code'. If we have useful methods for solving almost any cryptographic problem, may it not be that with proper interpretation we already have useful methods for translation? (Weaver 1955)

1.2 Evolution of MT

Although mathematical methods prove useful for cryptology, they turned out to be inadequate for more challenging and complex translation tasks. Accordingly, the systems that were subsequently developed were based on dictionaries and selectively used syntactic operations (this was the time when J.J. Becher's article on the universal language was republished with the subtitle "A programming approach from the year 1661"). From today's point of view, these approaches were remarkably naïve.

The constant threat of the Cold War caused euphoria in government and military circles regarding the anticipated possibilities of MT. Until 1966, large amounts of money were spent in order to develop MT systems, mostly for the English-Russian language constellation. But with the publication of the famous Automatic Language Processing Advisory Committee (ALPAC) report, on behalf of the US administration, the CIA and the National Science Foundation, funding decreased immediately, due to the anticipation that MT would be neither useful nor seemed to provide any considerable advance or meaningful progress (Hutchins 1996). With the exception of some practically-oriented teams in Europe and the USA, research and development of MT expired.

In order to react to the results of the ALPAC report and the reduction of resources, the discourse became more classically scientific and tried to integrate linguistic knowledge on a broader basis, above all, semantic analysis. The results that were achieved by these approaches were promising and so, in the middle of the 1970s and in the course of the rapid development of technology and the introduction of the first personal computers, MT research was revitalized and headed to a continuously increasing popularity from the beginning of the 1980s.

Ten years later, however, in the middle of a syntax- and semantics-based MT system era, an IBM research group led by Peter F. Brown published an article (Brown et al. 1988), which suggested the return to statistical methods for a new MT system. Technological advances and the increased availability of language resources such as machine readable parallel corpora had changed the underlying conditions significantly. Thus, the results seemed very promising, especially regarding the extremely condensed time that would be necessary in order to create a state of the art MT system. As a result, the majority of MT research switched to statistics-based MT in the following years, as it was possible to create comparable MT systems without years of work and the expertise of a team of linguists. A few days of time and a very good bilingual corpus ("bitext") were enough for a prototype.

Since then there has been a lot of development in statistical MT (SMT). While the first systems were only trained to compare the probabilities of co-occurring words, later approaches tried to use groups of words instead, n-grams of different sizes. But pure SMT seemed to hit its frontiers as there were several shortcomings and problems confusingly similar to those of rule-based MT systems and it seemed to be impossible to solve them by just using bigger corpora. Hence, the focus in MT research changed again. Actually, various trends were discussed simultaneously, e.g. SMT for lesser resourced languages or example-based methods. Since the middle of the 2000s hybrid approaches that combine SMT with linguistic knowledge ("context-based" or "knowledge-based" MT) were often seen and a new trend of the last years is to use corpora that are not parallel but at least comparable. One of the most recent interesting developments links back to the beginning of MT, i.e. as well to the famous memorandum by Warren Weaver as to the creators of secret languages mentioned above: After the success of Kevin Knight, Beáta Megyesi and Christiane Schaeferin in deciphering the Copiale codex (Knight et al. 2011), a German 18th century text with freemasonry background, the use of decipherment strategies in MT underwent a renaissance (Dou & Knight 2012).

2 Machine translation vs. computer-aided translation

An important distinction exists between MT and computer aided translation (CAT). While the (today not that often announced) goal of MT is a so-called FAHQT (fully automatic high quality translation), in CAT, tools and methods that assist human translators in the translation process are researched and developed. A well-known and widely used example of CAT is the use of translation-memory systems (TMS). A TMS combines a user friendly translator front end with a database that saves all translations that have been done in a certain project (the translation memory), as well as a component that analyzes the units that are still to be translated for similarities with the ones in the translation memory. If a similarity beyond a certain threshold is found, the system enables the translator to modify the translation or, in cases of 100% similarity, just replaces it. Without a doubt, this kind of tool turned out to be impressively useful for translators in the domains of technical documentation or software localization. But of course CAT is not designed for the translation of literary texts – the localization of video games seems to be situated in between these poles, as the texts are often combinations of technical and literary writing. Further components of a TMS may involve MT for units with lower similarities, the automatic transliteration of numbers, dates and other placeable elements, or the implementation of user-made dictionaries for terminology management (Seewald-Heeg 2002).

3 Typology

As described above, in the course of the years several approaches to the task of MT have evolved. Today, the most important ones are rule-based MT (RBMT) and SMT. Although they sometimes may still be understood as concurring approaches, the general view seems to be that both statistical as well as linguistic approaches may serve as tools in the machine translation toolkit that may be freely combined in order to improve results. In the next sections the two main representatives and the most common alternative approaches will be discussed (Jekat & Volk 2010).

3.1 Rule-based MT

RBMT today is often considered the "classical approach" and is still regularly used in commercial solutions, although with the withdrawal of Systrans "Babelfish", the most popular representative of this approach has disappeared. The results of RBMT systems range from useful to hilarious, depending on the concrete text and its complexity with regard to common problems such as resolution of anaphors or lexical ambiguities, as well as the language pair and even the translation direction, as well as if the text is in a certain domain or contains special terminology (which is, given a prepared system, easier to process than general language).

A loose distinction between three levels of complexity of MT is common and the results, as well as the expenses, differ significantly: direct, transfer and interlingual translation.

The majority of RBMT systems is based on the transfer method which processes text in three successive steps:

1. Analysis

2. Transfer

3. Generation/Synthesis

3.1.1 Direct translation

MT systems that are based on direct translation simply replace words on a word by word basis and only rely on a parallel dictionary – so they do neither analysis nor transfer or generation. Often, positional changes are also included in order to follow the word order of the target language. This approach is only of interest for a few possible application scenarios, but in general it may rather be considered a theoretical measure to demonstrate the benefits and advantages of a translation system. Historically, however, this is how the first systems were designed.

3.1.2 Transfer

Transfer translations define a set of rules ranging from morphology and syntax to semantics and context. Regarding the complexity of these rules there are no limits and tens of thousands of rules, combinations and exceptions may be coded. In practice, however, there seems to exist a point where higher complexity no longer yields better results. Instead, internal conflicts and contradicting rules produce arbitrary new errors. The majority of the existing RBMT systems can be considered a part of the transfer level.

3.1.3 Interlingua

The third level of complexity, Interlingua, is based on the utopia of a neutral language that would be able to represent all meaningful information of every utterance in every language. On the scale presented above for Interlingua systems there is no need to transfer from one language to another as they use a common metalanguage that is able to express the meaning of both in an unambiguous way. This universal language ("Interlingua") would be the target language for every translation in the first place and in the next step it would be the source for the composition of meaning in the target language. Unfortunately, such a language has not yet been found, although several attempts have been made, beginning with the thoughts of Llull and Leibnitz, over to "semantic primitive" as in the work of Anna Wierzbicka (Wierzbicka 1996) and later on in experiments using constructed languages such as Esperanto or Lojban. Although this approach is considered optimal, it should be noted that even a perfect interlingua could make things potentially even more complicated due to its abstraction (Nicholas 1996).

3.2 Statistics-based

As mentioned above, the new rise of SMT began in 1988 when IBM researcher Peter Brown presented a new approach to MT that was solely based on statistic measures (Brown et al. 1988) at the second TMI conference of the Carnegie Mellon University. The basic principle is that every translation decision is made based on conditional probabilities, i.e. the probability that an event will occur when another event is known to occur (or has already occurred). As a resource, instead of complex rule sets, large parallel corpora are needed.

3.2.1 Functioning

From a formal point of view, SMT works like this: In order to translate the arbitrary French sentence f to English, one can consider all possible and impossible English sentences e as potential translations of f. But some are more probable translations than others. *p(e|f)* is the probability that *e* is a valid translation of *f*. Philosophically speaking, we assume that the speaker of *f* initially conceived *e* and then internally translated *e* to *f* before uttering it. This construction is used to define the goal of SMT: Find the original sentence e which is the most probable translation. Please note that this assumption is similar to Weaver's remark about understanding Chinese as English that is encrypted with the Chinese code.

This ideal situation is confronted with the impossibility of accessing all sentences of a language. Therefore, SMT works with approximations, so-called models. A bilingual aligned corpus defines the translation model that represents all possible translations between two languages, i.e. the larger the translation model, the better the expected results. Generally, every word is considered a potential translation of all the others, but the probability is the highest for those with which they are aligned.

An additional monolingual corpus of the target language is defined as the language model. It represents all valid sentences (or better, words or word sequences, which is a more operable abstraction) of a language. A search algorithm then determines the sentence by finding the highest product of the values sentence for *validity* (language model), *word translation* and *word order* (translation model). The result is the most probable translation.

The concrete probabilities used by the computer are estimated with Bayes' Theorem.

$$Pr(e|f) = \frac{Pr(e) * Pr(f|e)}{Pr(f)}$$

This formula can be reduced to the search of the maximum value of the terms *Pr(e)* ("probability that *e* has been said by someone") and *Pr(f|e)* ("probability that someone would translate *e* to *f*").

$$\hat{e} = \frac{\arg\max_e Pr(e) * Pr(f|e)}{e}$$

Brown used the English-French parallel "Hansard" corpus, which consists of protocols from the Canadian parliament. Hence, this is where the example languages e and f derive from.

In the beginning SMT was mainly based on Brown's original model, i.e. the target language utterances were derived according to Shannon's Information Theorem out of a noisy channel translation model. But since 2002, when Och and Ney proposed a system in which the noisy channel was replaced by a discriminative log linear model (Och & Ney 2002), this approach became established as de facto standard as it allows to add additional features next to the language and translation model (Chiang 2012).

3.2.2 SMT types

The analysis of whole sentences makes little sense: How often is it possible to translate the exact same sentence that is already present in the translation model? As long as an SMT system does not have a corpus that indeed contains all (or at least almost all) possible sentences of a language, it is useful to reduce the considered unit. Therefore, there is the differentiation between word-based and phrase-based SMT.

3.2.2.1 Word-based SMT

The Word-based is the original approach and analyzes data on the level of simple lexical units. This means that one word in the source language has to correspond to one word in the target language. But unfortunately, it is quite often the case that a word has to be translated by more than one simple lexical unit, e.g. the English verb *slap* has to be translated to Spanish *dar una bofetada*. This is a construction that is possible to model with word-based SMT, but to perform a translation in the opposite direction, i.e. to translate from *dar una bofetada* to *slap*, is impossible. And as a matter of fact, so-called multi-word expressions (MWE) are by far the biggest part of the lexicon of any natural language – but that does not answer the question of which concepts are expressed through MWE in which language.

A related problem is that words may belong together although there are other words between them (e.g. so-alled separable verbs in German). It is impossible to translate them correctly when the relation between them is not considered, as with e.g. the word *ab* in the construction *reiste ... ab*, derived from the verb *abreisen*, in the German sentence in example 1.

(1) Ich reiste   schon nach vierzehn Tagen wieder ab
    I   checked yet   after fourteen days   again   out

    "I left after only fourteen days"

This is especially problematic for languages with a strongly deviating syntax, e.g. in regard to the position of the finite verb.

3.2.2.2 Phrase-based SMT

Phrase-based SMT is an approach that tries to solve the problems mentioned above and is common for actual SMT systems. But the term 'phrase' does not indicate that the systems are able to identify, analyze or separate linguistically motivated phrases, e.g. noun phrases that may be composed of (complex) determiners and (compound) nouns. It rather refers to sequences of successive words (n-grams) that are derived from data.

The use of n-gram-based phrases in SMT addresses some of the shortcomings of word-based SMT: it is possible to translate one word with many and vice versa? Additionally, the broadened context enables better disambiguation algorithms. For example, it is impossible to decide whether English *pretty* should be translated as German *schön* or as *ziemlich* without knowing if the next word is *flower* or *much*, and thus it cannot be translated properly by word-based SMT but by phrase-based. Depending on the size of the word sequences (i.e. the n-gram window) it might also be possible to address problems regarding differences in word order or other syntactical phenomena. Hierarchical phrase-based SMT, also known as syntax-based SMT, is an advanced approach that allows the use of tree-based syntax data in the phrase-model (Koehn 2010).

3.2.3 Pros and cons of SMT

The great advantage of SMT is the possibility to create a working MT system without any knowledge of the source or target languages and their special features. As a matter of fact, the translation quality of an unadapted (i.e. pure SMT) system is generally weak (mainly depending on the corpora used). However, SMT systems are still comparable to RBMT systems and – in the view of decades of language rule modeling – a ground-breakingly fast approach to proportionately robust MT systems, both in terms of time and money. So MT becomes within reach for languages that do not possess sufficient manpower to create a work-intensive RBMT system, but for which sufficient resources (i.e. bitexts) exist (which for instance is the case for most of the official languages of the European Union).

In terms of translation quality it can be stated that RBMT and SMT are similarly error-prone, but have some principal differences regarding the error types. Thus, one can easily observe that RBMT systems produce better sentences in terms of word order, syntax and coherence, but SMT systems produce better translations in terms of word choice, disambiguation, etc. Multi-word expressions or proverbs may also be translated without the effort of enumerating them beforehand (but only if they are present in sufficient number in the corpora to be identified statistically). Hence, one can state the basic philosophy of SMT as "bigger corpora means better results".

However, the disadvantages of SMT are closely related to the advantages. Due to the fact that every translation is produced by opaque calculation processes over gigantic text quantities, it is nearly impossible to identify the potential causes of failures. Therefore, manual correction efforts for systematic errors are laborious and may often result in just adding better examples manually in order to change the statistical measure of a misinterpretation. Additionally, it is necessary to mention that for certain language pairs immense problems may arise, especially if they involve a fundamentally different structure in terms of inflection, word order, use of pronouns, number and kind of temporal forms, etc. For instance, the translation of German separable verbs often results in a missing finite verb which is essential to a sentence's meaning. According to this, it becomes evident that the best translations are obtained when the SMT is created, trained and used for a special domain. The simple philosophy of SMT mentioned above also includes a disadvantage: If bigger corpora mean better results, this means that a corpus can be too small but never big enough.

3.2.4 Parallel, comparable and low-resource corpora

Another access point to improve SMT are the requirements of language data for training and translation purposes. As described above, the first approaches obligated the use of large parallel corpora, i.e. corpora in which every sentence is aligned to a translated version of itself – for every language pair. Nevertheless, large parallel corpora exist for many language pairs, the corpora generally consist of parliamentary proceedings and their professional translations or a similar text type, e.g. from the European Parliament or the already mentioned Canadian Hansard Corpus. Therefore, the use of political and economic terminology is highly overrepresented compared to corpora with standard language.

The creation of parallel corpora for other language domains constitutes a complex and laborious task even for languages with many speakers, but it is, as a third shortcoming, very hard to manage for lesser-resourced languages where the corpus not only needs to be compiled or translated, but simply written in first place. Due to this, a new approach is working with so-called comparable corpora, i.e. corpora that are not parallel but related to each other, such as Wikipedia articles. Changes in the processing of the translation model in another approach resulted in the use of larger monolingual corpora and smaller parallel ones. Bridging through similar, but better-resourced languages, e.g. in the case of using Spanish as a bridge to translate English to Catalan, is also a way to deal with this.

3.3 Hybrid systems

Hybrid approaches try to combine the advantages of several systems. This is especially the case for SMT: There are numerous articles describing the combination of SMT with syntactic preprocessing, semantic disambiguation or similar applications. Often the combination of approaches broadens the scope of research possibilities for unfavorable language pairs, sometimes due to strong divergence in terms of inflection and word order, or due to the fact that one or both of the languages in question are lesser-resourced ones. But although there has been quite a lot of effort in this research direction and most of the approaches have indeed improved the translation quality (at least a bit), there does not seem to be a breakthrough in sight.

3.4 Perspectives

MT research has experienced some highs and lows in its history. Although a FAHQT is no longer the single goal of MT, the last years have been characterized by increasing MT research funding and diversification of the topics of interest. This may be due to the fact that freely available state of the art MT systems, e.g. by Google or Microsoft, have demonstrated the high usability of MT, even though the systems are not perfect.

The combination of approaches to creating hybrid systems, e.g. the use of linguistic information and statistical data, has become one of the most researched fields in MT over the last decade. The integration of syntax into phrase-based SMT systems has reanimated the search for the right kind of linguistic data (e.g. multi-word expressions, linguistically motivated phrases, etc.) to be integrated as well as the kind of preprocessing that is needed for it (syntax trees, support of variables, etc.). This way, the type and state of resources are rated more appropriately than in the beginning of SMT research. This is also relevant in the context of domain adaption, i.e. the identification of data that are necessary to represent a closed domain and the expansion to new fields as it turns out that the automatic translation of specialized domains is more reliable.

Recently there has been a shift from the "traditional" language pairs in MT, namely English, Russian, German, French, Spanish and in the last years also Chinese and Japanese, to lesser-resourced ones. Especially the expansion of the European Union has been a starting point for growing research in this area as there are speakers of 23 languages that demand participation at every level and in their mother tongue for a growing amount of texts and offers such as ecommerce. The automatic translation between language pairs that do not include English also reinforces attempts to deal with complex problems of morphology.

Another topic of still growing interest is the automatic evaluation of translations – either with the focus on metrics that underline the currently standard metric BLEU (e.g. by using syntax information) or with the focus on reusing good translations as additional training data.

References

Becher, Johann Joachim. 1962. *Zur mechanischen Sprachübersetzung. Ein Programmierversuch aus dem Jahre 1661. Allgemeine Verschlüsselung der Sprachen.* Stuttgart: Kohlhammer.

Brown, Peter F., John Cocke, Stephen Della Pietra, Vincent J. Della Pietra, Frederick Jelinek, Robert L. Mercer & Paul S. Roossin. 1988. A statistical approach to French/English translation. In Christian Fluhr & Donald E. Walker (eds.), *Computer-assisted information retrieval (recherche d'information et ses applications) - RIAO 1988, 2nd international conference, massachusetts institute of technology, cambridge, ma, march 21-25, 1988. proceedings,* 810–829. Cambrigde, MA: CID.

Chiang, David. 2012. Hope and fear for discriminative training of statistical machine translation. *Journal of Machine Learning Research* 13(13). 1159–1187.

Dou, Qing & Kevin Knight. 2012. Large scale decipherment for out-of-domain machine translation. In *Proceedings of the 2012 joint conference on empirical methods in natural language processing and computational natural language learning (EMNLP-CoNLL '12),* 266–275. Jeju Island, Korea: Association for Computational Linguistics.

Gardt, Andreas. 1999. *Geschichte der Sprachwissenschaft in Deutschland: Vom Mittelalter bis ins 20. Jahrhundert.* Berlin: de Gruyter.

Hutchins, John W. 1996. ALPAC: The (in)famous report. In S. Nirenburg, H. Somers & Y. Wilks (eds.), *MT news international. Newsletter of the International Association for Machine Translation*, 9–12. Cambridge: International Association for Machine Translation.

Jekat, Susanne & Martin Volk. 2010. Maschinelle und computergestützte übersetzung. Deutsch. In *Computerlinguistik und Sprachtechnologie: Eine Einführung*. 3rd edn., 642–658. Heidelberg: Spektrum, Akad. Verl.

Knight, Kevin, Beáta Megyesi & Christiane Schaefer. 2011. The secrets of the Copiale cipher. *Journal for Research into Freemasonry and Fraternalism* 2(2). 314–324.

Koehn, Philipp. 2010. *Statistical machine translation*. Cambridge: Cambridge University Press.

Nicholas, Nick. 1996. Lojban as a machine translation Interlingua in the Pacific. In *Fourth Pacific Rim International Conference on Artificial Intelligence: Workshop on "future issues for multilingual text processing"*, 31–39. Cairns: University of Melbourne.

Och, Franz-Josef & Hermann Ney. 2002. Discriminative training and maximum entropy models for statistical machine translation. In *ACL 2002: Proceedings of the 40th annual meeting of the association for computational linguistics*, 295–302. Philadelphia: Association for Computational Linguistics Stroudsburg.

Seewald-Heeg, Uta. 2002. CAT: Intelligente Werkzeuge anstelle unzulänglicher Automaten. In Gerd Willée, Bernhard Schröder & Hans-Christian Schmitz (eds.), *Computerlinguistik: Was geht, was kommt? Computational Lingustics: Achievements and perspectives*, 263–267. Oxford: Gardez!

Weaver, Warren. 1955. Translation. In William N. Locke & Andrew D. Booth (eds.), *Machine translation of languages: Fourteen essays*, 15–20. New York: Technology Press of MIT.

Wierzbicka, Anna. 1996. *Semantics: Primes and universals*. Oxford: Oxford University Press.

Chapter 3

The META-NET strategic research agenda for language technology in Europe: An extended summary

Georg Rehm
DFKI GmbH

Recognising Europe's exceptional demand and opportunities for multilingual language technologies, 60 leading research centres in 34 European countries joined forces in META-NET, a European Network of Excellence. META-NET has developed a Strategic Research Agenda (SRA) for multilingual Europe – the complex planning and discussion process took more than two years to complete. While the complete SRA has been published elsewhere (Rehm & Uszkoreit 2013), this heavily condensed version provides an extended summary as an alternative mode of access and to enable interested parties to familiarise themselves with its key concepts in an efficient way.

1 Introduction

The multilingual setup of our European society imposes grand societal challenges on political, economic and social integration and inclusion, especially in the creation of the single digital market and unified information space targeted by the Digital Agenda (European Commission 2010). As many as 21 European languages are at risk of digital extinction (Rehm & Uszkoreit 2012). They could become victims of the digital age as they are under-represented online and under-resourced with respect to language technologies. Huge market opportunities remain untapped because of language barriers. If no action is taken, many European citizens will find that speaking their mother tongue leaves them at a social and economic disadvantage.

Georg Rehm. The META-NET strategic research agenda for language technology in Europe: An extended summary. In Georg Rehm, Felix Sasaki, Daniel Stein & Andreas Witt (eds.), *Language technologies for a multilingual Europe: TC3 III*, 19–41. Berlin: Language Science Press. DOI:10.5281/zenodo.1291926

Language technology is the missing piece of the puzzle that will bring us closer to a single digital market. It is the key enabler and solution to boosting future growth in Europe and strengthening our competitiveness. The key question is: Will Europe wholeheartedly decide to participate in this fast growing market?

Although we use computers to write, phones to chat and the web to search for knowledge, Information Technology (IT) does not yet have access to the meaning, purpose and sentiment behind our trillions of written and spoken words. Technology will bridge the rift separating IT and the human mind using sophisticated technologies for language understanding. Today's computers cannot understand texts and questions well enough to provide translations, summaries or reliable answers, but in less than ten years such services will be offered for many languages. Technological mastery of human language will enable a host of innovative IT products and services in commerce, administration, government, education, health care, entertainment, tourism and other sectors.

Recognising Europe's exceptional demand and opportunities, 60 leading research centres in 34 European countries joined forces in META-NET (http://www.meta-net.eu), a European Network of Excellence dedicated to the technological foundations of a multilingual, inclusive, innovative and reflective European society and partially supported through several projects funded by the European Commission (EC). META-NET assembled the Multilingual Europe Technology Alliance (META) with more than 700 organisations and experts representing multiple stakeholders. In addition, META-NET signed collaboration agreements and memoranda of understanding (see META-NET 2013) with more than 40 other projects and initiatives in the field such as CLARIN (Common Language Resources and Technology Infrastructure, http://www.clarin.eu) and FLaReNet (Fostering Language Resources Network, http://www.flarenet.eu).

Working together with numerous organisations and experts from a variety of fields, META-NET has developed a Strategic Research Agenda (SRA, Rehm & Uszkoreit 2013). Our recommendations for Multilingual Europe 2020, as specified in the SRA, are based on a thorough planning process involving more than one thousand experts.

We predict, in line with many other forecasts, that the next generation of IT will be able to handle human language, knowledge and emotion in competent and meaningful ways. These new competencies will enable an endless stream of novel services that will improve communication and understanding. Many services will help people learn about and understand things such as world history, technology, nature and the economy. Others will help us to better understand each other across language and knowledge boundaries. They will also drive many other services including programmes for commerce, localisation, and personal assistance.

Our ultimate goal is monolingual, crosslingual and multilingual technology support for all languages spoken by a significant population in Europe. To achieve this, we recommend focusing on three priority research topics connected to innovative application scenarios that will provide European research and development (R&D) in this field with the ability to compete with other markets and subsequently achieve benefits for European society and citizens as well as an array of opportunities for our economy and future growth. We are confident that upcoming EU funding programmes, specifically Horizon 2020 (European Commission 2012b) and Connecting Europe Facility (European Commission 2011a), combined with national and regional funding, can provide the necessary resources for accomplishing our joint vision.

A recent policy brief (Veugelers 2012) proposes that Europe specialises in new ICT (Information and Communications Technology) sectors as a means for post-crisis recovery. The European problem lies less in the generation of new ideas than in their successful commercialisation. The study identifies major obstacles: the lack of a single digital market, and the absence of ICT clusters and powerful platform providers. It suggests that the EU policy framework could overcome these barriers and leverage the growth potential of new ICT markets by extending research and infrastructure funding to pre-commercial projects, in particular those involving the creation of ICT clusters and platforms. This is exactly the goal we are trying to achieve. Our recommendations envisage five lines of action for large-scale research and innovation. First, there are three priority research themes: *Translingual Cloud*, *Social Intelligence and e-Participation* and *Socially Aware Interactive Assistants*. The other two themes focus upon *Core Technologies and Resources for Europe's Languages* and a *European Service platform for Language technologies*.

The objective of the priority research themes is to turn our joint vision into reality and allow Europe to benefit from a technological revolution that will overcome barriers of understanding between people of different languages, people and technology, and people and the digitised knowledge of mankind.

2 Multilingual Europe: Facts and opportunities

During the last 60 years, Europe has become a distinct political and economic structure. Culturally and linguistically it is rich and diverse. However, everyday communication between Europe's citizens, enterprises and politicians is inevitably confronted with language barriers. They are an invisible and increasingly problematic threat to economic growth (Economist 2012). The EU's institutions spend about *one billion Euros per year* on translation and interpretation to maintain their policy of multilingualism (European Commission 2012c) and the overall European market for translation, interpretation, software localisation and website globalisation was estimated at 5.7 billion Euros in 2008.

The only – unacceptable and rather un-European – alternative to a multilingual Europe would be to allow a single language to take a predominant position and replace all other languages in transnational communication. Another way to overcome language barriers is to learn foreign languages. Given the 23 official EU languages plus 60 or more other languages spoken in Europe (European Commission 2012a), language learning alone cannot solve the problem. Without technological support, our linguistic diversity will be an insurmountable obstacle for the entire continent. Only about half of the 500 million people who live in the EU speak English. There is no such thing as a lingua franca shared by the vast majority of the population.

Less than 10% of the EU's population are willing or able to use online services in English, which is why multilingual technologies are badly needed to support and to move the EU online market from more than 20 language-specific sub-markets to one unified single digital market with more than 500 million users and consumers. The current situation with "many fragmented markets" is considered one of the main obstacles that seriously undermine Europe's efforts to exploit ICT fully (European Commission 2010).

Language technology is a key enabler for sustainable, cost-effective and socially beneficial solutions to overcome language barriers. It will offer European stakeholders tremendous advantages, not only within the European market, but also in trade relations with non-European countries, especially emerging economies.

In the late 1970s the EU realised the relevance of language technology as a driver of European unity and began funding its first research projects, such as EUROTRA. After a longer period of sparse funding (Joscelyne & Lockwood 2003; Lazzari 2006), the European Commission set up a department dedicated to language technology and machine translation a few years ago. Selective funding efforts have led to a number of valuable results. For example, the EC's translation services now use Moses, which has been mainly developed in European research projects. However, these never led to a concerted European effort through which the EU and its member states systematically pursue the common goal of providing technology support for all European languages.

Europe now has a well-developed research base. Through initiatives such as CLARIN and META-NET the community is well connected and engaged in a long term agenda that aims gradually to strengthen language technology's role. What is missing in Europe is awareness, political determination and political will that would take us to a leading position in this technology area through a concerted funding effort. This major dedicated push needs to include the political determination to modify and to adopt a shared, EU-wide language policy that foresees an important role for language technologies.

Europe's more than 80 languages are one of its richest and most important cultural assets, and a vital part of its unique social model (European Commission 2008; 2012a). While languages such as English and Spanish are likely to thrive in the emerging digital marketplace, many European languages could become marginal in a networked society. This would weaken Europe's global standing and run counter to the goal of ensuring equal participation for every European citizen regardless of language. A recent UNESCO report on multilingualism states that languages are an essential medium for the enjoyment of fundamental rights, such as political expression, education and participation in society (UNESCO 2007; 2008; 2011b; Vannini & Crosnier 2012).

Many Europeans find it difficult to interact with online services and participate in the digital economy. According to a recent study, only 57% of internet users in Europe purchase goods and services in languages that are not their native language. Fifty-five percent of users read content in a foreign language while only 35% use another language to write e-mails or post comments on the web (European Commission 2011c). A few years ago, English might have been the lingua franca of the web but the situation has now drastically changed. The amount of online content in other European as well as Asian and Middle Eastern languages has exploded (Ford & Batson 2011). Already today, more than 55% of web-based content is not in English.

The European market for translation, interpretation and localisation was estimated to be 5.7 billion Euros in 2008. The subtitling and dubbing sector was at 633 million Euros, while language teaching at 1.6 billion Euros. The overall value of the European language industry was estimated at 8.4 billion Euros and expected to grow by 10% per year, i. e., resulting in ca. 16.5 billion Euros in 2015 (European Commission 2009b; 2011b). Yet, this existing capacity is not enough to satisfy current and future needs, e. g., with regard to translation (DePalma & Kelly 2009). Already today, Google Translate translates the same volume per day that all human translators on the planet translate in one year (Och 2012).

Despite recent improvements, the quality, usability and integration of machine translation into other online services is far from what is needed. If we rely on existing technologies, automated translation and the ability to process a variety of content in a variety of languages will be impossible. The same applies to information services, document services, media industries, digital archives and language teaching. The most compelling solution for ensuring the breadth and depth of language usage in tomorrow's Europe is to use appropriate technology. Still, the quality and usability of current technologies is far from what is needed. Especially the smaller European languages suffer severely from under-representation in the digital realm.

Drawing on the insights gained so far, today's hybrid language technology mixing deep processing with statistical methods could be able to bridge the gap between all European languages and beyond. In the end, high-quality language technology will be a must for all of Europe's languages for supporting the political and economic unity through cultural diversity. The three priority research themes are mainly aimed at Horizon 2020 (European Commission 2012b). The more infrastructural aspects, platform design and implementation and concrete language technology services are aimed at CEF (European Commission 2011a). An integral component of our strategic plans are the member states and associated countries: it is of utmost importance to set up, under the umbrella of the SRA, a coordinated initiative both on the national (member states, regions, associated countries) and international level (EC/EU), including research centres as well as small, medium and large enterprises who work on or with language technologies.

3 How can language technology help?

We believe that *Language Technology made in Europe for Europe* will significantly contribute to future European cross-border and cross-language communication, economic growth and social stability while establishing for Europe a worldwide, leading position in technology innovation, securing Europe's future as a worldwide trader and exporter of goods, services and information. There are many societal changes and challenges as well as economic and technological trends that confirm the urgent need to include sophisticated language technology in our European ICT infrastructure. Among these changes and challenges are language barriers (European Commission 2009a), an ageing population, people with disabilities, immigration and integration, personal information services and customer care, operation and cooperation on a global scale, preservation of cultural heritage, linguistic diversity (WSIS 2003; UNESCO 2011a), social media and e-participation as well as market awareness and customer acceptance.

Multilingualism has become the global norm rather than the exception (Vannini & Crosnier 2012). Future applications that embed information and communication technology require sophisticated language technologies. Fully speech-enabled autonomous robots could help in disaster areas by rescuing travellers trapped in vehicles or by giving first aid. Language technology can significantly contribute towards improving social inclusion and can help us provide answers to urgent social challenges while creating genuine business opportunities. Language technology can now automate the very processes of translation, content production, and knowledge management for all European languages. It can also empower intuitive language/speech-based interfaces for household electronics, machinery, vehicles, computers and robots.

4 Language technology 2012: Current state

Answering the question on the current state of a whole R&D field is both difficult and complex. For language technology, even though partial answers exist in terms of business figures, scientific challenges and results from educational studies, nobody has collected these indicators and provided comparable reports for a substantial number of European languages yet. In order to arrive at a comprehensive answer, META-NET prepared the White Paper Series "Europe's Languages in the Digital Age" (Rehm & Uszkoreit 2012) that describes the current state of language technology support for 30 European languages (including all 23 official EU languages). This immense undertaking has been in preparation since mid 2010 and was published in the Summer of 2012. More than 200 experts participated to the 30 volumes as co-authors and contributors.

The differences in technology support between the various languages and areas are dramatic and alarming. In all of the four areas we examined (machine translation, speech processing, text analytics, language resources), English is ahead of the other languages but even support for English is far from being perfect. While there are good quality software and resources available for a few larger languages and application areas, others, usually smaller or very small languages, have substantial gaps. Many languages lack even basic technologies for text analytics and essential language resources. Others have basic resources but the implementation of semantic methods is still far away. Currently no language, not even English, has the technological support it deserves. Also, the number of badly supported and under-resourced languages is unacceptable if we do not want to give up the principles of solidarity and subsidiarity in Europe.

The META-NET White Paper Series is fully available online at http://www.meta-net.eu/whitepapers. On this website we also present the press release "At least 21 European Languages in Danger of Digital Extinction" which was circulated on the occasion of the European Day of Languages 2012 (Sept. 26), and also its impact around the world. The echo generated by our press release shows that Europe is very passionate and concerned about its languages and that it is also very interested in the idea of establishing a solid language technology base for overcoming language barriers.

5 Language technology 2020: The META-NET technology vision

We believe that in the next IT revolution computers will master our languages. Just as they already understand measurements and formats for dates and times, the operating systems of tomorrow will *know* human languages. They may not reach the linguistic performance of educated people and they will not yet know enough about the world to understand everything, but they will be much more useful than they are today and will further enhance our work and life.

The broad area of COMMUNICATION AMONG PEOPLE will see a dramatically increased use of sophisticated language technology (LT). By the year 2020, with sufficient research effort on high-quality automatic translation and robust accurate speech recognition, reliable dialogue translation for face-to-face conversation and telecommunication will be possible for at least hundreds of languages, across multiple subject fields and text types, both spoken and written. Authoring software will check for appropriate style according to genre and purpose and help evaluate comprehensibility. It will flag potential errors, suggest corrections, and use authoring memories to suggest completions of started sentences or even whole paragraphs. By 2020 tele-meetings will be the norm for professional meetings. LT will be able to record, transcribe, and summarise them. Brainstorming will be facilitated by semantic lookup and structured display of relevant data, proposals, pictures, and maps. Business email will be embedded in semantic process models to automate standardised communication. Even before 2020, email communication will be semantically analysed, checked for sentiment indicators, and summarised in reports. Semantic integration into work processes, threading, and response management will be applied across channels, as will machine translation and analytics.

Human language will become the primary medium for COMMUNICATION BE-TWEEN PEOPLE AND TECHNOLOGY. The voice-control interfaces we see today for smartphones and search engines are just the modest start of overcoming the communication barrier between humankind and the non-human part of the world. Only a few years ago the idea of talking to a car to access key functions would have seemed absurd, yet it is now commonplace. Recently the concept of a personal digital assistant has increased in popularity. We will soon see much more sophisticated virtual personalities with expressive voices, faces, and gestures. They will become an interface to any information provided online. The metaphor of a personal assistant is powerful and extremely useful, since such an assistant can be made sensitive to the user's preferences, habits, moods, and goals. By the year 2020 we could have a highly personalised, socially aware and interactive virtual assistant. Having been trained on the user's behaviour and communication space, it will proactively offer advice and it will be able to speak in the language and dialect of the user but also digest information in other natural and artificial languages and formats. The assistant will translate or interpret without the user even needing to request it. By 2020 there will be a competitive landscape of intelligent interfaces to all kinds of objects and services employing human language and other modes for effective communication.

In the context of the Semantic Web, Linked Open Data and the general semantification of the web as well as knowledge acquisition and ontology population, LT can perform many tasks in the PROCESSING OF KNOWLEDGE AND INFORMATION. It can sort, categorise, catalogue, and filter content and it can deliver the data for data mining in texts. LT can connect web documents with meaningful hyperlinks and it can produce summaries of larger text collections. Opinion mining and sentiment analysis can find out what people think about products, personalities, or problems and analyse their feelings about such topics. In the next few years we will see considerable advances for all these techniques. For large parts of research and application development, language processing and knowledge processing will merge. The predicted and planned use of language and knowledge technologies for social intelligence applications will involve text and speech analytics, translation, summarisation, opinion mining, sentiment analysis, and several other technologies. In 2020, LT will enable forms of knowledge evolution, transmission and exploitation that speed up scientific, social, and cultural development. The effects for other knowledge-intensive application areas such as business intelligence, scientific knowledge discovery, and multimedia production will be immense.

The wide range of novel or improved applications in our shared vision represents only a fragment of the countless opportunities for LT to change our work and everyday life. Language-proficient technology will enable or enhance applications wherever language is present. It will change the production, management, and use of patents, legal contracts, medical reports, recipes, technical descriptions, and scientific texts, and it will permit many new voice applications such as automatic services for the submission of complaints and suggestions, for accepting orders, and for counselling in customer-care, e-government, education, community services, etc.

6 Language technology 2020: The META-NET priority research themes

In ten years or less, basic language proficiency is going to be an integral component of any advanced IT. It will be available to any user interface, service and application. Additional language skills for semantic search, knowledge discovery, human-technology communication, text analytics, language checking, e-learning, translation and other applications will employ and extend the basic proficiency. The shared basic language competence will ensure consistency and interoperability among services. Many adaptations and extensions will be derived and improved through sample data and interaction with people by powerful machine learning techniques.

In the envisaged big push toward realising this vision by massive research and innovation, the technology community is faced with three enormous challenges:

Richness and diversity. A serious challenge is the sheer number of languages, some closely related, others distantly apart. Within a language, technology has to deal with dialects, sociolects, registers, jargons, genres and slangs.

Depth and meaning. Understanding language is a complex process. Human language is not only the key to knowledge and thought, it also cannot be interpreted without shared knowledge and active inference. Computational language proficiency needs semantic technologies.

Multimodality and grounding. Human language is embedded in our daily activities. It is combined with other modes and media of communication. It is affected by beliefs, desires, intentions and emotions and it affects all of these. Successful interactive language technology requires models of embodied and adaptive human interaction with people, technology and other parts of the world.

It is fortunate for research and economy that the only way to effectively tackle the three challenges involves submitting the evolving technology continuously to the growing demands and practical stress tests of real world applications. Only a continuous stream of technological innovation can provide the economic pull forces and the evolutionary environments for the realisation of the grand vision. We propose five major action lines of research and innovation:

- Three Priority Research Themes along with application scenarios to drive research and innovation. These will demonstrate novel technologies in show-case solutions with high economic and societal impact. They will open up numerous new business opportunities for European language-technology and -service providers.

    1. **Translingual Cloud:** generic and specialised federated cloud services for instantaneous reliable spoken and written translation among all European and major non-European languages.

    2. **Social Intelligence and e-Participation:** understanding and dialogue within and across communities of citizens, customers, clients and consumers to enable e-participation and more effective processes for preparing, selecting and evaluating collective decisions.

    3. **Socially Aware Interactive Assistants** that learn and adapt and that provide proactive and interactive support tailored to specific situations, locations and goals of the user through verbal and non-verbal multi-modal communication.

- The other two themes focus upon base technologies and a service platform:

    4. **Core technologies and resources for Europe's languages:** a steadily evolving system of shared, collectively maintained interoperable core technologies and resources for the languages of Europe and selected other languages. These will ensure that our languages will be sufficiently supported and represented in the next generations of IT.

    5. **A European service platform for language technologies** for supporting research and innovation by testing and showcasing research results, integrating various services, even including professional human services, will allow small to medium enterprise (SME) providers to offer component and end-user services, and share and utilise tools, components and data resources.

These priority themes have been designed with the aim of turning our vision into reality and to letting Europe benefit from a technological revolution that will overcome barriers of understanding between people of different languages, between people and technology and between people and the knowledge of mankind. The themes connect societal needs with LT applications.

6.1 Priority theme 1: Translingual cloud

The goal is a multilingual European society, in which all citizens can use any service, access all knowledge, enjoy all media and control any technology *in their mother tongues*. This will be a world in which written and spoken communication is not hindered anymore by language barriers and in which even specialised high-quality translation will be affordable. The citizen, the professional, the organisation, or the software application in need of cross-lingual communication will use a single access point for channelling text or speech through a gateway that will instantly return the translations into the requested languages in the required quality and desired format. Behind this access point will be a network of generic and special-purpose services combining automatic translation or interpretation, language checking, post-editing, as well as human creativity and quality assurance.

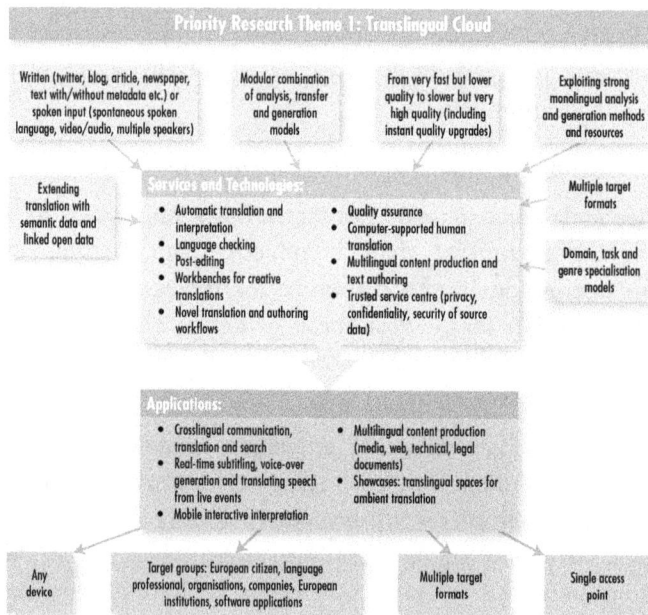

Figure 1: Priority Research Theme 1: Translingual Cloud

One key component of this service (see Figure 1) is a use and provision plat-form for providers of computer-supported top-quality human translation, multi-lingual text authoring and quality assurance by experts. Other important compo-nents are trusted service centres as certified service providers fulfilling highest standards for privacy, confidentiality and security of source data and translations and quality upscale models embedded into services permitting instant quality up-grades if the results of the requested service levels do not yet fulfil the quality requirements.

6.2 Priority theme 2: Social Intelligence and e-Participation

The central goal behind the second theme is to use information technology and the digital content of the web for improving effectiveness and efficiency of deci-sion-making in business and society (see Figure 2). Social intelligence builds on improved text analytics methodologies but goes far beyond the analysis. One goal is the analysis of large volumes of social media, comments, blogs, forum postings etc. of citizens, customers, consumers and other stakeholder communities. Part of the analysis is directed to the status, opinions and acceptance associated with the individual information units. As the formation of collective opinions and attitudes is highly dynamic, new developments need to be detected and trends analysed. As emotions play an important part in individual actions such as voting, buying, supporting, donating and in collective opinion formation, the analysis of sentiment is a crucial component of social intelligence.

Social intelligence can also support collective deliberation processes. Today any collective discussion processes involving large numbers of participants are bound to become intransparent and incomprehensible rather fast. By recording, grouping, aggregating and counting opinion statements, pros and cons, support-ing evidence, sentiments and new questions and issues, the discussion can be summarised and focussed. Decision processes can be structured, monitored, doc-umented and visualised, so that joining, following and benefitting from them becomes much easier. The efficiency and impact of such processes can thus be greatly enhanced.

A key enabler will be technologies that can map large, heterogeneous, and, to a large extent, unstructured volumes of online content to actionable representa-tions that support decision making and analytics tasks. Such mappings can range from the relatively shallow to the relatively deep, encompassing coarse-grained topic classification at the document or paragraph level or the identification of named entities, as well as in-depth syntactic, semantic and rhetorical analysis at the level of individual sentences and beyond or the resolution of co-reference

Georg Rehm

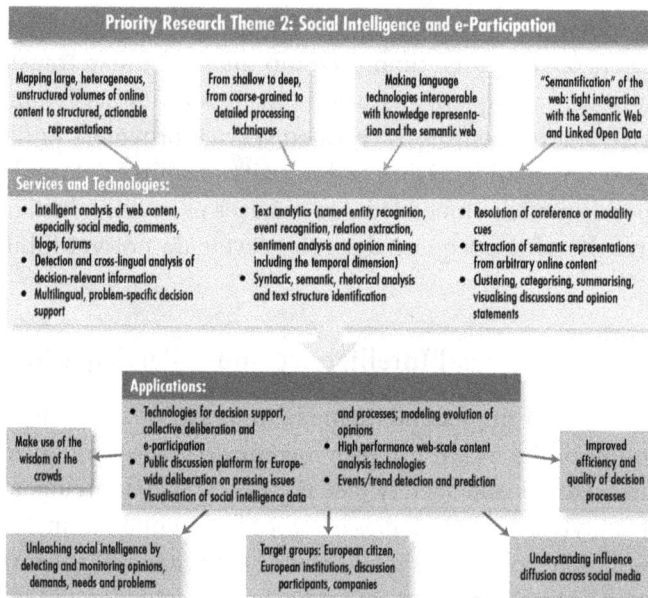

Figure 2: Priority Research Theme 2: Social Intelligence and e-Participation

or modality cues within and across sentences. Technologies such as, e. g., information extraction, data mining, automatic linking and summarisation have to be made interoperable with knowledge representation and semantic web methods. Drawing expertise from related areas such as knowledge management, information sciences, or social sciences is a prerequisite to meet the challenge of modelling social intelligence (Généreux & Hamon 2012).

6.3 Priority theme 3: Socially aware interactive assistants

Socially aware interactive assistants are conversational agents (see Figure 3). Their socially-aware behaviour is a result of combining analysis methods for speech, non-verbal and semantic signals. They support people interacting with their environment, including human-computer, human-agent/robot, and computer-mediated human-human interaction. The assistants must be able to act in various environments, both indoor, outdoor and virtual environments, and also be able to communicate, exchange information and understand other agents' intentions. They must be able to adapt to the user's needs and environment and have the capacity to learn incrementally from all interactions and other sources of information.

32

The ideal socially aware multilingual assistant can interact naturally with humans in any language and modality. It can adapt and be personalised to individual communication abilities, including special needs (for the visual, hearing, or motor impaired), affections, or language proficiencies. It can recognise and generate speech incrementally and fluently. It is able to assess its performance and recover from errors. It can learn, personalise itself and forget. It can assist in language training and education, and provide synthetic multimedia information analytics.

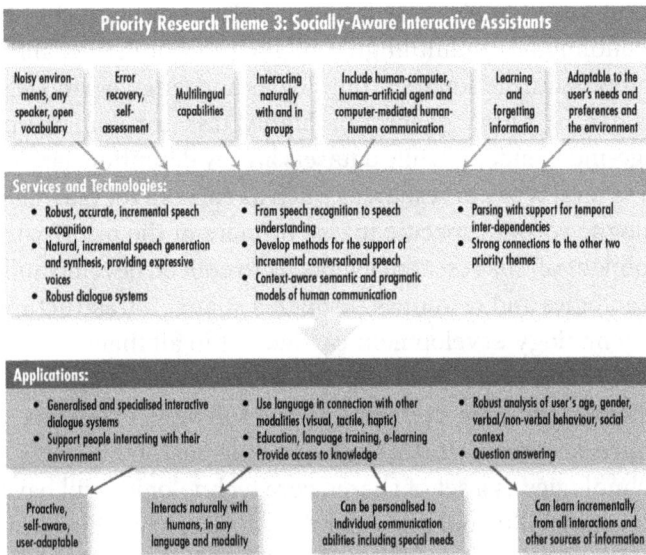

Priority Research Theme 3: Socially-Aware Interactive Assistants

| Noisy environments, any speaker, open vocabulary | Error recovery, self-assessment | Multilingual capabilities | Interacting naturally with and in groups | Include human-computer, human-artificial agent and computer-mediated human-human communication | Learning and forgetting information | Adaptable to the user's needs and preferences and the environment |

Services and Technologies:

- Robust, accurate, incremental speech recognition
- Natural, incremental speech generation and synthesis, providing expressive voices
- Robust dialogue systems

- From speech recognition to speech understanding
- Develop methods for the support of incremental conversational speech
- Context-aware semantic and pragmatic models of human communication

- Parsing with support for temporal inter-dependencies
- Strong connections to the other two priority themes

Applications:

- Generalised and specialised interactive dialogue systems
- Support people interacting with their environment

- Use language in connection with other modalities (visual, tactile, haptic)
- Education, language training, e-learning
- Provide access to knowledge

- Robust analysis of user's age, gender, verbal/non-verbal behaviour, social context
- Question answering

| Proactive, self-aware, user-adaptable | Interacts naturally with humans, in any language and modality | Can be personalised to individual communication abilities including special needs | Can learn incrementally from all interactions and other sources of information |

Figure 3: Priority Research Theme 3: Socially Aware Interactive Assistants

In addition to significantly improving core speech and language technologies, the development of socially aware interactive assistants requires several research breakthroughs. With regard to speech recognition, accuracy and robustness have to be improved. Methods for self-assessment, self-adaptation, personalisation, error-recovery, learning and forgetting information, and also for moving from recognition to understanding have to be developed. Concerning speech synthesis, voices have to be made more natural and expressive, control parameters have to be included for linguistic meaning, speaking style, emotion, etc. They also have to be equipped with methods for incremental conversational speech, including filled pauses and hesitations.

6.4 Theme 4: Core language resources and technologies

The three priority research themes share a large and heterogeneous group of core technologies for language analysis and production that provide development support through basic modules and datasets (see Figure 5). To this group belong tools and technologies such as, among others, tokenisers, part-of-speech taggers, parsers, tools for building language models, information retrieval tools, machine learning toolkits, speech recognition and speech synthesis engines, and integrated architectures. Many of these tools depend on specific datasets (i. e., language resources), for example, very large collections of linguistically annotated documents (monolingual or multilingual, aligned corpora), treebanks, grammars, lexicons, terminologies, dictionaries, ontologies and language models. Both tools and resources can be rather general or highly task- or domain-specific, tools can be language-independent, while datasets are, by definition, language-specific. There are also several types of resources, such as corpora for machine translation or spoken dialogue corpora specific to one or more of the priority themes.

A key component of this research agenda is to collect, develop and make available core technologies and resources through a shared infrastructure so that the research and technology development carried out in all themes can make use of them. Over time, this approach will improve the core technologies, as the specific research will have certain requirements on the software, extending their feature sets, performance, accuracy, etc. through dynamic push-pull effects. Conceptualising these technologies as a set of shared core technologies will have positive effects on their sustainability and interoperability. Also, many European languages other than English are heavily under-resourced (Rehm & Uszkoreit 2012).

The European academic and industrial technology community is fully aware of the need for sharing resources such as language data, language descriptions, tools and core technology components as a basis for the successful development and implementation of the priority themes. Initiatives such as FLaReNet (Calzolari et al. 2011) and CLARIN have prepared the ground for a culture of sharing, META-NET's open resource exchange infrastructure, META-SHARE, is providing the technological platform as well as legal and organisational schemes (see http://www.meta-share.eu). All language resources and basic technologies will be created under the core technologies umbrella.

6.5 Theme 5: A European service platform for language technologies

We recommend the design and implementation of an ambitious large-scale platform as a central motor for research and innovation in the next phase of IT evolution and as a ubiquitous resource for the multilingual European society. The platform will be used for testing, showcasing, proof-of-concept demonstration, avant-garde adoption, experimental and operational service composition, and fast and economical service delivery to enterprises and end-users (see Figure 4). The creation of a cloud platform for a wide range of services dealing with human language, knowledge and emotion will not only benefit the individual and corporate users of these technologies but also the providers. Large-scale ICT infrastructures and innovation clusters such as this one are foreseen in the Digital Agenda for Europe (European Commission 2010: 24).

A top layer consists of LANGUAGE PROCESSING such as text filters, tokenisation, spell, grammar and style checking, hyphenation, lemmatising and parsing. At a deeper level, services will be offered that realise some degree and form of LANGUAGE UNDERSTANDING including entity and event extraction, opinion mining and translation. Both basic language processing and understanding will be used by services that support HUMAN COMMUNICATION or realise human-machine interaction. Part of this layer are question answering and dialogue systems as well as email response applications. Another component will bring in services for processing and storing KNOWLEDGE gained by and used for understanding and communication. This part will include repositories of linked data and ontologies. These in turn permit a certain range of rational capabilities often attributed to a notion of intelligence. The goal is not to model the entire human intelligence but rather to realise selected forms of INFERENCE that are needed for utilising and extending knowledge, for understanding and for successful communication. These forms of inference permit better decision support, pro-active planning and autonomous adaptation. A final part of services will be dedicated to HUMAN EMOTION. Since people are largely guided by their emotions and strongly affected by the emotions of others, truly user-centred IT need facilities for detecting and interpreting emotion and even for expressing emotional states in communication.

All three priority areas will be able to contribute to and at the same time draw immense benefits from this platform. There are strong reasons for aiming at a single service platform for the three areas and for the different types of technologies. They share many basic components and they need to be combined for many valuable applications, including the selected showcase solutions of the three areas.

6.6 Languages to be supported

The SRA has a much broader scope in terms of languages to be supported than our study "Europe's Languages in the Digital Age" (Rehm & Uszkoreit 2012). The set of languages to be reflected with technologies include not only the 23 official

Providers of operational and research technologies and services

| Research Centres | National Language Institutions | Language Service Providers | Universities | Language Technology Providers | European Institutions | Other companies (SMEs, startups etc.) |

Priority Research Theme 1: **Translingual Cloud**

Priority Research Theme 2: **Social Intelligence & e-Participation**

Priority Research Theme 3: **Socially Aware Interactive Assistants**

Language Processing

European Service Platform for Language Technologies
(Cloud or Sky Computing Platform)

Language Understanding

| Text analytics | Multilingual technologies | Text generation | Information and relation extraction |

Knowledge

| Language checking | Sentiment analysis | Named entity recognition | Summarisation | Knowledge access and management |

Emotion/ Sentiment

Features
- Data protection
- Tools
- Data Sets
- Resources
- Components
- Metadata
- Standards
- Interfaces
- APIs
- Catalogues
- Quality Assurance
- Data Import/Export
- Input/Output
- Storage
- Performance
- Availability
- Scalability

Interfaces (web, speech, mobile etc.)

Beneficiaries/users of the platform

| European Institutions | Research Centres | Public Administrations | European Citizens | Enterprises | LT User Industries | Universities |

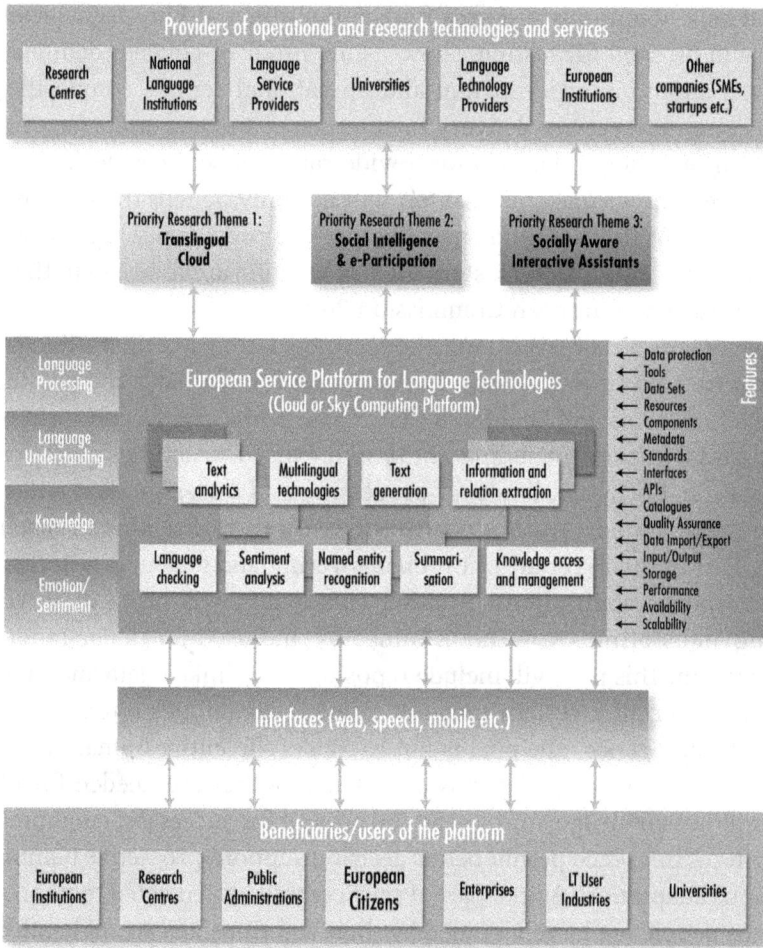

Figure 4: European Service Platform for Language Technologies

languages of the EU but also recognised and unrecognised regional languages and the languages of associated countries or non-member states. Equally important are the minority and immigrant languages that are in active use by a significant population in Europe (for Germany, these are, among others, Turkish and Russian; for the UK, these include Bengali, Urdu/Hindi and Punjabi). An important set of languages outside our continent are those of important political and trade partners such as Chinese, Japanese, Korean, Russian, and Thai. META-NET already has good working relationships with several of the respective official bodies, especially EFNIL (European Federation of National Institutions for Language), NPLD

(Network to Promote Linguistic Diversity), and also the Maaya World Network for Linguistic Diversity. The concrete composition of languages to be supported by this agenda's research programme up until the year 2020 and beyond depends on the composition of participating countries and regions and also on the specific nature of the funding instruments used and combined for realising the ambituous plan.

6.7 Structure and principles of research organisation

The three proposed priority research themes overlap in technologies and challenges. The overlap reflects the coherence and maturation of the field. At the same time, the resulting division of labour and sharing of resources and results is a precondition for the realisation of this highly ambitious programme. The themes need to benefit from progress in core technologies of language analysis and production such as morphological, syntactic and semantic parsing and generation. But each of the three areas will concentrate on one central area of language technology: the Translingual Cloud will focus on cross-lingual technologies such as translation and interpretation; the Social Intelligence strand will take care of knowledge discovery, text analytics and related technologies; the research dedicated to Interactive Assistants will take on technologies such as speech and multimodal interfaces (see Figure 5).

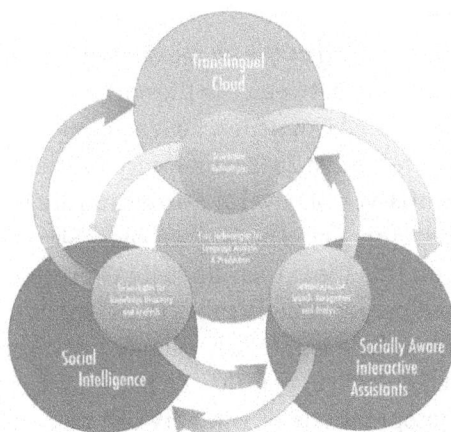

Figure 5: Scientific cooperation among the three priority research themes

The final model for the organisation of collaboration will have to be guided by a thoughtful combination of the following basic approaches. The collaboration will be interdisciplinary, flexible, evolutionary and analytical. It will be staged in two major phases (2015–2017, 2018–2020). We will make heavy use of improving systems by bootstrapping earlier systems and prototypes and by collaborating very closely with relevant areas of service and technology industries.

7 Towards a shared European programme

In the Strategic Research Agenda META-NET recommends setting up a large, multi-year programme on language technologies to build the technological foundations for a truly multilingual Europe. The research strands and associated sets of applications we suggest to build in the next ten years are of utmost importance for Europe. Through these technologies we will be able to overcome language barriers in spoken and written communication, we will be able to carry out country- and language-border-crossing debates and we will enable new forms and means of communication. We are confident that the impact of our technologies will be so immense that they will be able to help establishing a sense of a European identity in the majority of European citizens. The research plan described in the SRA will generate a countless number of opportunities, it will significantly participate to Europe's future growth and will secure Europe's position in many global markets.

Due to the scope and duration of the suggested action, our preferred option is to set up a shared programme between the European Commission and the Member States as well as Associated Countries. First steps along those lines have been taken at META-NET's META-FORUM 2012 conference in Brussels, Belgium, on June 21, 2012, when representatives of several European funding agencies (Bulgaria, Czech Republic, France, Hungary, The Netherlands, Slovenia) who participated in a panel discussion on this topic unanimously expressed the urgent need for setting up such a shared programme (META-NET 2012a).

The programme will include a carefully planned governance structure. Here, first steps have been taken as well: META-NET has an Executive Board with currently 12 members, the operations of the network and its bodies are specified in its Statutes (META-NET 2012b). Furthermore, a legal person for META-NET was established. This legal person, META-TRUST AISBL, is an international non-profit organisation under Belgian law (META-NET 2012c). These proven and established structures can be used as starting points for the governance structure of a future programme.

Acknowledgements

This extended summary of the META-NET *Strategic Research Agenda for Multilingual Europe 2020* (Rehm & Uszkoreit 2013) is, first and foremost, based on joint work with the SRA's other co-editor, Hans Uszkoreit. The work presented in this article would not have been possible without the dedication and commitment of our colleagues Aljoscha Burchardt, Kathrin Eichler, Tina Klüwer, Arle Lommel and Felix Sasaki (all DFKI), the 60 member organisations of the META-NET network of excellence, the ca. 70 members of the Vision Groups, the ca. 30 members of the META Technology Council, the more than 200 authors of and contributors to the META-NET Language White Paper Series (Rehm & Uszkoreit 2012) and the ca. 200 representatives from industry and research who contributed to the META-NET Strategic Research Agenda. The author would also like to thank the reviewers of this paper for their helpful comments.

META-NET is co-funded by the 7th Framework Programme of the European Commission through the following grant agreements: T4ME Net (no. 249 119), CE-SAR (no. 271 022), METANET4U (no. 270 893) and META-NORD (no. 270 899).

More information is available at http://www.meta-net.eu and via office@meta-net.eu.

References

Calzolari, Nicoletta, Nuria Bel, Khalid Choukri, Joseph Mariani, Monica Monachini, Jan Odijk, Stelios Piperidis, Valeria Quochi & Claudia Soria. 2011. *Language Resources for the Future – The Future of Language Resources.* http://www.flarenet.eu/sites/default/files/FLaReNet_Book.pdf.

DePalma, Donald A. & Nataly Kelly. 2009. *The Business Case for Machine Translation. How Organizations Justify and Adopt Automated Translation.* Common Sense Advisory. http://www.commonsenseadvisory.com.

Economist, Economist Intelligence Unit: The. 2012. *Competing across borders. How cultural and communication barriers affect business.* http : / / www . managementthinking.eiu.com/competing-across-borders.html.

European Commission. 2008. *Multilingualism: An Asset for Europe and a Shared Commitment.* http://ec.europa.eu/languages/pdf/comm2008_en.pdf.

European Commission. 2009a. *Report on cross-border e-commerce in the EU.* http://ec.europa.eu/consumers/strategy/docs/com_staff_wp2009_en.pdf.

European Commission. 2009b. *Size of the language industry in the EU.* http://ec.europa.eu/dgs/translation/publications/studies.

European Commission. 2010. *A Digital Agenda for Europe.* http://ec.europa.eu/ information_society/digital-agenda/publications/.

European Commission. 2011a. *Connecting Europe Facility: Commission adopts plan for 50 billion Euros boost to European networks.* http://europa.eu/rapid/ pressReleasesAction.do?reference=IP/11/1200.

European Commission. 2011b. *Languages mean business.* http://ec.europa.eu/ languages/languages-mean-business/.

European Commission. 2011c. *User Language Preferences Online.* Directorate-General Information Society & Media of the European Commission. http:// ec.europa.eu/public_opinion/flash/fl_313_en.pdf.

European Commission. 2012a. *Europeans and their Languages.* European Commission. Special Eurobarometer 386/77.1. http://ec.europa.eu/languages/ languages-of-europe/eurobarometer-survey_en.htm.

European Commission. 2012b. *Horizon 2020: The Framework Programme for Research and Innovation.* http://ec.europa.eu/research/horizon2020/.

European Commission. 2012c. *Languages.* http://ec.europa.eu/languages/.

Ford, Daniel & Josh Batson. 2011. *Languages of the world (wide web).* http:// googleresearch.blogspot.com/2011/07/languages-of-world-wide-web.html.

Généreux, Michel & Thierry Hamon (eds.). 2012. *Workshop on Language Technology for Decision Support at the Fourth Swedish Language Technology Conference.* http://permalink.gmane.org/gmane.science.linguistics.corpora/15911.

Joscelyne, Andrew & Rose Lockwood. 2003. *The EUROMAP Study. Benchmarking HLT progress in Europe.* http://cst.dk/dandokcenter/FINAL_Euromap_rapport. pdf.

Lazzari, Gianni. 2006. *Human Language Technologies for Europe.* http://cordis. europa.eu/documents/documentlibrary/90834371EN6.pdf.

META-NET. 2012a. *META-FORUM 2012: A Strategy for Multilingual Europe. Panel discussion "Plans for LT Research and Innovation in Member States and Regions".* Videos available at http://www.meta-net.eu/events/meta-forum-2012/ programme.

META-NET. 2012b. *META-NET Statutes. Version 1.1.* http://www.meta-net.eu/META-NET-Statutes.pdf.

META-NET. 2012c. *META-TRUST AISBL (Association internationale sans but lucratif).* http://www.meta-trust.eu.

META-NET. 2013. *META-NET: Collaborations with other projects and initiatives.* http://www.meta-net.eu/collaborations.

Och, Franz. 2012. *Breaking down the language barrier – six years in.* http : / / googleblog. blogspot.de/2012/04/breaking-down-language-barriersix-years. html.

Rehm, Georg & Hans Uszkoreit (eds.). 2012. *META-NET White Paper Series: Europe's Languages in the Digital Age.* Heidelberg / New York / Dordrecht / London: Springer. 31 volumes on 30 European languages. More details and full text available at http://www.meta-net.eu/whitepapers.

Rehm, Georg & Hans Uszkoreit (eds.). 2013. *The META-NET Strategic Research Agenda for Multilingual Europe.* Heidelberg / New York / Dordrecht / London: Springer. Presented by the META Technology Council. More details and full text available at http://www.meta-net.eu/sra and http://link.springer.com/book/10.1007/978-3-642-36349-8.

UNESCO. 2007. *Intersectoral Mid-term Strategy on Languages and Multilingualism.* Paris. http://unesdoc.unesco.org/images/0015/001503/150335e.pdf.

UNESCO. 2008. *UNESCO Information for All Programme: International Conference Linguistic and Cultural Diversity in Cyberspace: Final Document. Lena Resolution.*

UNESCO. 2011a. *Information for All Programme (AFP).* http://www.unesco.org/new/en/communication-and-information/intergovernmental-programmes/information-for-all-programme-ifap/.

UNESCO. 2011b. *UNESCO Information for All Programme: Second International Conference Linguistic and Cultural Diversity in Cyberspace: Final Document. Yakutsk Call for Action.* http://www.maayajo.org/IMG/pdf/Call_for_action_Yakutsk_EN-2.pdf.

Vannini, Laurent & Hervé Le Crosnier (eds.). 2012. *Net. Lang: Towards the Multilingual Cyberspace.* Paris: C&F éditions. The Maaya World Network for Linguistic Diversity. http://net-lang.net.

Veugelers, Reinhilde. 2012. *New ICT Sectors: Platforms for European Growth?* Issue 2012/14. http://www.bruegel.org/publications/.

WSIS. 2003. *World Summit on the Information Society: Declaration of Principles – Building the Information Society: A global challenge in the new Millennium.* http://www.itu.int/wsis/docs/geneva/official/dop.html.

Chapter 4

Metadata for the multilingual web

Felix Sasaki

DFKI and W3C Fellow

We describe the Internationalization Tag Set (ITS) 2.0, an upcoming standard to foster the development of the multilingual Web. ITS 2.0 provides metadata to integrate workflows for content production, localization and language technology. The technical goal is to achieve better results in content creation and other language-related processes; the goal in terms of community building is to raise awareness of needs in multilingual workflows. This aim is also supported by providing re-usable software components for various use cases.[1]

1 Introduction

Content in languages other than English is growing on the Web. But so far a lot of content resides in "language silos". A study by Ford & Batson (2011) reveals that Web pages rarely have links to other languages even of neighbouring countries. Also, the links to English web pages are rather few. This demonstrates that English has not developed into the "lingua franca" of the Web. This has a huge economic impact. A *Flash Eurobarometer* (2011) study indicates for example that 51% of European retailers sell via the Internet, but only 21% support cross-border transactions.

The situation of language silos is also given on the Semantic Web. Ell et al. (2011) have analysed human-readable labels in the Semantic Web. Less than 5% of Uniform Resource Identifiers (URIs) have a language tag, and less than 1% contain labels in several languages. One might argue that in the Semantic Web human readable labels are not needed. But to query the Semantic Web across

---

[1]The work described in this paper was funded by the European Commission (project name MultilingualWeb-LT) through the Seventh Framework Programme (FP7) Grant Agreement No. 287815.

Felix Sasaki. Metadata for the multilingual web. In Georg Rehm, Felix Sasaki, Daniel Stein & Andreas Witt (eds.), *Language technologies for a multilingual Europe: TC3 III*, 43–53. Berlin: Language Science Press. DOI:10.5281/zenodo.1291928

languages, query authors need to work with labels or inter-language links leading to resources in their own languages; otherwise non-Japanese speakers, for instance, cannot make use of URIs like http://ja.dbpedia.org/page/講談社 to formulate adequate queries across languages in the Semantic Web.

Translation and creation of cross-language links between (Semantic) Web resources can improve the situation. The challenge here is scalability and cost. Language technology like cross-lingual search and machine translation has gained widespread adoption (e.g. as part of search-engine interfaces). But the translation quality often is rather poor, especially if "distant" languages like German and Japanese are processed, or languages with smaller speaker communities are in scope. As Kornai (2012) discusses, such languages rarely have a lobby on the Web: they lack basic language resources for creating multilingual applications and might even face a "digital extinction".

This paper explores how standardization can help to address challenges faced by the multilingual Web. The upcoming standard "Internationalization Tag Set (ITS) 2.0"[2] fills a gap that hinders better quality in translation on the Web: the availability of metadata to influence multilingual content authoring, translation and localization workflows, using humans and/or language technology.

2 Background

2.1 The MultilingualWeb community

The standardization of ITS 2.0 has emerged from the MultilingualWeb project[3]. Funded by the European commission and lead by the W3C (World Wide Web Consortium), the project started in 2010 with two aims. First, MultilingualWeb brings together stakeholders who are interested in the multilingual Web: language technology researchers, localization service providers, Web technology developers and standardization experts, users from various communities and policy makers who support various regions and their linguistic diversity.

Second, MultilingualWeb has the aim of detecting gaps that hinder the adoption of the multilingual Web. The focus here is gaps related to standardization. Since MultilingualWeb is lead by the W3C, which is the main provider of Web technology standardization building blocks, MultilingualWeb is in a good position to discuss standardization related gaps and to help closing these.

---

[2]The latest draft of ITS 2.0 is available at http://www.w3.org/TR/its20/ The predecessor ITS 1.0 is available at http://www.w3.org/TR/its/
[3]See http://multilingualweb.eu/ for further information.

MultilingualWeb is running workshops as the main instrument to achieve its goals. Since the start of the first underlying EU project, the EU thematic network MultilingualWeb, four workshops have taken place. Due to the success of the workshops, the MultilingualWeb brand was continued: the successor project called MultilingualWeb-LT (MLW-LT)[4] is supporting the standardization of ITS 2.0 within W3C and the continuation of the MultilingualWeb workshop series and its community. The creation of the MLW-LT EU project and the related W3C group working on ITS 2.0 was a direct result of community building at MultilingualWeb workshops.

2.2 Metadata for the MultilingualWeb: A simple example

At the MultilingualWeb workshops, the topic of metadata for supporting multilingual content creation and related processes came up frequently. Some metadata items like language or character encoding information have been in use for quite some time and are available in various parts of the Web architecture, e.g. HTML Web content or HTTP server settings. One concrete metadata item has been lacking for a long time: a means to identify pieces of content as non-translatable.

Such translation metadata is useful both for language technology, i.e. machine translation systems, and human translators. A standardized means to convey the metadata can ease the creation of high quality localization workflows. The metadata is created by content producers in one language, taken up by localization service providers, and brought to various (human) translators. Here the metadata helps to create a better translation result.

The predecessor of ITS 2.0, that is ITS 1.0, provides a "Translate" metadata item. Metadata items in ITS 1.0 and ITS 2.0 are so-called "data categories". Discussion about adding a "translate" attribute implementing the "Translate" metadata category in HTML5 started in 2008; the attribute eventually was added to the HTML5 draft in 2012. The MultilingualWeb community helped significantly to raise awareness about the topic, see e.g. the presentation of Ishida & Kosek (2011).

2.3 From "Translate" to enhanced metadata

Soon after adding the attribute to HTML5, two online machine translation services provided support: Bing Translator and Google Translate. [5] This demonstrated the usefulness of metadata for multilingual Web content processing.

---

[4]See http://www.w3.org/International/multilingualweb/lt/ for further information.

[5]Test results and example files demonstrating the functionality are available at http://www.w3.org/International/tests/html-css/translate/results-online

However, the "Translate" data category is only the tip of the iceberg: already ITS 1.0 provides further data categories like "Terminology" markers for terms, "Elements within Text" indicators of nested text flows (e.g. embedded footnotes) and others.

The scope of ITS 1.0 is XML content; for ITS 2.0, the aim is to provide the data categories also for HTML5 or other flavours of HTML. In addition, ITS 2.0 provides further data categories that support workflows between Web content authoring environments, language technology applications and localization tools.

3 Introduction to ITS 2.0

3.1 Basic principles

Both ITS 1.0 and ITS 2.0 share the same basic principles. Metadata items, that is the "data categories", are defined independently of their usage or "implementation". An example is the "Translate" data category. Its purpose is to convey two kinds of information: a piece of content is translatable or not. The implementation of "Translate" can happen via a "translate" attribute as in HTML5. Adding ITS markup directly into a document is called the ITS "local approach".

In many workflows, data categories are not set by content creators locally for each piece of information. The metadata is rather introduced by information architects working on a document format or project template basis. For this scenario, ITS provides an XML approach of "global rules". The following ITS file contains a rule demonstrating this functionality for the "Translate" data category.

```
<its:rules ...>
  <its:translateRule translate="no" selector="//code"/>
</its:rules>
```

The "its:rules" element serves as a wrapper. The "its:translateRule" element contains a "selector" attribute. Via an XPath expression, all "code" elements are selected. The "translate" attribute set to "no" expresses that these elements should not be translated.

ITS global rules are independent of a given document, that is: what "code" elements are matched depends on the actual content being processed.

In addition to global rules and local markup, ITS provides further data category specific definitions, like inheritance behaviour of ITS information (e.g. inheriting "Translate" information to child elements of selected element nodes) or defaults. For example the default for "Translate" is that elements are translatable and attribute values are not translatable.

3.2 Types of content: from XML to HTML

As described above, ITS 1.0 was defined with a focus on XML content. This raises the question how XML specific technologies like XPath can be used to process other types of Web content. A few years ago the focus of web technology development was on XHTML, the XML version of HTML. Today HTML5 needs to be taken into account. It provides an XML form too, but also a widely used, non-XML serialization.

The ITS 2.0 approach to accommodate this development has four aspects. First, data categories that are available natively in HTML are mapped to ITS 2.0 definitions, so that an ITS 2.0 processor can take the HTML markup into account. This approach is taken e.g. for the "Translate" data category and the "Language Information"data category, which conveys language information in the same way as the HTML "lang" or XHTML "xml:lang" attributes.

Second, ITS 2.0 provides counterparts of ITS local markup in a manner that easily can be integrated into Web content. The below example shows local ITS markup for "Terminology" information in an arbitrary XML format, using a "term" attribute in the ITS namespace.

```
<p ...>
 And he said: you need a new
 <quote its:term ="yes">motherboard</quote>
</p>
```

The HTML counterpart replaces the XML namespace mechanism with a hard-wired prefix its-*.

```
<p ...>
 And he said: you need a new
 <quote its-term="yes">motherboard</quote>
</p>
```

The HTML validation service validator.nu,[6] which is the basis for the HTML5 part of the w3c markup validator, already provides a preset (HTML5 + SVG1.1 + MathML3.0 + ITS2.0) for validating this kind local ITS 2.0 in HTML5 markup.

Third, to be able to re-use global rules with various serialization flavours of HTML5, ITS 2.0 foresees a processing chain that takes the serializations as input and creates one common DOM (document object model) in memory representation. This representation can be processed with XPath. The output then can be serialized into different forms. The aforementioned validator.nu service provides an HTML5 parser to realize both the DOM generation and the output serializations.

---

[6]See http://validator.nu/ for more information.

Finally, in ITS 2.0, the selection mechanism of global rules, that is XPath, can be replaced by CSS selectors. Various libraries to convert CSS selectors into XPath expressions exist; in this manner, content authors and content managment system (CMS) template editors can use the selectors technology of their preference and convert the CSS selectors into XPath before actual processing. This approach helps to make ITS data categories accessible for a wide range of users.

3.3 A birds eye view on ITS data categories

ITS 1.0 provides data categories with a focus on two areas. The first is translation and localization processes. "Translate" or "Term" are examples of relevant data categories. The second area is called "internationalization". In ITS 1.0, internationalization related data categories encompass metadata needed for content authoring in specific cultural or language regions. The main data categories here are: "Ruby", used to add among others pronunciation information to texts e.g. in the Japanese script; and "Directionality", used to specify the base writing direction for e.g. the Arabic or Hebrew script.

In ITS 2.0, localization related data categories are being extended and language technology related metadata is provided. An example for new localization related data categories is "Locale Filter". It identifies content that is relevant (or not relevant) for a given locale. "Allowed characters" defines characters that are permitted to appear in a piece of content, e.g. in certain parts of a user interface.

Language-technology related data categories help to create workflows including e.g. machine translation process. An example here is "Domain", see the following its:domainRule element.

```
<its:rules ...>
 <its:domainRule selector="/h:html/h:body" domain
  Pointer="/h:html/h:head/h:meta[@name='keywords']/ @content" />
</its:rules>
```

The "selector" attribute selects the body of the HTML content via an XPath expression, in the same manner as the selector described above for the "translateRule" element. The "domainPointer" attribute selects keywords available in the HTML content: a certain "meta" element. Such domain information then can be used e.g. by machine translation systems to choose the appropriate subsystem being trained for certain text domains.

Another language-technology related data category is "MT Confidence". A machine translation system can use it to express confidence information about the translation. For other data categories like "Terminology", which may be created via automatic annotation processes, such confidence information is provided as well.

4 Metadata versus, for or in linguistic annotation?

Annotating textual content as a resource for language related processing is not new. Linguistic corpora including annotations have been developed for decades. Efforts in a forum like ISO TC 37 / SC4 have led to standards for linguistic annotation. ITS both 1.0 and 2.0 are different with respect to their main focus. They do not focus on adding information about linguistic categories on various levels (e.g. morphology, syntax, semantics) to textual content, but non-linguistic, mostly process related metadata (e.g. start time, end time, CPU seconds used etc.).

However, some data categories for ITS 2.0 have a close relation to linguistic annotations. An example is the aforementioned "Terminology". A data category that has been added to ITS 2.0 is called "Text Analysis". It uses the prefix "its-ta" in HTML. The aim is to represent the output of an automatic annotation process. In the below example it is assumed that the string "Dublin" has been annotated as a result of such a process.

```
<span
  its-ta-confidence="0.7"
  its-ta-class-ref="http://nerd.eurecom.fr/ontology#Place"
  its-ta-ident-ref="http://dbpedia.org/resource/Frankfurt_(Oder)">Frankfurt
</span>
```

"ta-confidence" provides tool-generated confidence information, similar to "MT Confidence" or confidence information for "Terminology". "ta-class-ref" contains a reference to the class of unit being annotated, here making use of the NERD ontology, see Rizzo et al. (2012). "ta-ident-ref" is a unique identifier of the unit, here taken from the DBpedia structured information source, see Kobilarov et al. (2007).

Making this kind of metadata available beyond the realm of language technology has great promises. Localization workflows can convey information to translators and speed up translation. In the above example, the "its-ta-ident-ref" attribute helps to disambiguate the reference of *Frankfurt* in the given text.

Before providing real value, however, challenges have to be addressed. Some tools may assign different ta-ident-ref attributes to the same unit. This leads to a need for annotating the same content with competing pieces information. Many approaches to realizing this requirement exist[7] – but should ITS 2.0 try to adopt these?

Such topics are currently under discussion. The direction seen on the horizon is along the lines of "divide and conquer": ITS 2.0 will keep the focus on simple inline annotations, providing mostly container attributes for the output of text analysis tools. In case of conflicting information or decisions to be taken about how to categorize concurrent annotations, ITS 2.0 is only a starting point for further linguistic processing.

The decision about what formats are to be used here is out of scope for ITS 2.0. Nevertheless, the current ITS 2.0 draft provides an algorithm to convert ITS 2.0 annotated documents into the NIF format, see Rizzo et al. (2012). Using a NIF wrapper, more complex linguistic processing can take place, and the output can be integrated into ITS 2.0 "ta-*" representations again.

5 Use cases and reference implementations

ITS 2.0 by no means tries to solve all issues of metadata for the multilingual Web. As the previous section has shown, areas like linguistic annotation are rather left to other technology areas and standardization efforts. ITS 2.0 focuses on certain use cases. These also have driven the definition of the standard itself. Below is a short summary of major use cases. Additional information is provided by Lieske (2013).

5.1 Simple machine translation

In this use case, XML or HTML5 documents are translated using a machine translation service. The textual content is extracted based on ITS 2.0 data categories. The extracted content is then sent to the machine translation service. The translated content is finally merged back into the original format.

For this use case, "Translate" and "Locale Filter" are useful data categories. "Elements within Text" helps to drive the extraction process as well, e.g. for separating footnotes from the overall text flow. Another data category is "Preserve space": it helps to assure proper handling of whitespace in the translated text. Depending on the capabilities of the machine translation system, "Domain" information can be taken into account as well.

---

[7]The TEI provides an overview of these approaches, see http://www.tei-c.org/release/doc/tei-p5-doc/en/html/NH.html

5.2 Translation package creation

The aim here is to convert input text into a translation package format like XLIFF. Like in the machine translation use case, ITS 2.0 metadata drives the extraction process. Compared to that use case, additional data categories are taken into account, like "Allowed Characters" or "Terminology". During the extraction process, the ITS 2.0 metadata is transformed into an XLIFF representation. The actual role of the metadata then depends on the translation tool being used.

5.3 Integration of CMS and TMS systems

Often Web content is created via a CMS. Hence, the integration of a CMS with translation managment systems TMS is a major task for creating localization workflows. In this use case, ITS 2.0 data categories help to streamline the localization workflow.

The same data categories as in the translation package creation are relevant for this use case. The main difference is that no dedicated package format like XLIFF is being used.

5.4 Terminology and text analysis annotation

These use cases encompass the automatic services to create ITS 2.0 annotations described above.

5.5 Reference implementations

The use cases are demonstrated by various reference implementations. These are being developed within the EU project underlying the MLW-LT group. The output mostly will be open source implementations, to foster the widespread adoption of the metadata.

6 Conclusion and future work

This paper described ITS 2.0, an upcoming standard that provides metadata to integrate workflows for content production, localization and language technology. We discussed the MultilingualWeb community whose efforts led to the creation of ITS 2.0. Then we introduced the basic principles of the upcoming standard and technical details.

Various metadata items, so-called "data categories", are being provided by ITS 2.0. We discussed some of them; the area of text analysis annotation has challenges and promises and may help to apply language-technology based, linguistic annotations within localization tool chains. Finally, we discussed some use cases that demonstrate the application of ITS 2.0 metadata, and reference implementations.

The metadata definitions of ITS 2.0 were finalized during 2013, and reference implementations helped to foster their adoption. The publication of the final ITS 2.0 standard was issued on 29 October 2013.

The work undertaken for ITS 2.0 has focused on basic infrastructure for the multilingual Web. Currently detailed topics of the next decade for research in the area of language technology are being defined. The META-NET Strategic Research Agenda (SRA), described by Rehm in this volume, played a major role in shaping these topics. Among these are areas like multilingual Semantic Web, which has been discussed in the introduction of this paper. One future challenge will be how to use such data from or for the multilingual Semantic Web in localization or language technology applications, while also taking ITS 2.0 metadata into account.

References

Ell, Basil, Denny Vrandečic & Elena Simperl. 2011. Labels in the web of data. In *Proceedings of ISWC 2011*, 162–176.

Flash Eurobarometer. 2011. http://ec.europa.eu/public%5C_opinion/flash/fl%5C_313%5C_en.pdf. User Language Preference Online. Report, May 2011.

Ford, Daniel & Josh Batson. 2011. *Languages of the world (wide web).* http://googleresearch.blogspot.com/2011/07/languages-of-world-wide-web.html.

Ishida, Richard & Jirka Kosek. 2011. *HTML5 i18n: A report from the front line.* http://www.multilingualweb.eu/en/documents/luxembourg-workshop/luxembourg-workshop-report%5C#ishida.

Kobilarov, Georgi, Piet Hensel, Richard Cyganiak & Christian Bizer. 2007. *DBpedia: A nucleus for a web of open data.* Poster presentation at CSSW07.

Kornai, András. 2012. *Language death in the digital age.* http://www.meta-net.eu/events/meta-forum-2012/report#kornai_presentation. Presentation at META-FORUM 2012, Brussels.

Lieske, Christian. 2013. *Metadata for the multilingual web: usage scenarios and implementations.* http://www.w3.org/TR/mlw-metadata-us-impl/. W3C Working Draft 7 March 2013.

Rizzo, Giuseppe, Troncy Raphaël, Hellmann Sebastian & Bruemmer Martin. 2012. NERD meets NIF: Lifting NLP extraction results to the linked data cloud. In Christian Bizer, Tom Heath, Tim Berners-Lee & Hausenblas Michael (eds.), *LDOW, 5th Workshop on Linked Data on the Web*, 1–10. Lyon, France: Linked Data on the Web (LDOW2012).

Chapter 5

State of the art in Translation Memory Technology

Uwe Reinke
Cologne University of Applied Sciences

Commercial Translation Memory systems (TM) have been available on the market for over two decades now. They have become the major language technology to support the translation and localization industries. The following paper will provide an overview of the state of the art in TM technology, explaining the major concepts and looking at recent trends in both commercial systems and research. The paper will start with a short overview of the history of TM systems and a description of their main components and types. It will then discuss the relation between TM and machine translation (MT) as well as ways of integrating the two types of translation technologies. After taking a closer look at data exchange standards relevant to TM environments, the focus of the paper then shifts towards approaches to enhance the retrieval performance of TM systems looking at both non-linguistic and linguistic approaches.

1 Introduction

Translation Memory (TM) systems are the most widely used software applications in the localization of digital information, i.e. the translation and cultural adaptation of electronic content for local markets. The idea behind its core element, the actual "memory" or translation archive, is to store the originals and their human translations of e-content in a computer system, broken down into manageable units, generally one sentence long. Over time, enormous collections of sentences and their corresponding translations are built up in the systems. TMs allow translators to recycle these translated segments by automatically proposing a relevant translation from the memory as a complete ("exact match") or partial solution ("fuzzy match") whenever the same or a similar sentence occurs again

Uwe Reinke. State of the art in Translation Memory Technology. In Georg Rehm, Felix Sasaki, Daniel Stein & Andreas Witt (eds.), *Language technologies for a multilingual Europe: TC3 III*, 55–84. Berlin: Language Science Press. DOI:10.5281/zenodo.1291930

in their work. This increases the translator's productivity and helps ensure that the same terminology and expressions are consistently used across translations. Thus, TMs facilitate and speed-up the translation of a rapidly growing amount of specialised texts.

No other technology has changed the general conditions of translation as a professional service as radically as TM systems have done over the past 20 years. This might be due to the fact that TMs mainly support professional translators in their routine work without radically influencing cognitive translation processes in those situations that require the creativity and knowledge of the human translator.

Today most professional translators use TM technology on a regular basis Massion (2005); Lagoudaki (2006). The most well-known commercial systems are *Across, Déjà Vu, memoQ, MultiTrans,* SDL *Trados, Similis, Transit* and *Wordfast*.[1]

2 Translation memory systems

2.1 History

The basic idea of computer-assisted reuse of human translations can be traced back to the 1960s, when the European Coal and Steel Community (ECSC) developed and used a computer system to retrieve terms and their contexts from stored human translations by identifying those sentences whose lexical items most closely matched the lexical items of a sentence to be translated.

The translation of the sentence (i.e. the sentence stored in the database) is not done by the computer, but by a human translator. However, since the data produced by each query are added to the database, the more the system is in use, the greater is the probability of finding sentences that have the desired term in the proper context (ALPAC 1966: 27).

Yet, modern TM systems differ considerably from the former ECSC application. As the quote below from the ALPAC report shows, the latter was rather something like a bilingual keyword in context (KWIC) retrieval tool that mainly served the purpose of showing source language terms and their target language equivalents in their respective contexts. Retrieving previous translation units for reuse was, if at all, a secondary goal:

> The system utilized at CECA is one of automatic dictionary look-up with context included. [...] [T]he translator indicates, by underlining, the words

---

[1]For a brief overview on TM technology see also Somers (2003) and Reinke (2006). Comprehensive investigations can be found in Reinke (2004).

with which he desires help. The entire sentence is then keypunched and fed into a computer. The computer goes through a search routine and prints out the sentence or sentences that most nearly match (in lexical items) the sentences in question. The translator then receives the desired items printed out with their context and in the order in which they occur in the source. (ALPAC 1966: 27)

A much broader reuse of existing machine-readable human translations with a clear focus on facilitating and accelerating revision processing by identifying unchanged passages was envisaged in a model developed by the translation service of the German Federal Army in the early 1970s (Krollmann 1971). Apart from using several lexical databases this model also envisaged subsystems for storing and analysing text corpora and translation archives stored on magnetic tape:

> [...] via descriptors or keywords, large batches of text could automatically be searched for particular passages and then be displayed on video screens as an aid to the translator; [...] For revised new editions of translations only the changed passages would have to be retyped. Insertion of changes and corrections into the old text would automatically be done by computer [...]. (Krollmann 1971)

At the end of the 1970s European Comission translator Peter Arthern (1979) proposed even more far reaching computer-assisted support for the translator. His suggestions have to be seen in the context of a discussion led at that time within the European Commission about the use of terminology databases and the feasibility of introducing the MT system *Systran*. While Krollmann's (1971) model only seemed to include the reuse of identical text fragments (today known as "exact matches"), Arthern suggests a system that can also retrieve from the reference material similar source language sentences and their translations (today known as "fuzzy matches"):

> This would mean that, simply by entering the final version of a text for printing, as prepared on the screen at the keyboard terminal, and indicating in which languages to compare the new text, probably sentence by sentence, with all the previously recorded texts prepared in the organization in that language, and to print out *the nearest available equivalent for each sentence* in all the target languages, on different printers.
>
> The result would be a complete text in the original language, plus at least partial translations in as many languages as were required, all grammati-

cally correct as far as they went and all available simultaneously. Depending on how much of the new original was already in store, the subsequent
work on the target language texts would range from the insertion of names
and dates in standard letters, through light welding at the seams between
discrete passages, to the translation of large passages of new text with the
aid of a term bank based on the organization's past usage. (Arthern 1979:
94f. my emphasis)

While Arthern did not tackle the issue of "the nearest available equivalent" –
or "similarity" – in more detail, he even envisaged the possibility of integrating
TM and machine translation (MT):

Since this form of machine-assisted translation would operate in the context of a complete text-processing system, it could very conveniently be
supplemented by 'genuine' machine translation, perhaps to translate the
missing areas in texts retrieved from the text memory. (Arthern 1979: 95)

Yet, it took another decade before the ideas sketched by Krollmann and Arthern became part of real applications and market-ready systems. The notion of automatically retrieving "exact matches" was first implemented in the early 1980s
by ALPS Inc. (later ALPNET Corporation) in a simple component called "Repeti-
tions Processing" as part of the company's commercial MT system called *Translation Support System* (TSS) (Seal 1992). The reuse of similar sentences ("fuzzy
matching") was supported by the first commercial TM systems like *IBM Translation Manager*, and *Trados Translator's Workbench II* that did not appear in the
market before the early 1990s.[2]

2.2 Components

Apart from the "memory" or translation archive as its core element, a typical
TM system consists of an array of tools and functionalities to assist the human
translator. These usually include:

- a MULTILINGUAL EDITOR for reading source texts and writing translations
  in all relevant file formats of different word processing programs, DTP systems, etc., protecting the layout tags of these formats against accidentally
  being deleted or overwritten

---

[2]Hutchins (1998) and Reinke (2004: 36–41) provide further information on the history of TM
systems.

- a TERMINOLOGY MANAGEMENT PROGRAM for maintaining termbases to store, retrieve, and update subject-, customer-, and project-specific terminology

- an AUTOMATIC TERM RECOGNITION FEATURE for automatically looking up in the termbase all terms that occur in the source text segment the translator is currently working on

- a CONCORDANCE TOOL allowing users to retrieve all instances of a specific search string (single words, word groups, phrases, etc.) from a TM and view these occurrences in their immediate context

- a STATISTICS FEATURE providing a rough overview of the amount of text that can be reused from a TM for translating a new source document

- an ALIGNMENT TOOL to create TM databases from previously translated documents that are only available as separate source and target text files by comparing a source text and its translation, matching the corresponding segments, and binding them together as units in a TM.

In addition, a few TM systems offer terminology extraction as an optional or an integrated feature to assist in populating termbases and setting up the terminology for an e-content localization project by extracting mono- or bilingual lists of potential terms from a selection of electronic (source and/or target) texts. Today, many TM suites also include support for machine translation, either by offering interfaces with MT systems or even by integrating their own MT component. Finally, some kind of project management (PM) support is built into most TM systems. These PM features may support:

- file handling and management (specification of all source language files, project-relevant termbases and TM databases, assistance in defining folder structures)

- management of client and translator data (addresses, contact persons, translators' skills, equipment, availability, etc.)

- workflow management (deadlines, project progress, etc.).

Figure 1 provides an overview of how the major components of a standard TM environment interact, while Figure 2 gives an example for a typical user interface of a commercial TM system.

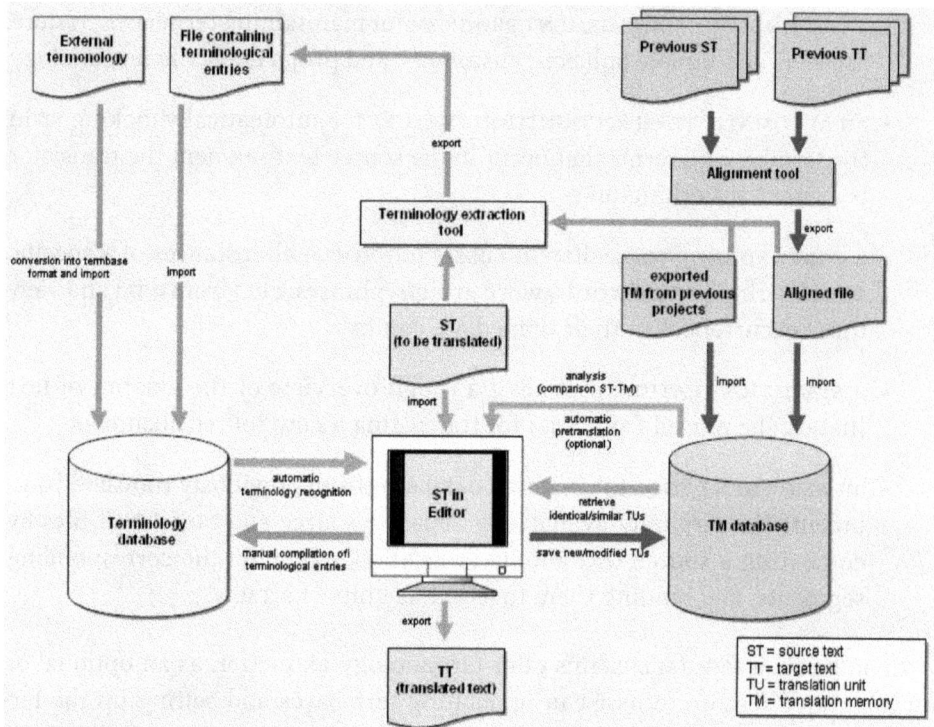

Figure 1: Components and processes in a translation memory (TM) system (excluding project management and machine translation functionalities)

Although professional translators often stress the need to constantly adjust to rapid technological changes in the field (some complaining about this constant pressure, others rather regarding it as a professional necessity and a challenge), it must be said that all in all the core functionalities of commercial TM systems have remained very much the same since the first – mostly still MS-DOS-based – applications became available at the beginning of the 1990s. Even the first versions contained a translation memory, a terminology management system and a (multilingual) editor, providing features like exact and fuzzy matching, pretranslation[3], concordance lookup, terminology recognition, etc. (Figure 3). Of course, the matching algorithms – although still being based on simple character match-

---

[3]Pre-translation refers to the batch process "of comparing a complete source text to a Translation Memory database and automatically inserting the translations of all exact matches found in the database. The result is a hybrid text containing pretranslated and untranslated segments." (eCoLoRe 2012)

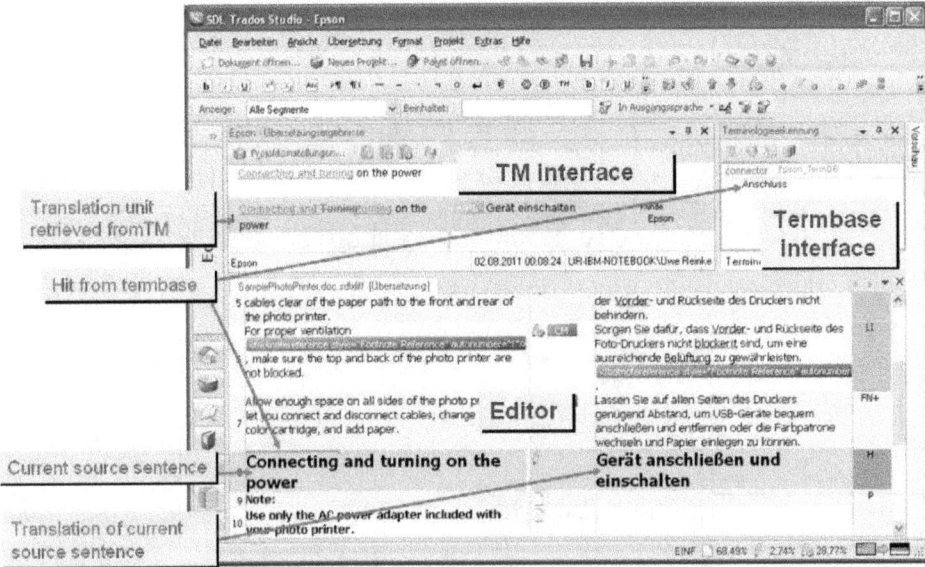

Figure 2: User interface of SDL Trados Studio

ing procedures – have been altered and modified to a considerable extent, and many additional features and functionalities have been added, so that a growing number of scholars, professionals and application providers now prefer to call TM systems "translation environments" or "translation environment tools (TEnT)" (CERTT 2012: 8).

What has changed dramatically indeed during the last two decades is the translation workflow, i.e. the way the translation processes are organized and the way the parties involved in these processes interact and collaborate. The introduction of client/server solutions after the turn of the millennium enabled new ways of real-time collaboration among distributed teams but led to even more controversial discussions about intellectual property rights on TM data collections and liability issues. The near future will reveal to which extent new buzzword technologies and forms of collaboration like "cloud computing" and "crowd sourcing" will actually affect translation workflows and work situations.

2.3 Types of TM systems

In most systems available on the market the TM is a database. Each record in a TM database contains a translation unit (TU) consisting of a pair of source and target

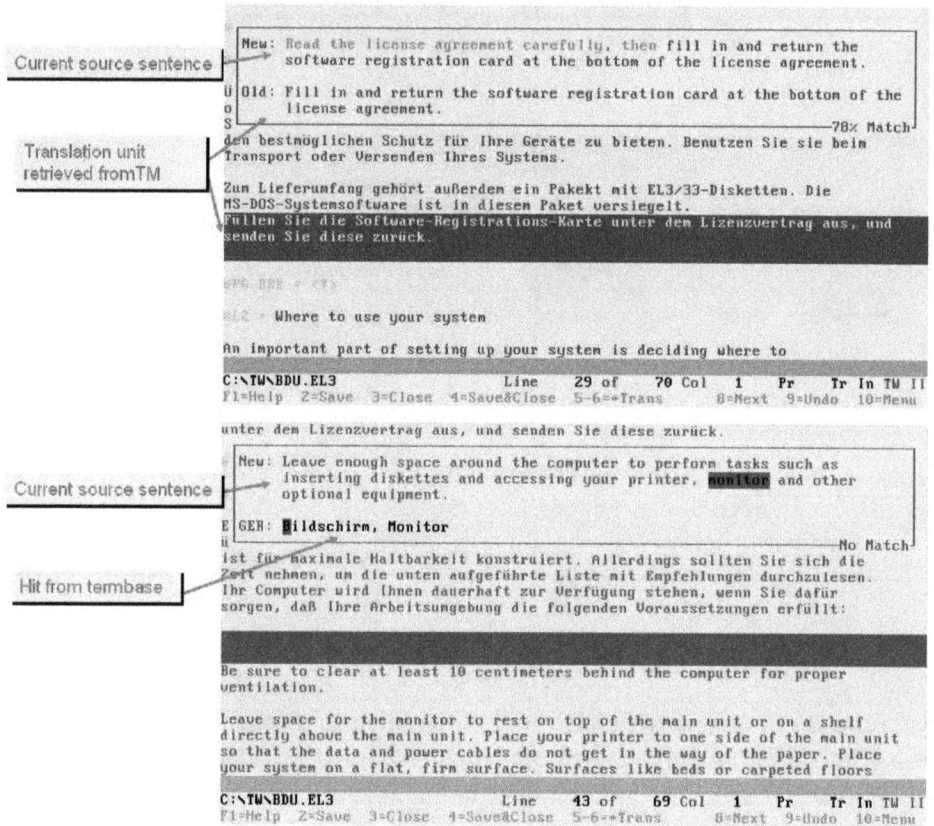

Figure 3: Fuzzy matching and terminology recognition in TRADOS Translator's Workbench II

text segments.[4] In addition to the TU, there may be further information on the creation and modification dates, the person who created or modified the entry, the project(s) or customer(s) the TU is used for, etc.

A major feature of a typical TM database is the fact that it grows incrementally. The database is 'dynamic' because new TUs – regardless of whether they are created from scratch or by adjusting the translation of a similar TU retrieved from the TM – are added during the translation process.

---

[4]In most TMs, translation units consist of source language sentences and their target language equivalents. Apart from 1:1 equivalences, where a sentence from the source text is transferred into one sentence in the target text, this can also include 1:n and n:1 relations, depending on the decisions taken by the individual translator. Moreover, smaller TUs having the size of clauses or phrases, larger units based on paragraphs, or nested units starting at paragraph level and then assigning further relations at sentence level may also occur.

Basically, there are three ways of feeding a TM:

- While translating: When translating a text using a TM database each segment from the source text will be automatically stored in the database along with its translation.

- By importing another TM database: This can either be a TM created with the same TM system or a TM available in the Translation Memory eXchange format (TMX), which is supported by all commercial systems.

- By aligning existing translations and their original texts: With the help of an alignment tool it is possible to create TM databases from the source and target text files of previous translation projects.

Some TM systems do not make use of the database approach but store entire source and target text pairs in their proprietary formats as reference material for future reuse in related translation projects. While TM databases constitute an amalgamation of translation units that isolates each segment from its context, the reference text approach makes it easier to take context into account during the matching process. On the other hand, this approach is rather static, i.e. it is not possible to immediately reuse TUs that have just been created. Therefore, systems based on the reference text approach also create a so called temporary "fuzzy index", which is a kind of temporary database providing access to recently created TUs as well as fuzzy-match functionality. In turn, TM systems following the database approach have tried to overcome the complete decontextualisation of their TUs by adding so-called "context matches" or "perfect matches", where an exact match is preceeded and/or followed by another exact match, i.e. the segment to be translated and the match retrieved from the TM have the same textual environment. This is achieved by simply storing in the TM database the relevant context segments together with the actual TUs and sometimes by additionaly taking into account information obtained from style sheets, document templates or structural document markup (Chama 2010). Some database-oriented TM systems have also included the reference text approach as an additional option to retrieve translaslation units for reuse by allowing to specify bilingual files from previous translation projects and combining them with TM databases. In general, it seems that the developers of commercial TM systems more and more try to combine the advantages of both the database-oriented and the reference text-oriented approaches.

Another major issue in TM technology is the retrieval of fragments below sentence level. Most commercial TM systems now offer some kind of subsegment matching. The simplest form of subsegment matching is to look for complete TM database and termbase units that are part of the current souce language segment and automatically insert their target language sections, thus usually creating suggestions that form a mix of source and target language fragments and require further adaptation ("fragment assembly"). A more complex way of finding subsegments is to retrieve longest common substrings (LSCs) from TM database units (Figure 4). Finally, a third – and probably the most productive – way of subsegment matching that can be found in commercial TM systems is to automatically suggest target language fragments while typing a translation (auto-completion; Figure 5). These fragments are retrieved from bilingual lexicons that were statistically generated from TM databases (Chama 2010).

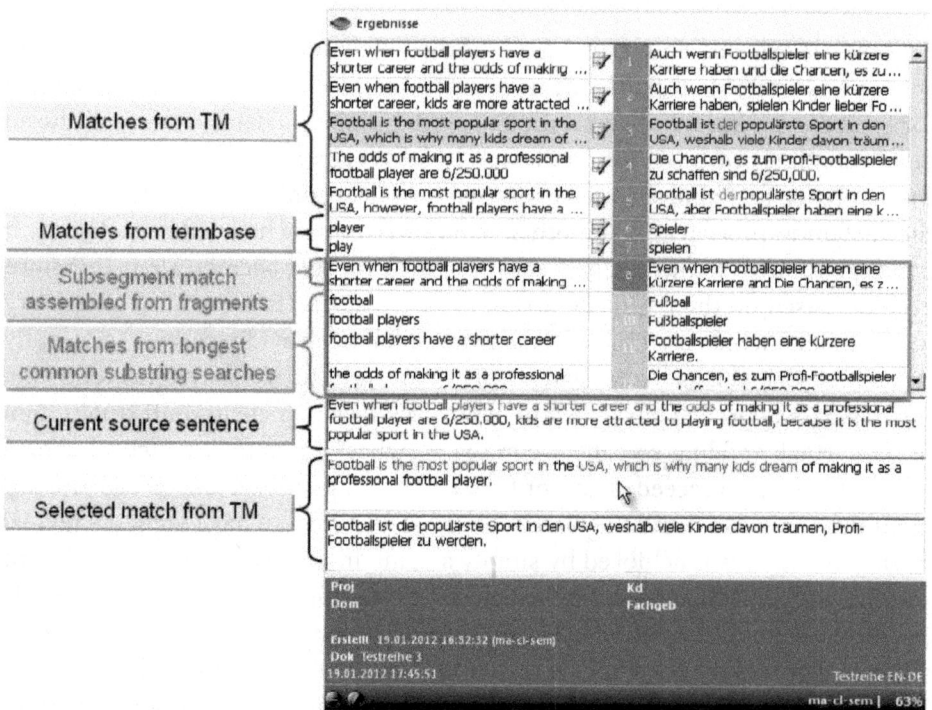

Figure 4: Subsegment matching in Kilgray MemoQ

| Dieses Abkommen - abgefasst in zwei Urschriften in dänischer, deutscher, englischer, französischer, griechischer, italienischer, 24 niederländischer, portugiesischer und spanischer Sprache, wobei jeder Wortlaut gleichermaßen verbindlich ist - tritt am Tag seiner Unterzeichnung in Kraft. Abgefasst in zwei Urschriften in dänischer, deutscher, englischer, französischer, griechischer, italienischer, niederländischer, | T This Agreement is drawn up in duplicate This Agreement shall enter into force This Agreement This That TWO Two |

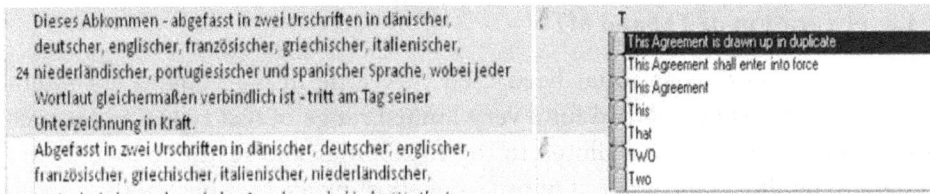

Figure 5: Subsegment matching in SDL Trados Studio

2.4 Translation memory and machine translation

2.4.1 Distinction between TM and MT

TM technology is not to be confused with machine translation. Whereas MT translates without human intervention, TM systems provide features and tools to store and retrieve segments translated by a human translator. Despite this essential distinction between TM and MT, TM technology shares certain commonalities with both example-based machine translation (EBMT), an approach first suggested in Japan in the early 1980s (Nagao 1984), and statistical machine translation (SMT), an approach developped at IBM in the late 1980s (Brown et al. 1988) that did not have its breakthrough before the turn of the millenium and is considered the state-of-the art paradigm in MT today (Koehn 2010: 17f). Both TM and EBMT/SMT try to retrieve "best matches" for the sentences of the text to be translated from a bilingual text archive or database containing sentence-level alignments of existing translations and their original texts.[5] Yet, there are fundamental differences between the purposes of EBMT/SMT and TM systems. A TM is mainly an information retrieval application that leaves decisions about whether and how to reuse and adjust the retrieved results – and thus the actual translation task – to the human translator. EBMT and SMT produce translations by automatically selecting suitable fragments from the source language side of the retrieved TUs and building the translation from the corresponding elements of the target language side. Due to the complexity of this recombination task, not every TU contained in a translation archive is equally suited for reuse in TM systems and EBMT or SMT environments.

---

[5]Both EBMT and SMT are corpus-based approaches, so that the term corpus-based MT (CBMT) is used as an umbrella for both as opposed to rule-based MT (RBMT) (Carl & Way 2003: xviii). The major difference between EBMT and SMT is that SMT considers translation as a "statistical optimization problem" (Koehn 2010: 17) and is based on probability calculations over large bilingual corpora, while EBMT tries to find analogies between an input sentence and examples from a bilingual corpus applying more "traditional" linguistic means like (morpho-)syntactic analysis and thesauri. For an extensive overview on EBMT see Carl & Way (2003) and Somers (2001). A comprehensive introduction to SMT can be found in Koehn (2010).

2.4.2 Integration of TM and MT

For good reason MT has so far been used very little in high quality e-content localization. MT is only suited for a very limited range of text types, and source texts have to be carefully tailored to the capabilities and restrictions of an MT system to minimize the amount of time and effort needed for post-editing.

Nevertheless, TM suites increasingly offer support for MT. Basically, there are two possible ways of combining MT and TM:

1. Batch processing (usually during data preparation): In a batch scenario, all segments of the source text that do not produce an exact or high percentage "fuzzy match" when being compared with the TM database may be exported for processing by MT. After the unknown segments have been translated by the MT application, the new translation units can be merged into the TM database. When the translator works on the text, the units generated by the MT system will be presented as candidate translations, possibly with a predefined matching penalty.

2. Interactive processing (during the translation stage proper): In an interactive scenario, translators can invoke the MT system each time there is no match with the TM database. If the result from the MT system proves helpful, it can be edited as necessary. The resulting translation unit will then be stored in the TM database for future reuse.

Commercial TM systems like *Across* or *SDL Trados Studio* offer interfaces to both RBMT and SMT systems. Large MT companies like *Sybase* report productivity gains by combining SMT and TM, provided that the MT system has been trained with a large-enough company-specific bilingual corpus (cf. Bier 2012). Like other large companies *Sybase* has carried out experiments using the freely available SMT system *Moses* (Koehn et al. 2007) interactively together with a TM system. Bier (2012) mentions faster turnaround (delivery time decreased by an average of 50%), 20–30% cost reductions for updates, stable translation quality (no visible impact on style with full post-editing, fewer content errors, slight increase in minor linguistic errors) and a rise in productivity between 5 and 70% (depending on the kind of source texts, the terminology used and the performance of individual translators).[6]

---

[6]For a comparison of TM and SMT output see also Offersgaard et al. (2008). Offersgaard et al. report high productivity gains of more than 65% for certain domains and for situations in which the TM database does not produce matches for two thirds or more of the sentences

2.5 Data exchange standards for TM systems

2.5.1 Overview

A versatile TM system must be able to handle the full range of proprietary and standard file formats in which e-content can be produced and exchanged. One of the major metastandards that play a central role in technical documentation is the eXtensible Markup Language (XML) (W3C 2008). XML provides a framework for the creation of markup languages for all kinds of individual document types, and there is a growing number of XML-based standards and formats to support various aspects of the documentation and localization process. While standards like DocBook (OASIS 2006), DITA (OASIS 2007), and XLIFF (OASIS 2008) are related to the creation and exchange of localizable content, TMX (LISA 2005), SRX (LISA 2008) and TBX (ISO 2008) serve the purpose of facilitating the exchange of reference material (TM databases and termbases).

Current efforts like Linport (Language Interoperability Portfolio, Linport 2012) and TIPP (Translation Interoperability Protocol Package, InteroperabilityNow! 2012) focus on the development of a standard for the exchange of complete translation projects between different translation environments.

2.5.2 Supporting standards for the exchange of localizable e-content

For public XML-based standards like DocBook, DITA und XLIFF, TM systems should include import routines that provide an automatic distinction between so-called "external" XML markup elements, that need not be modified during the translation process, and "internal" elements, which the translator may need to move, add or delete. Translatable and non-translatable attribute values should be distinguished automatically as well.

For proprietary XML-based formats, TM systems should provide a feature to create import routines from a combination of various sources, i.e. XML document type definitions (DTDs), XML schema definition files (XSDs) and localizable XML content files, keeping the effort for manually correcting translation-related settings for the indiviudal XML elements and attributes as small as possible.

Content in formats like XLIFF, which mainly serve the purpose of exchanging bilingual files during the localization process, must be diplayed correctly in the TM system's multilingual editor, i.e. for editors using separate windows or table

---

to be translated. Guerberof (2009) also reports higher processing speed for post-editing SMT output compared with TM matches, but also points to the fact that deviation between individual subjects is very high.

columns for source and target languages, the <source> and <target> elements of an XLIFF file must be placed into the correct windows or columns (Figure 6). Moreover, metadata like translation comments and information on the processing status of translation units should be adequately imported, displayed and exported without any loss of information (Figure 7).

Finally, it must be taken into account that XLIFF is a kind of hybrid format, because apart from localizable content XLIFF files can also contain bilingual reference material from previous versions or related documents. TM systems must be able to recognize this reference material in an XLIFF file and store it in a TM database together with relevant metadata also contained in the XLIFF file, like information on match values, authors, systems used to create the material, etc. (Figure 8).

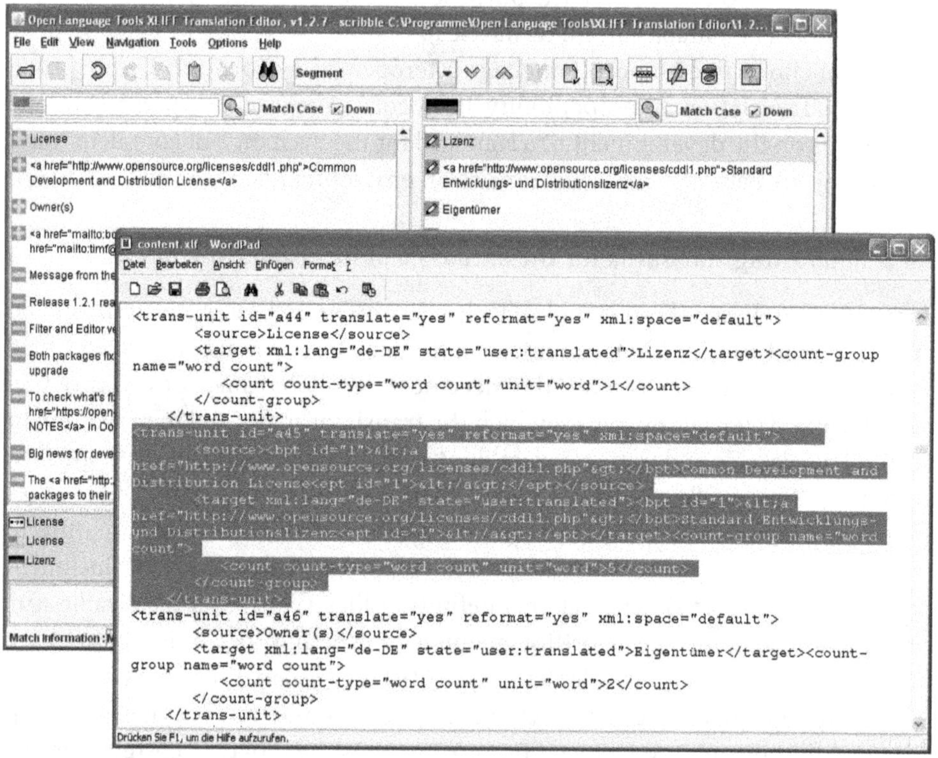

Figure 6: Fragment from an XLIFF file in a text editor and in an XLIFF translation editor

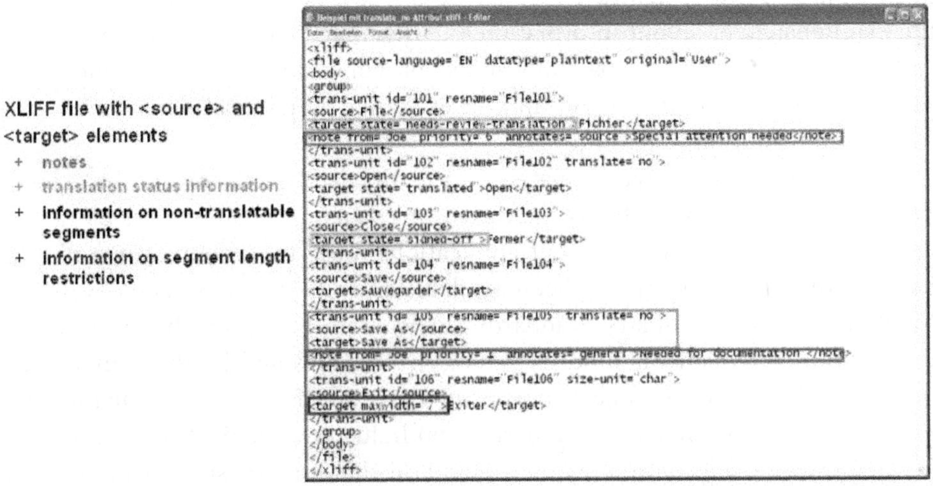

XLIFF file with <source> and
<target> elements

+ notes
+ translation status information
+ **information on non-translatable segments**
+ **information on segment length restrictions**

Figure 7: Complex XLIFF file containing various metadata

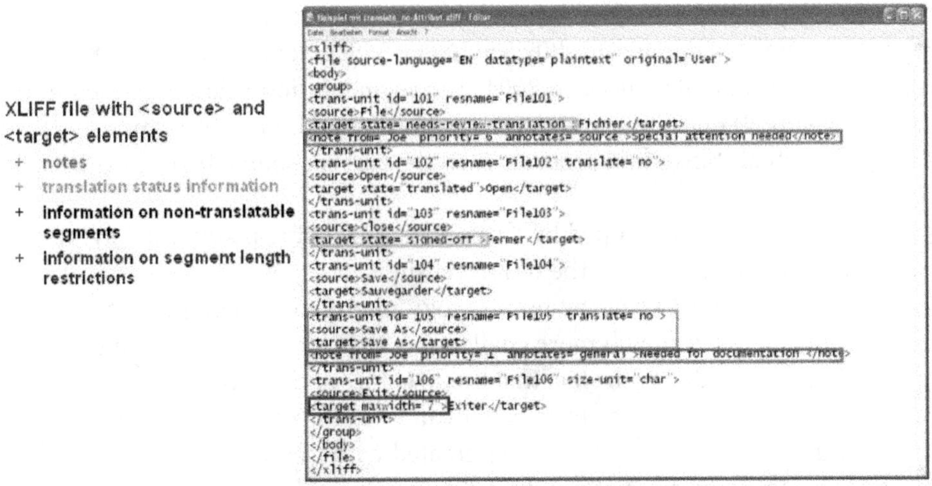

XLIFF file with <source> and
<target> elements

+ notes
+ translation status information
+ **information on non-translatable segments**
+ **information on segment length restrictions**

Figure 8: XLIFF file containing various reference material

2.5.3 Supporting standards for the exchange of reference material

The exchange of TM database elements mainly causes problems with respect to the maintenance of layout information and dynamic fields (i.e. placeholders for embedded objects and automatically adjustable content like cross-references and other variables) contained in TUs and the exchange of information on rules used for the segmentation of text into TUs.

To keep the loss of layout-related information and placeholders for embedded objects and dynamic fields contained in TUs as minimal as possible when exchanging TMs between different applications most TM systems support TMX Level 2. The TMX standard has been available since 1998. It has been developed by the Localization Industry Standards Association (LISA), which was an interest group of major information technology companies and localization service providers. After LISA became insolvent in 2011. TMX is now being maintained by the Localization Industry Standards (LIS) Industry Specification Group (ISG) of the European Telecommunications Standards Institute (ETSI) (GALA 2012) and the standard is freely available from the website of the Globalization and Localization Association (GALA).[7]

Breaking up text into smaller TUs requires segmentation rules that may differ between languages as well as text types and file formats. Examples include individual punctuation characters like the quotation mark in Spanish or the different treatment of colons, semi-colons and other characters depending on language and text type. In order to overcome a loss in reusability of TUs due to different segmentation rules applied in different TMs the Segmentation Rules eXchange (SRX) standard was introduced in 2004. The segmentation rules contained in an SRX file (Figure 9) must be applied when exporting and importing TMs as well as during the actual translation process when the current source text has to be split up into TUs.

Like TMX, SRX was developed by LISA and is now being maintained by ETSI. It can also be downloaded from the GALA website.

Exchanging data between the terminology management components of various TM systems can be much more challenging than sharing TMs among various applications. This is due to the fact that the structure and complexity of termbases may differ severely from system to system and – in the case of user-definable entry structures – even among termbases created with the same application. It has taken a long time since the efforts to define a universal exchange format for ter-

---

[7]GALA is a non-profit organization of localization and translation service providers, language technology developers and other companies involved in language services or technology. The former LISA standards can be found at http://www.gala-global.org/lisa-oscar-standards.

```
<?xml version="1.0"?>
<srx version="2.0"
    xmlns="http://www.lisa.org/srx20"
    xsi:schemaLocation="http://www.lisa.org/srx20 srx20.xsd"
    xnlns:xsi="http://www.v3.org/2001/XMLSchena-instance">
  <header segmentsubflows="yes" cascade="yes">
    <formathandle type="start" include="no"/>
    <formathandle type="end" include="yes"/>
    <formathandle type="isolated" include="yes"/>
  </header>
  <body>
    <languagerules>
      <languagerule languagerulename="Default">
      <!-- Common rules for most languages -->
      <rule break="no">
          <beforebreak>^\s*[0-9]+\.</beforebreak>
          <afterbreak>\s</afterbreak>
      </rule>
      <rule break="yes">
          <afterbreak>\n<afterbreak> '
      </rule>
      <rule break="yes">
          <beforebreak>[\.\?!]+</beforebreak>
          <afterbreak>\s</afterbreak>
      </rule>
      </languagerule>
      <languagerule languagerulename="English">
        <!-- Some English abbreviations -->
        <rule break"-no'>
          <beforebreak>\s[Ee][Tt][Cc]\.</beforebreak>
          <atterbreak>\s[a-z]</afterbreak>
        </rule>
        <rule break="no">
            <beforebreak>\sMr\.</beforebreak>
            <afterbreak>\s</afterbreak>
        </rule>
        <rule break="no">
            <beforebreak>\sU\.K\.</beforebreak>
            <afterbreak>\s</afterbreak>
        </rule>
        </languagerule>
```

Figure 9: Section from an SRX file

minological data have lead to the Termbase eXchange Standard (TBX). Although TBX has become an ISO standard in 2008 (cf. ISO 2008) the format is still not properly supported by all TM systems.

2.6 Advantages and limitations of TM systems

The advantages of using TM systems are fairly obvious: they increase the translator's productivity and enhance translation quality by ensuring that terminology and expressions are used consistently within and across translations. Users in industry and international organizations usually claim a 25% to 60% rise in productivity (Reinke 2004: 113f.). However, at least in some industries productivity gains seem to come to an end after a certain time. Thus, at Sybase "[t]raditional TM technology [is] almost fully exploited" with "ca. 80% of costs spent on 'new' words" and "only 20% spent on recycling" (Bier 2012). Bier also states that there are "[n]o more improvements in turnaround times" as the average productivity of translators has remained at a maximum level of 2.400 words per day for years.

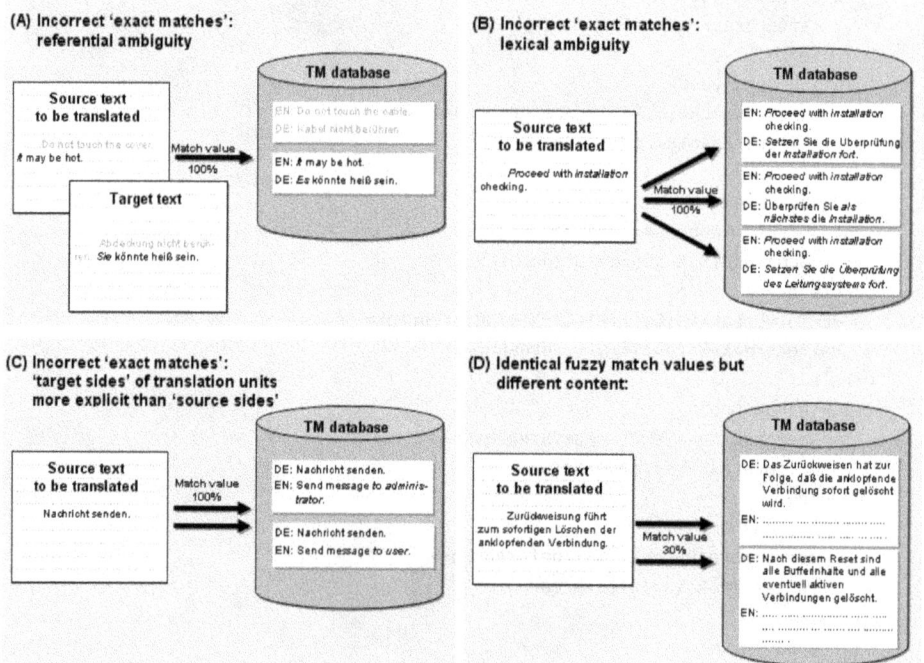

Figure 10: Examples in English (EN) and German (DE), demonstrating shortcomings of fuzzy match algorithms (Reinke 2006: 64)

Furthermore, it must be stated that the use of TM systems may also have negative effects on translation quality. One of the major disadvantages of TM systems is that they usually operate at sentence level. Thus, there is a serious danger that the translator will focus too much on isolated sentences, possibly disregarding the contexts they are embedded in (Reinke 2004: 136f.).

Examples (A) and (B) in Figure 10 examplify this problem with respect to referential and lexical ambiguity. In example (A) the pronoun *it* is an anaphoric reference to the noun phrase *the cover* in the previous sentence. As the German translation *die Abdeckung* is female, the pronoun should be female as well (i.e. *sie*). In the same English sentence in the TM the pronoun *it* refers to a different noun phrase with a German translation using a neuter noun like *das Kabel,* so that *it* has to become *es.* Thus, an exact match for *It can be hot* yields a translation that does not fit the current context. In example (B) terms like *installation* or general language words like *proceed* are lexically ambiguous. *Installation* could, for instance, refer the installation of a piece of software or to a piping system, while *to proceed with s.th.* might mean *to continue a process that has been interrupted* or *to go on with the next step of a process.* These different meanings require different translations in German. Therefore, an exact match from the TM might produce an incorrect translation.

The matching algorithms of TM systems are based on very simple formal criteria like the similarity of character strings. Thus, the human translator's notion of the degree of similarity between a segment to be translated and a segment retrieved from the database may differ considerably from the degree of similarity calculated by the TM system. This may lead to situations where "exact matches" yield wrong translations (examples A to C in Figure 10) or one translation of a "fuzzy match" requires little or no adjustment, while another "fuzzy match" with the same similarity value is not useful at all, e.g., because the content belongs to a different (sub-)domain (example D in Figure 10).

Despite these drawbacks, it should be noted that TM systems generally integrate into the translation workflow comparatively smoothly. As opposed to MT, they leave human translators in control of the actual translation process, while relieving them from routine work and maintaining translation as a creative act whenever the linguistic resourcefulness of a human being is required.

3 Approaches to enhance the information retrieval performance of TM systems

3.1 Approaches not applying "linguistic knowledge"

Although commercial TM systems have been available for over two decades, their retrieval performance has not improved considerably in terms of quality and quantity. Of course, the matching algorithms have been altered and modified over time, but they still rely on simple character- or token-based matching procedures without taking into account linguistic aspects like morphosyntactic, syntactic or semantic features that may determine the "similarity" of translation units.[8] Even rather straightforward approaches that do not rely on "linguistic knowledge" but could, for instance, easily improve the retrieval performance for TUs containing so-called placeable and localizable elements[9] are not yet a matter of course in commercial TM systems.

Azzano (2011) presents a detailed analysis of the question at what extent the occurrence of placeable and localizable elements influence the retrieval performance of commercial TM systems. He found that placeable elements sometimes lead to comparatively low fuzzy match values because some systems treat them like standard text when comparing the lengths of source language segments (SegSL) to be translated and source language segments from a TM (SegSL$_{TM}$). Instead, it would be more reasonable to use a fixed penalty when SegSL and SegSL$_{TM}$ only differ with respect to the placeable elements they contain while the remaining standard text is identical.

Azzano (2011) also reports that some systems yield exact matches when SegSL and SegSL$_{TM}$ contain both identical text and identical placeable elements and just differ in the order or position of the placeable elements. This is a serious mistake because in most cases these modifications will also be relevant to the new translation if the target language segment from the TM (SegTL$_{TM}$) will be reused.

---

[8]For a brief overview on similarity measures relevant to TM systems see Trujillo (1999: 61–68), Reinke (2004: 193–198), Sikes 2007.

[9]Placeable elements like tags, inline graphics and dynamic fields usually do not contain translatable text. They can often be copied ("placed") into the target text without any need for further modifications. Tags are markup elements in HTML and XML files; inline graphics and dynamic fields typically occur in DTP formats and Microsoft Word files. Localizable elements like numbers, dates, URLs or e-mail addresses, in turn, consist of plain text following a certain pattern, so that they can be identified without any "linguistic knowledge". The localization of these elements follows given rules and often does not influence the remaining parts of a TU.

Comparatively simple methods could also be applied to improve the retrieval of TM segments containing localizable elements. Instead of treating them like plain text they should be seen as special elements that follow certain patterns. These patterns can be recognized with the help of regular expressions. For the calculation of match values the same principles already suggested for placeable elements could be applied (i.e. using a fixed penalty if SegSL and SegSL$_{TM}$ differ in terms of localizable elements). Azzano (2011) found that to a certain extent commercial TM systems do apply regular expressions to identify localizable elements, but for some elements like complex numerical patterns they still show severe weaknesses, whereas other elements are not recognized at all. Although there are useful and well-known regular expressions, e.g. for identifying URLs in plain text (Goyvaerts & Levithan 2009), these are hardly implemented in commercial TM systems. Azzano (2011) suggests a number of regular expressions to improve the recognition of various localizable elements.

3.2 Approaches applying "linguistic knowledge"

3.2.1 Current approaches in commercial and research systems

Linguistics-driven efforts on enhancing retrieval in TM systems are basically motivated by two different goals:

1. improving recall and precision of (monolingual) retrieval, i.e. enhancing quantity, quality and ranking of matches, at segment level and at subsegment level (retrieval of "chunks", (complex) phrases, clauses) by enriching the retrieval algorithms of TM systems with "linguistic knowledge"

2. automated adjustment of fuzzy matches to enhance reusability and reduce postediting efforts by integrating SMT technology into TM systems.

With *Similis* the French company *Lingua et Machina* produces one of the very few commercial TM systems that do not only rely on character-based matching algorithms but also try to integrate linguistic methods by using morphosyntactic analysis and shallow parsing to identify fragments below segment level (Planas 2005). Planas (2005) describes his system as "second generation translation memory software". Of course, this kind of linguistically enhanced application is only available for a restricted number of language pairs.[10] Investigations indicate that

---

[10] Currently *Similis* supports combinations between English, German, French, Italian, Spanish, Portugese and Dutch (http://similis.org/linguaetmachina.www/index.php?afficher=10&sel=40&info=Spezifikationen).

at least for certain language combinations like English-German the system only identifies rather short phrases like simple NPs but cannot retrieve larger syntactical units, which would be desirable for the support of professional computer-assisted human translation (Kriele 2006; Macken 2009). Figures 11 and 12 illustrate these findings for an English-German example shown the *Similis* translation and alignment editors.

Linguistically enhanced TM systems have mainly been developed and tested as research systems (Gotti et al. 2005; Hodász & Pohl 2005; Mitkov & Corpas 2008). Like *Similis* they mostly integrate morphosyntactic analysis and shallow syntactic parsing. However, there are even efforts to include semantic information to improve the retrieval of sentence-level praraphrases that differ lexically and syntactically (Mitkov & Corpas 2008). Due to the rather restricted availability of semantic data in relevant subject areas, the relevance of these approaches within commercial implementations is still rather small.

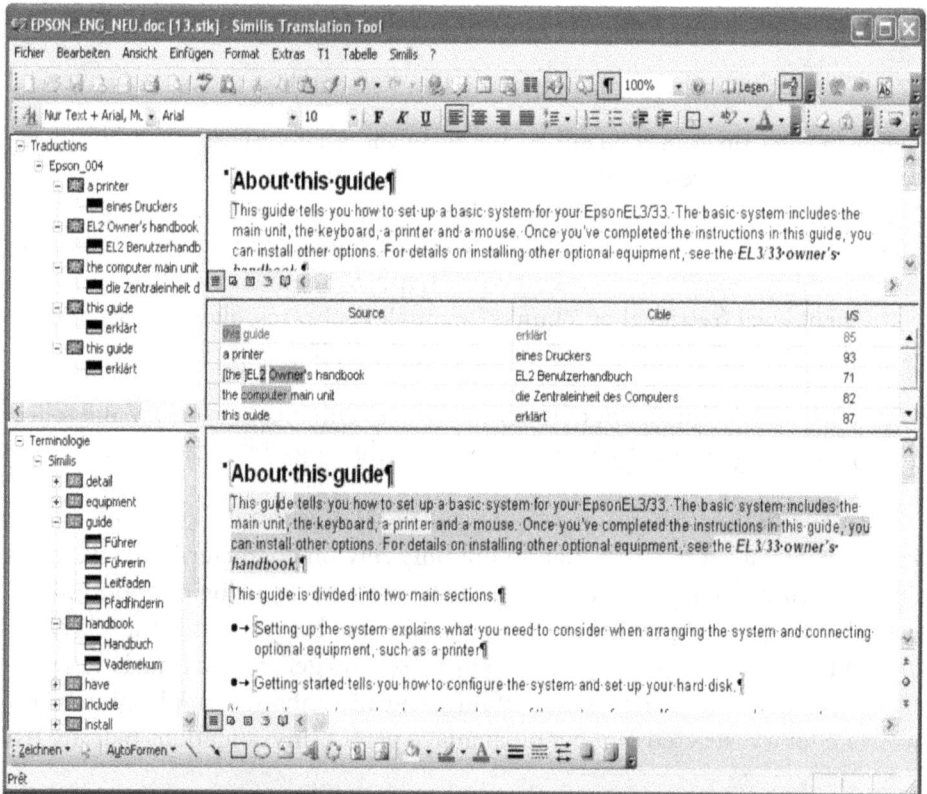

Figure 11: English-German example for subsegment retrieval in Similis

Alignment Edition - 12 - EPSON_ENG.doc

Ursegmente (136)	Stelle	Ergebnis	Stelle	Zielsegmente (138)
Then read the section called Getting started.	5(1)	65	5(1)	Lesen Sie danach das Kapitel mit der Überschrift Inbetriebnahme des Systems.
It contains details of how to turn on the computer and the procedure for installing DOS 3.3.	5(2)	100	5(2)	Es enthält Einzelheiten über das Einschalten des Computers und über das Vorgehen bei der Installation von DOS 3.3.
If you encounter words that are unfamiliar, you can find a glossary in EL2.Owner's Handbook.	6(1)	100	6(1)	Wenn Sie auf Ausdrücke stoßen, die Ihnen unbekannt sind, finden Sie ein Glossar im EL2 Benutzerhandbuch.
You can find a list of conventions used in this guide on the following page.	7(1)	75	7(1)	Eine Liste von in diesem Handbuch verwendeten Schreibweisen finden Sie auf der folgenden Seite.
Conventions used in this guide	8(1)	60	8(1)	In diesem Handbuch verwendete Schreibweisen
This table explains the symbols and typefaces	9(1)	99	9(1)	In dieser Tabelle werden die in diesem Handbuch

Urchunks	Stelle	Ergebnis	Stelle	Zielchunks
you encounter	2	75	2	Sie auf Ausdrücke
that are unfamiliar	4	75	6	unbekannt sind
you can find	6	75	8	finden Sie
a glossary	7	75	9	ein Glossar

Figure 12: Subsegment alignment in Similis

More recent research on enhancing retrieval in TM systems mainly seems to focus on improving the reusability of fuzzy matches by applying methods from SMT (Biçici & Dymetman 2008; Zhechev & van Genabith 2011; Koehn & Senellart 2010). The aim is to identify those fragments that make the difference between a segment to be translated and a fuzzy match retrieved from a TM database and adjust their translations automatically using SMT procedures. Ideally, for the human translator there would be no additional post-editing effort for these matches. However, one should have a careful "empirical look" at the question how this "fusion" of human translation and machine translation at segment level actually affects the post-editing of fuzzy matches and at what extent it really enhances the productivity of human translators as well as text quality.

3.2.2 Integrating robust linguistic procedures into existing commercial systems

Ways of integrating standard methods and procedures known from computational linguistics into commercial TM systems are currently analyzed at Cologne University of Applied Sciences in a research project supported by the German Federal Ministry of Education and Research (BMBF) (Azzano et al. 2011). The focus of the project lies on enhancing the performance of commercial TM systems with respect to the retrieval of paraphrase patterns and subsegment fragments as well as on improving term recognition and validation with the help of robust procedures for morphosyntactic and sentence syntactic analysis. The goal is to develop interface models and prototypical interfaces between commercial TM systems and "lingware" using SDL Trados Studio 2009 and the morphosyntactic analysis tool MPRO (Maas et al. 2009) as a prototypical environment and German and English as prototypical languages to gain experiences for the development of further language modules and for applying the results to other TM systems.

At first, relevant similarity patterns were identified and classified using authentic multilingual technical documentation (user manuals and operating instructions from various areas). For this purpose, TM databases were created and compared with "related" texts (updates, texts on closely related items of communication, texts belonging to related text types and dealing with the same topic of communication). Currently the master TM database contains 51.000 segments. Both the segments from the TM databases and the texts "related" to the TM material were morphosyntactically annotated with MPRO. To identify relevant similarity patterns the "related" texts were automatically matched with the TM databases using the pretranslate function. In many cases the resulting match values and the similarity judgments of human translators differed considerably. In a further step, the linguistic differences between the segments of the new, "related" texts and the matches from the TM were described and categorized in order to identify linguistic features that may help to enhance the retrieval performance of commercial TM systems.

To integrate morphosyntactical information into the commercial TM a standalone SQL database was developed. This "linguistic TM" is built from the morphosyntactically annotated segments of the commercial TM and – apart from the tokens of the text surface – mainly contains information obtained from lemmatization, compound analysis and word class recognition. The segments of the "linguistic TM" are linked to the "originals" in the commercial TM via unique IDs. To accelerate the retrieval of relevant TUs from the SQL database the data is stored in the form of suffix arrays (Aluru 2004).

When looking up TUs in the "linguistic TM" during the translation process each SLSeg first need to be morphosyntactically analyzed and annotated. The actual retrieval process then consists of two steps. First, the tokens found in the SLSeg to be translated are compared with the tokens in the SLSeg$_{TMling}$ to determine whether one or more SLSeg$_{TMling}$ completely or partially contain SLSeg. A second query searches the "linguistic TM" for all SLSeg$_{TMling}$ with morphosyntactic patterns similar to those of the SL_{Seg} to be translated. For all results of both queries the Longest Common Substrings (LCS) between SL_{Seg} and $SLSeg_{TMling}$ are calculated using Generalized Suffix Arrays (GSA) (Rieck et al. 2007). In order to rank the results a formula is developed that combines the matches obtained from the two queries taking into consideration the number and the length of LCS as well as their position in SL_{Seg} and $SLSeg_{TMling}$ (Hawkins & Giraud-Carrier 2009).

4 Conclusions and outlook

This paper has given an overview of the state of the art in TM technology, explaining the major concepts and looking at recent trends in both commercial systems and research. As TM and MT "have been developed very much in isolation" because "different communities played a role in each technology's development" (Koehn & Senellart 2010) and computational linguistics has long ignored the relevance of TM as a major language technology used in professional translation, there is still ample scope for further research as well as for closer collaboration between academia and the language translation industry.

An important field that could not be touched upon in this paper for reasons of space and time is empirical research on how TM and MT and the combination of both actually integrate into the translation workflow and how they influence the work of the translator. Paulsen Christensen & Schjoldager (2010: 99), identified three different areas of empirical TM research, namely "technology-oriented", "workflow-oriented" and "translation-theoretical", and conclude that

> Empirically documented knowledge about the nature and applications of TM systems and translators' interaction with them is both scarce and fragmented. In particular, more research is needed on how translators interact with TM technology and on how it influences translators' cognitive processes. The translation profession itself will also welcome more knowledge about the translators' perspective on TM technology. (Paulsen Christensen & Schjoldager 2010: 99)

Research into these areas has only just begun and it is to be hoped that in the near future more funding will be made available in this direction, because language technology for a multilingual society must, like any technology, serve the needs of its users.

References

ALPAC. 1966. *Language and machines. Computers in translation and linguistics. A report by the Automatic Language Processing Advisory Committee, Division of Behavioral Sciences, National Academy of Sciences, National Research Council.* ALPAC Automatic Language Processing Advisory Committee (ed.). Washington, D.C. Publication1416.

Aluru, Srinivas. 2004. Suffix trees and suffix arrays. In Dinesh P. Mehta & Sartaj Sahni (eds.), *Handbook of data structures and applications*, 29-1–29-21. Boca Rayton: Chapman & Hall/ CRC.

Arthern, Peter J. 1979. Machine translation and computerized terminology systems: A translator's viewpoint. In Barbara M. Snell (ed.), *Translating and the computer, proceedings of a seminar. London, 14th November, 1978*, 77–108. Amsterdam: North-Holland.

Azzano, Dino. 2011. *Placeable and localizable elements in translation memory systems.* Ludwig-Maximilians-Universität München dissertation.

Azzano, Dino, Uwe Reinke & Melanie Sauer. 2011. Ansätze zur Verbesserung der Retrieval-Leistung kommerzieller Translation-Memory-Systeme. In Hanna Hedeland, Thomas Schmidt & Kai Wörner (eds.), *Multilingual resources and multilingual applications. Proceedings of the Conference of the German Society for Computational Linguistics and Language Technology (GSCL) 2011*, 123–128. Hamburg: Universität Hamburg, Sonderforschungsbereich Mehrsprachigkeit.

Biçici, Ergun & Marc Dymetman. 2008. Dynamic Translation Memory: Using Statistical Machine Translation to improve Translation Memory Fuzzy Matches. In Alexander F. Gelbukh (ed.), *Computational Linguistics and Intelligent Text Processing: Lecture Notes in Computer Science 4919*, 454–465. Berlin, Heidelberg: Springer.

Bier, Kerstin. 2012. An MT journey: MT in use at Sybase, a SAP company. In *TAUS open source machine translation showcase. Paris, June 4, 2012.* http://www.slideshare.net/TAUS/4-june--taus-moses-open-source-mt-showcase-paris-kerstin-bier-sybase.

Brown, Peter F., John Cocke, Stephen A. Della Pietra, Vincent J. Della Pietra, Fredrick Jellinek, John D. Lafferty, Robert L. Mercer & Paul S. Roossin. 1988. A statistical approach to language translation. In *In Proceedings of the 12th International Conference on Computational Linguistics (COLING-88), Budapest, August 1988*, 71–76.

Carl, Michael & Andy Way (eds.). 2003. *Recent advances in Example-Based machine translation.* Dodrecht, Boston, London: Kluwer.

CERTT. 2012. Glossary of translation tool types. In *Collection of electronic resources in translation technologies*. Ottawa: University of Ottawa, School of Translation & Interpretation. http://aix1.uottawa.ca/~certt/Glossary%20of%20translation%20tool%20types_FINAL.pdf.

Chama, Ziad. 2010. Vom Segment zum Kontext. *technische kommunikation* 32(2). 21–25.

eCoLoRe. 2012. *Glossary of terms related to econtent localisation*. http://ecolore.leeds.ac.uk/xml/materials/overview/glossary.xml?lang=en.

GALA. 2012. *LISA OSCAR STANDARDS*. http://www.gala-global.org/lisa-oscar-standards.

Gotti, Fabrizio, Philippe Langlais, Elliott Macklovitch, Didier Bourigault, Benoit Robichaud & Claude Coulombe. 2005. 3GTM: A third-generation translation memory. In *Proceedings of the 3rd Computational Linguistics in the North-East (CLiNE) Workshop, Gatineau, Québec, August 2005*. http://www.iro.umontreal.ca/%7B~%7Dfelipe/Papers/paper-cline-3gtm-2005.pdf.

Goyvaerts, Jan & Stephen Levithan. 2009. *Regular expressionscookbook*. Sebastopol: O'Reilly.

Guerberof, Ana. 2009. Productivity and quality in MT post-editing. In *MT Summit XII – Workshop: Beyond Translation Memories: New Tools for Translators MT, August 29, 2009*. Ottawa, Ontario, Canada.

Hawkins, Brian E. & Christophe G. Giraud-Carrier. 2009. Ranking search results for translated content. In Kang Zhang & Reda Alhajj (eds.), *IRI '09 – Proceedings of the 10th IEEE international conference on Information Reuse Integration*, 242–245. Piscataway, NJ: IEEE Press.

Hodász, Gábor & Gábor Pohl. 2005. MetaMorpho TM: A linguistically enriched translation memory. In *International Workshop: Modern Approaches in Translation Technologies*, 26–30. Borovets, Bulgaria. http://www.mt-archive.info/RANLP-2005-Hodasz.pdf.

Hutchins, John W. 1998. The origins of the translator's workstation. *Machine Translation* 13(13). 287–307.

InteroperabilityNow! 2012. *The TMS Interoperability Protocol Package (TIPP). Version 1.4.1*. http://code.google.com/p/interoperability-now/downloads/detail?name=The_TMS_Interoperability_Protocol_Package-1.4.1.pdf&can=2&q=.

ISO. 2008. *ISO 30042:2008: Systems to manage terminology, knowledge and content – TermBase eXchange (TBX)*. Genf.

Koehn, Philipp. 2010. *Statistical machine translation*. Cambridge: Cambridge University Press.

Koehn, Philipp, Hieu Hoang, Alexandra Birch, Chris Callison-Burch, Marcello Federico, Nicola Bertoldi, Brooke Cowan, Wade Shen, Christine Moran, Richard Zens, Chris Dyer, Ondřej Bojar, Alexandra Constantin & Evan Herbst. 2007. Moses: Open source toolkit for statistical machine translation. In *ACL 2007, Proceedings of the Interactive Poster and Demonstration Sessions*, 177–180. Prague, Czech Republic.

Koehn, Phillip & Jean Senellart. 2010. Convergence of translation memory and statistical machine translation. In Ventsislav Zhechev (ed.), *Proceedings of the Second Joint EM+/CNGL Workshop Bringing MT to the User: Research on Integrating MT in the Translation Industry*, 21–31. http://www.mt-archive.info/JEC-2010-Koehn.pdf. Workshop at AMTA 2010: the Ninth conference of the Association for Machine Translation in the Americas, Denver, CO, 4 November 2010.

Kriele, Christian. 2006. *Vergleich der beiden Translation-Memory-Systeme TRADOS und SIMILIS*. Saarbrücken: Saarland University MA thesis.

Krollmann, Friedrich. 1971. Linguistic data banks and the technical translator. *Meta* 16(1-2). 117–124.

Lagoudaki, Elina. 2006. Translation Memories Survey 2006: Users' perceptions around TM use. Englisch. In. London: Imperial College.

Linport. 2012. http://www.linport.org/.

LISA. 2005. *Translation Memory eXchange (TMX), version 1.4b*. http://www.galaglobal.org/oscarStandards/tmx/tmx14b.html.

LISA. 2008. *Segmentation Rules eXchange (SRX), version 2.0*. http://www.gala-global.org/oscarStandards/srx/srx20.html.

Maas, Heinz-Dieter, Christoph Rösener & Axel Theofilidis. 2009. Morphosyntactic and semantic analysis of text: The MPRO tagging procedure. In Cerstin Mahlow & Michael Piotrowski (eds.), *State of the art in computational morphology: Workshop on Systems and Frameworks for Computational Morphology. SFCM 2009, Zurich, Switzerland, September 4, 2009, proceedings*, 76–87. New York: Springer.

Macken, Lieve. 2009. In search of the recurrent units of translation. In Walter Daelemans & Véronique Hoste (eds.), *Evaluation of translation technology*, 195–212. Brussels: Academic & Scientific Publishers.

Massion, François. 2005. *Translation Memory Systeme im Vergleich*. ger. Reutlingen: doculine Verl. OCLC: 181512570.

Mitkov, Ruslan & Gloria Corpas. 2008. Improving third generation translation memory systems through identification of rhetorical predicates. In *Proceedings of LangTech 2008, Rom, 28-29 Februar 2008.* http://langtech.fub.it/en/poster/ 07%5C_MITKOV.pdf.

Nagao, Makoto. 1984. A framework of a mechanical translation between Japanese and English by analogy principle. In Alick Elithorn & Ranan Banerji (eds.), *Artificial and human intelligence. Edited review papers presented at the International NATO Symposion on artificial and human intelligence, Lyon, 1981*, 173–180. Amsterdam, New York, Oxford: North Holland.

OASIS. 2006. *The DocBook document type.* Billerica, MA. http://www.oasis-open. org/docbook/specs/docbook-4.5-spec.html.

OASIS. 2007. *DITA Version 1.1. Architectural specification.* Billerica, MA. http:// www.oasisopen.org/committees/download.php/24944/dita1.1.zip.

OASIS. 2008. Billerica, MA. http://docs.oasis-open.org/xliff/xliff-core/xliff-core.html.

Offersgaard, Lene, Claus Povlsen, Lisbeth Almsten & Bente Maegaard. 2008. Domain specific MT in use. In John Hutchins & Walter Hahn von (eds.), *Proceedings of the Twelfth EAMT conference, 22-23 September 2008*, 148–157. Hamburg: HITEC e.V.

Paulsen Christensen, Tina & Anne Schjoldager. 2010. Translation-Memory (TM) research: What do We know and how do We know it? *Hermes – Journal of Language and Communication Studies* 44(44). 89–101.

Planas, Emmanuel. 2005. SIMILIS: Second-generation translation memory software. In *Translating and the computer 27: Proceedings of the Twenty-seventh International Conference on Translating and the Computer.* London: Aslib.

Reinke, Uwe. 2004. *Translation memories: Systeme Konzepte linguistische Optimierung.* Frankfurt am Main: Lang.

Reinke, Uwe. 2006. Translation memories. In Keith Brown (ed.), *Encyclopedia of language and linguistics*, 61–65. Oxford: Elsevier.

Rieck, Konrad, Pavel Laskov & Sören Sonnenburg. 2007. Computation of similarity measures for sequential data using generalized suffix trees. In Bernhard Schölkopf, John Platt & Thomas Hoffman (eds.), *Advances in neural information processing systems 19*, 1177–1184. Cambridge, MA: MIT Press.

Seal, Thomas. 1992. ALPNET and TSS: The commercial realities of using a computer-aided translation system. In *Translating and the computer 13. Proceedings from the Aslib conference 1991*, 120–125. London: Aslib.

Sikes, Richard. 2007. Fuzzy matching in theory and practice. *MultiLingual* 18(6). 39–43.

Somers, Harold L. 2001. Review article: Example-based machine translation. *Machine Translation* 14(14). 113–157.

Somers, Harold L. 2003. Translation memory systems. In Harold L. Somers (ed.), *Computers and translation: A translator's guide*, 31–47. Amsterdam & Philadelphia: John Benjamins. Amsterdam and Philadelphia.

Trujillo, Arturo. 1999. *Translation engines: Techniques for machine translation.* London: Springer.

w3c. 2008. *Extensible markup language (XML) 1.0 (fifth edition) w3c recommendation 26 november 2008. World Wide Web Consortium.* http://www.w3.org/TR/REC-xml/.

Zhechev, Ventsislav & Josef van Genabith. 2011. Languages of the World (Wide Web). In *Proceedings of the Ninth Conference of the Association for Machine Translation in the Americas.* http://googleresearch.blogspot.de/2011/07/languages-of-world-wide-web.html. Google Research Blog entry, July 2011.

Chapter 6

Authoring support for controlled language and machine translation: A report from practice

Melanie Siegel

Hochschule Darmstadt

Automatic authoring support for controlled language on the one hand and machine translation on the other have previously been seen as two distinct tools in the text processing process. This paper describes methods for the close integration of both, resulting in better written documents as well as machine translation output of higher quality. The methods were implemented in an existing tool for automatic authoring support.

1 Introduction

With the internationalization of the market for technology products and technologies, the demand for translation of technical documentation is increasing. Especially in the European Union there is a raising awareness that it is not sufficient to provide English language documentation, but that documentation needs to be translated into the native language of the users. These translations must be quickly available, upgradable, available in multiple languages simultaneously, and of high quality. At the same time there are significant technological advances in machine translation: there are rule-based and statistical systems, but also hybrid translation methods. More and more companies are supporting their translation efforts with machine translation. Nevertheless, there are several problems:

- Users are not familiar with the possibilities and limitations of machine translation. This is why their expectations are not met and they are left disappointed.

Melanie Siegel. Authoring support for controlled language and machine translation: A report from practice. In Georg Rehm, Felix Sasaki, Daniel Stein & Andreas Witt (eds.), *Language technologies for a multilingual Europe: TC3 III*, 85–102. Berlin: Language Science Press. DOI:10.5281/zenodo.1291932

- To evaluate and test the systems, inappropriate texts, such as prose, are used.

- Technical documentation that is translated using machine translation often lacks sufficient quality comparable to texts that are sent to human translators. However, human translators can compensate for this lack of quality in the source document while machine translation systems cannot.

- Statistical machine translation systems must be trained on parallel data. Often translation memory data files[1] are used for training. However, since this data is often accumulated over a number of years and has been originally translated by various different translators, it contains erroneous or inconsistent translations. The machine translation systems trained on this data reflect the heterogeneity of their training data which consequently leads to translations of bad quality.

Authoring support with language technology methods aims to support authors in the writing process. Tools based on methods from computational linguistics such as Acrolinx (www.acrolinx.com) are often used by authors of technical documentation. These tools provide support in checking spelling, grammar, and style, as well as in terminology extraction, terminology checking, and sentence clustering.[2] Users of authoring support software, on the other hand, make use of translation memory tools, such as TRADOS (www.trados.com). These tools provide access to previously translated sentences, based on fuzzy matching algorithms. Users of authoring support tools are currently starting to try out machine translation software. Often enough, they are not aware of the possibilities and restrictions of different machine translation methods and tools, which causes them to give up on these tools altogether. For the aforementioned reasons these tools remain distinct, although users already combine them in their daily work.

With the exception of some experiments such as Roturier (2006), authoring support and machine translation have generally been considered two distinct areas. We want to show that both of these areas can benefit from a combination of methods.

The first goal is to specify some of the possibilities and limitations of machine translation, to deduce options for the authoring of source language documents and to support these through automated processes.

---

[1] Translation memory data contains human-translated parallel sentences that professional translators store in a database in order to reuse the translations. For a more detailed description, see §3.3.

[2] For a detailed description, see §3.1.

The second goal is to reduce manual post-editing effort by enhancing the quality of the machine translation output, since experiments (such as Allen 2001 and Plitt & Masselot 2010) have shown that manual post-editing on high-quality machine translation output is much faster than the process being completed entirely by humans.

We combine methods from machine translation and authoring support and thus enhance the writing as well as the translation process. Methods and processes need to interfere, as authors and translators need to understand the other's way of structuring and processing work.

To this end we will give an overview of related work that our methods and ideas build upon. We will introduce relevant methods of authoring support, machine translation, and human translation. We will describe how methods from authoring support help users of machine translation to get better performance while explaining at the same time how methods from machine translation can be used in authoring support.

Experiments and evaluations on which this paper is based have mostly been conducted on German language examples. Rules and methods are implemented using the Acrolinx authoring support software and tested on Google Translate, Langenscheidt T1, and Systran machine translation systems.

2 Related work

Banerjee et al. (2012) investigate the effect of normalizing source language text, through for example, spell checking, in comparison to data supplementation. They conclude that "[f]or more noisy datasets [...] normalization does improve translation quality more effectively than data supplementation" (2012: 175).

Thurmair (2009) lists several pre-editing methods for statistical machine translation: compounding analysis, syntactic pre-processing (well-formed phrases are the only ones that are allowed in the phrase table) and reordering of source language words in a sentence. Our approach to pre-editing is similar to Thurmair's, but focuses on pre-editing rather than on pre-processing, and it tries to find a set of rules that are efficient for pre-editing.

In Siegel & Bredenkamp (2011) we have shown the impact of controlled language writing on the understandability and translatability of text, as was also done by Reuther (2003). This research focused on human understanding and translation. Inspired by these ideas, this paper takes a closer look at machine understanding and translation.

Genzel (2010) and others reorder the words in the source language sentence, so that it better fits the word order of the target language. They can show an improvement on the BLEU score of the translation. In contrast, we focus on pre-editing mechanisms that tend to have a positive effect on readability, correctness, and consistency of the source language text, as well as on machine translation.

Hutchins (2005) gives examples for controlled English rules that might affect machine translation quality. He does not refer to automatic checking of these rules.

Thicke (2011) describes the effect of using rules described in the Global English Style Guide (Kohl 2008) for pre-editing and terminology adaptations in the machine translation system: "untrained MT is two times faster to post-edit than to translate from scratch; trained MT is three times faster; and trained MT with source control is four times faster." We follow a similar approach to pre-editing, but also include rules that are specific for machine translation, while the Global English Style Guide was assumed for human translation and non-native English.

Various studies, including O'Brien & Roturier (2007) and Aikawa et al. (2007) have shown that pre-editing of the source language text could lead to machine translation quality improvements (in terms of either comprehensibility or post-editing efficiencies). These studies already take automatic rules into account.

Plitt & Masselot (2010) evaluate the productivity of using statistical machine translation and post-editing in comparison to human translation. They found that "the post-editing of statistical machine translation [...] allows translators to substantially increase their productivity" (2010: 15). Even more surprising was the result of the quality check: "To our surprise, translation jobs contained a higher number of mistakes than post-editing jobs" (2010: 14). The use of machine translation therefore did not only lead to productivity increase, but also to better translation quality. We go one step further and try to support productivity and translation quality with automatic authoring support in the post-editing process.

Simard et al. (2007) describe an automatic post-editing method in which a rule-based machine translation system is enhanced with statistical post-editing. This method copes with translation errors concerning terminology. This approach is similar to our idea to use statistical machine translation methods for multilingual terminology extraction and to use the results for terminology checking on the machine translation output in the post-editing phase. However, we propose to leave the post-editing process in the hands of human experts while supporting them with necessary information from the authoring support tool.

3 Basic methods in authoring support, machine translation, and human translation

In this section, we describe the methods in authoring support, machine translation, and human translation that are relevant to our approach. Experiments, implementations, and evaluations are based on these methods.

3.1 Methods in authoring support

Examples for linguistically-based authoring support are Acrolinx (www.acrolinx. com) and LanguageTool (www.languagetool.org). These systems first analyse the input using language technology methods, such as tokenization, morphology analysis, and part-of-speech tagging. This linguistic annotation of language data is the basis for further processing steps. We implemented the ideas described in this paper as part of the Acrolinx software and were thus able to build on existing language technology in this tool.

SPELL CHECKING AND GRAMMAR CHECKING can be based on morphology information and rules that detect spelling and grammar errors. Thus, rules that require context information can be implemented, such as in Example 3.1:

(1)   a.   "Meine Muttersprache ist Englisch."
           "My native language is English."

      b.   "Das Auto ist englisch."
           "This car is English."

The words "Englisch" and "englisch" are written with a capital or a lowercase letter, depending on the context they are used in, and on their syntactic category (POS): it is a noun in the first case and an adjective in the second.

Using the same mechanisms, STYLE RULES are defined. Style rules mark language constructions that are not wrong as such, but difficult to understand or not exactly adequate for the respective text type. For example, passive constructions can be hard to understand and should not be used in technical documentation. Kohl (2008) describes style rules for Global English and their implementation in authoring support software.

Closely connected to spell checking is TERMINOLOGY CHECKING. Again, while spell checking marks errors, terminology checking marks words that are not adequate for the text in the domain. The users (who generally work in a group of authors) define a list of terms in a term bank, which are important for the domain and the texts. They also define a list of words that should not be used in that domain. Connecting this user-given information to the general language analysis means that inflectional variants of these terms can be found and marked, such as plural forms. A term variant detection algorithm makes sure that further variants (such as writing a compound with and without a hyphen) are marked as deprecated. In order to set up such a term bank, the user is supported by terminology extraction methods. The aim of terminology extraction is to automatically detect domain terminology in a given corpus. Terminology extraction is carried out using rules that build upon POS information and lemmatization that makes use of morphology information.

The last relevant method is SENTENCE CLUSTERING. The authoring support is able to analyze a large amount of text data and find formulation variants, such as "Stellen Sie die Maschine jetzt an" and "Stellen Sie jetzt die Maschine an" ('turn on the machine'). Here, the word order is distinct but there is no difference in meaning. The user gets the suggestion to always pick one of these variants in order to make the documents more consistent and therefore better translatable.

3.2 Methods in machine translation

First we look at two basically distinct approaches to machine translation: the statistical approach and the knowledge-based (or rule-based) approach. There are also quite a few attempts to combine the ideas of both, as in Eisele (2009) and in Thurmair (2009), but a clear distinction at this point makes it easier to evaluate the influence authoring support has on each of the two methods. Some of the processes we propose can contribute to a hybrid machine translation system.

The KNOWLEDGE-BASED APPROACH to machine translation makes use of linguistic information and dictionaries to define translation rules based on this information. Examples for such systems are Lucy (www.lucysoftware.com), Langenscheidt T1 (www.langenscheidt.de), and SYSTRAN (www.systransoft.com). We expect an effect on the machine translation output when source language texts are more correct and therefore easier to analyze with language rules.

The STATISTICAL APPROACH to machine translation analyzes large amounts of parallel data, sets up phrase tables in the source and in the target language and combines the phrases in the translation task. This kind of parallel data is, for example, available in translation memories. Examples for this approach are Google Translate (translate.google.de) and Moses (Koehn et al. 2007). We expect an effect on the machine translation output when source texts are standardized, giving less variation in formulations of text and training data.

3.3 Methods in human translation

Most technical translations are carried out with the help of translation memories. TRANSLATION MEMORIES are databases of sentences that have been professionally translated in previous work. While translating, the translator uses the translation memory database that tries to find sentences similar to the one he or she is about to translate. If a similar sentence is found in the database, it can be re-used in the new translation. Somers & Diaz (2004) show that the technology of translation memories is similar to example-based translation – a method that is essential for statistical machine translation which is in widespread use today. This is why it can be said that many translators already use machine translation technology today when using translation memories without realizing that they do.

The databases that gradually develop from the work of translators are a valuable data source for statistical machine translation. They provide parallel sentences, translated by professional translators.

4 Authoring support for better machine translation results

The language analysis technologies of intelligent authoring support tools provide a basis for improving machine translation: automatic authoring support takes over the tasks of tokenization, POS-tagging, morphology analysis, decomposition, and shallow grammar analysis.

Authoring support provides rules concerning monolingual texts. In the process of translation these rules can be applied to the source language text (pre-editing) and to the target language text (post-editing). Further, authoring support rules and methods can help in the evaluation of machine translation results.

4.1 Pre-editing: Optimization of source language documents

Often enough, users test machine translation engines using texts that are not suited for that task. Sometimes they run tests with prose texts, such as excerpts from historical literature. Prose typically contains a lot of metaphorical language that is difficult to translate even for human translators. Sometimes they process texts of low quality, full of errors.

Using authoring support in the pre-editing process means to correct spelling and grammar errors in the source document. This example of a translation (of an instructive text) using Langenscheidt T1 demonstrates the effect on data cleaning, as in Example 4.1:

Melanie Siegel

(2) a. "Achten Sie darauf das der LNB fest am Arm des Spiegels montiert ist."
"You pay attention to that that the LNB firmly at the arm of the mirror is mounted."

   b. "Achten Sie darauf, dass der LNB fest am Arm des Spiegels montiert ist."
"Pay attention to the LNB being firmly mounted at the arm of the mirror."

Consistent and precise terminology helps the machine translation process. If a terminology database is available, checking for terminological consistency supports the machine translation process. For example, in our experiments, the imprecise term "Kerzenschlüssel" was translated to "candle key" while the precise term "Zündkerzenschlüssel" was correctly translated to "sparking-plug wrench". Authoring support provides not only methods for terminology checking, but also methods for terminology extraction in order to set up a terminology database, as described in Section 3.1. Terminology extraction rules in software like Acrolinx are based on linguistic information and run on data in the relevant domain. Thus, the extracted terms are more useful than, for example, a general domain-independent ontology.

Authoring support also contains style rules. These are defined along the lines of consistency, clarity, understandability, and translatability of text. Many of these rules are also useful for machine translation pre-editing. Here is an example of a complex sentence structure where the general authoring rule for reformulation is also helpful for machine translation, as in Example 4.1:

(3) a. "Eine zu lose Zündkerze hat Wärmestau und schlechte Abdichtung zur Folge, ein zu kräftiges Anziehen hingegen kann das Kerzengewinde und sogar den Zylinderkopf beschädigen."
"A too loose spark plug has been able to damage accumulation of heat and bad seal for the consequence a too strong pickup on the other hand the candle thread and even the cylinder head."

   b. "Eine zu lockere Zündkerze führt zu Wärmestau und schlechter Abdichtung. Eine zu fest angezogene Zündkerze kann das Gewinde und den Zylinderkopf beschädigen."
"A too loose spark plug leads to accumulation of heat and bad seal. A too firmly absorbed spark plug can damage the thread and the cylinder head."

Another area of authoring support that can be of help in machine translation is sentence normalization. Given a large amount of text data in the domain, sentence clustering can find similar sentences and help standardize them. Example 4.1 shows an English sentence cluster found in technical documentation:

(4) a. For more information, consult our web page.
     b. For more information, consult the web page.
     c. Go to our web page to find more info.

Authoring support can make sure that in contexts like this only one specific variant is used. If the variant selection is trained on machine translation training data, it can be ensured that in case of variants in the source language text these are changed to 100% matches in the machine translation training data.

These methods of pre-editing can, on the one hand, be applied by authors, as is usually done in the technical documentation authoring process. Errors are marked so that the author can come up with reformulations. Further, the author gets a better understanding of the abilities and limits of machine translation as such.

On the other hand, it is possible to automatically apply many of these reformulations. In contrast to authoring support of technical documents, the main focus here is on better machine translation results. Automatic application of rules is much faster. It can be the case, however, that the writing style used in the source language text will deteriorate when automatically applying rules without any human intervention whatsoever.

4.2 Post-editing: Optimization of machine translation output

The authoring support tool works on and processes monolingual text. Therefore, using the same mechanisms as in pre-editing, we can correct spelling, grammar and style errors on the target language text. In order to collect errors to correct in automatic post-editing, we conducted experiments with professional translators performing post-editing on machine translation output. On top of spelling and grammar corrections, we identified rules for automatic post-editing of German machine translation output on this basis. Here are examples of these rules:

- correct terminology

- correct standard expressions

- correct word order

- convert future tense to present tense

- convert indicative to causative

- convert "man" to passive

- convert series of "von"+ noun

Terminology correction is a major part of the corrected errors and thus requires a specific focus. Allen (2001) shows tools that support humans in manually adding unknown words to a dictionary and in domain-adaptation by manually selecting the best translations of words in a certain domain. We propose to do multilingual term extraction (a method that is part of authoring support), and make use of term bank organization (with domains and linked terms) for the organization of the domain-dependent selection of translations. The terminology can be adapted to the domain by extraction methods working on the training data; a term bank is set up with information about the domain and used for terminology checking on the source and target language texts.

4.3 Evaluation of machine translation

The authoring tool can also be used to evaluate machine translation results. Already in the project Verbmobil (Wahlster 2000) the idea came up to run different machine translation machines in parallel and to choose the best result. What result can be seen as best is dependent on the translation task. In the Verbmobil environment, picking the best result was often enough guided by time restriction because this was a spoken dialogue translation situation, where processing time is crucial. In translating technical documentation, a few seconds more or less are not that important. More important, however, is the actual quality of the machine translation result. The quality can be determined using authoring support along the areas of spelling, grammar, style, and terminology checking of the target language text. Checking results are combined in an evaluation value that can directly be used to choose the best translation.

5 Machine translation methods for better authoring support

The benefit of combining authoring support and machine translation is bidirectional because authoring support can also benefit from methods developed for machine translation. The first connection is very basic: some of the rules developed in authoring support for machine translation pre-editing can also be used in authoring support of technical documentation writing. Technical documentation often enough has to be translated to other languages. If the source language document is organized such that it is easier to translate for machine translation systems, it is also easier to translate (and to understand) for humans. Consider the rules concerning reduction of ambiguity, for example. One of these rules requires avoiding anaphoric pronouns. MT translates single sentences and is mostly unable to take care of anaphora resolution. Human translators use translation memories that also consist of single sentences. Therefore, this rule is useful for both.

Another area is the set-up of a term bank for terminology checking. Using paradigms from statistical machine translation, we extract phrase tables from multilingual data. These phrase tables create a foundation to linking both terms between languages, and terms within a particular language. The result is that we have within each language synonyms of the extracted terms because these terms were translated in the same way. For example, in German – English parallel data we found this cluster of words for English because all of these were translated to the German word "Grundstellung": starting position, basic position, home position, basic setting, initial position, starting pos., normal position. This word cluster actually builds a synonym cluster. These synonyms can be imported into the term bank and then linked. This information can be used in terminology checking, but also in sentence clustering as a similarity measure.

Finally, the multilingual term extraction results (with statistical machine translation methods) can again be used for rule-based machine translation to enhance the domain-specific dictionaries and for statistical machine translation to make the training data more consistent.

6 Experiments and evaluations

6.1 First experiment: Evaluate what type of authoring support is useful for MT

The goal of the first set of experiments we conducted was to find out how to set up the authoring support system in order to get the best results on machine translation output. We started with only three documents and one rule-based machine translation system, Langenscheidt T1. We applied several existing rules of authoring support and inspected the machine translation behavior. Here spelling and grammar correction on the source text turned out to be an important factor. Further, we found out that rules concerning lexical items, such as the avoidance of ambiguous words, have an important impact on the quality of machine translation.

Table 1: Application of rules and the effect on Google Translate and SYSTRAN for German–English and German–Italian translation. Adapted from Klausner (2011: 43).

	Google Translate		SYSTRAN	
	English	Italian	English	Italian
Avoiding *man*	3	3	nn	nn
Separation of verb components	2	2	2	1
Fillers	1	1	3	3
Prepositions	1	1	nn	nn
Word order	3	3	nn	nn
can	3	3	nn	nn
Simple list	nn	nn	nn	nn
Enumerations	3	2	2	2
One relative clause	3	3	3	3
Two relative clauses	3	3	2	2
Passive	3	3	3	2
Conditional clauses	2	2	2	2
Prepositional phrases	2	1	2	1
Questions	2	1	1	1
Swapping subject-object arguments	nn	nn	3	3

3: strong improvement, 2: slight improvement, 1: no improvement, nn: improvement not necessary

6.2 Second experiment: Different MT systems and target languages

The next step was to take into account a statistical machine translation system (Google Translate) and a rule-based system (SYSTRAN) in order to find out if pre-editing rules have more influence on one or the other. Furthermore, we compared the translations German – English and German – Italian in order to investigate whether source language correction methods should be dependent on the target language. For the results of this experiment, see Table 1. We identified style rules that have a similar effect on both machine translation systems. These include, for example, 'do not place two parts of a verb too far away from each other in the sentence' ("separation of verb components"), or rules that have a bigger impact on the statistical system, such as 'avoid the impersonal pronoun *man*' as well as rules that have an influence on the rule-based-system, such as 'use standard word order'. Simple lists can be handled by both machines and both target languages and need not to be converted, while enumerations seem to be a problem in MT.

In this experiment,[3] we could not find any differences in the influence of authoring support rules on machine translation results that can be explained by the structure of English or Italian as a target language. However, the results of the experiment could be used to produce a linguistic resource for authoring support checking, i.e., the 52 style rules used in the following experiments.

Table 2: Classification of errors in MT output of original text compared to text, where pre-editing rules are applied

	Evaluation (original text)	Evaluation I (pre-edited)	Evaluation II (pre-edited)	Evaluation III (pre-edited)	Average evaluations (pre-edited)
content words wrong	42	81	77	37	65
incorrect punctuation	11	4	8	4	5.33
incorrect word forms	17	27	7	3	12.33
incorrect word order	32	50	30	42	40.67
missing content words	16	1	17	3	7
other error	27[a]	15	27	19	20.33[b]
wrong functional words	26	34	40	21	31.67
TOTAL	171	212	206	129	182.33

[a]15.79%
[b]11.15%

6.3 Third experiment: Evaluate the effect of implemented rules on MT results

The aim of the next round of experiments was to evaluate the effect of these rules on machine translation results. To this end, a German text from the Open Office documentation (http://opus.lingfil.uu.se/OpenOffice3.php) was corrected along the lines of the authoring support checking results. Original and corrected

---

[3]The experiment was supported by Katharina Klausner. For further information see Klausner (2011).

text (about 100 sentences each) were translated using Lucy (rule-based), Moses, and Google Translate (both statistically-based) and their results were classified by translators according to the identified translation errors.

The error classification (see Table 2) showed that the translation of the pre-processed text contained more errors that could be classified by professional technical translators. The category "other error" contained 15.79% for the machine translation without pre-editing and only 11.15% for the machine translation with pre-editing.[4] It could also be shown that the results contained fewer grammar errors (punctuation, word forms) if pre-editing was performed with the authoring support rules.

Table 3 shows that there were no machine translation results categorized as correct translations for the non-pre-edited texts, while with pre-edited machine translation, 20% of the translations were correct.

Table 3: Comparison of sentences classified as correct translations, original and pre-edited sentences

	Evaluation (original text)	Evaluation I (pre-edited)	Evaluation II (pre-edited)	Evaluation III (pre-edited)	Average evaluations (pre-edited)
1.1. Lucy	0	1%	5%	10%	5.33%
1.2. Moses	0	1%	3%	9%	4.33%
Google Translate	0	4%	7%	7%	6%
TOTAL	0	7%	20%	33%	20%

6.4 Fourth experiment: Human post-editing of MT results

In another task (see Table 4), translators were asked to post-edit machine translation results. We calculated the total word-level Levenshtein distances between machine translation output and post-edited machine translation output. Pre-editing using authoring support before machine translation processing lead to the reduction of distance (15.82%) which indicates that post-editing is much less effort when pre-editing was involved as well.

---

[4]Other errors could be very different, such as untranslated words as in "By clicking of this symbol you add a hyperlink of the current URL to your document ein." or translation close to the (German) source text, such as "Did you split the page into columns or the cursor is in a multi-column text frame, ...".

Table 4: Total word-level Levenshtein distances between machine translation output and post-edited machine translation output

(Original)	2225
I (pre-edited)	2113
II (pre-edited)	1924
III (pre-edited)	1582
average pre-edited	1873

6.5 Fifth experiment: Automatic evaluation of rule impact

In Roturier et al. (2012), we introduced a framework to analyze the impact of source re-formulations on machine translation quality using automatic metrics (see Figure 1). This approach will enable us to automatically evaluate the effect of pre-editing rules on machine translation quality and therefore to get evaluations on more data. First results show that grammar reformulations (leading to correct grammar) seem to have a large influence on translation quality.

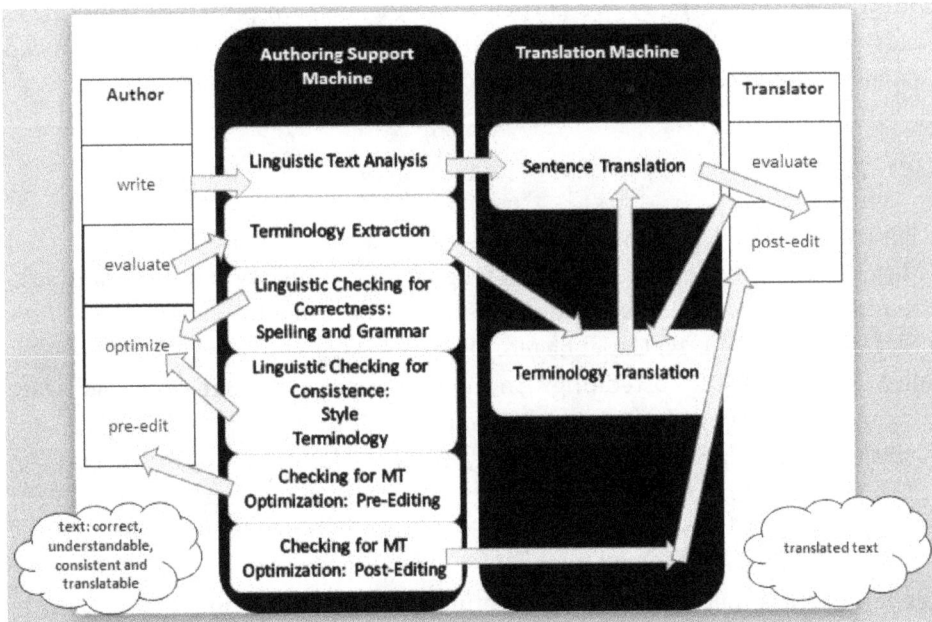

Figure 1: Workflow and Interdependencies in a Combined System

7 Summary

We have shown that methods from automatic authoring support and machine translation can be applied to both tasks. Thus, authoring support and machine translation should be integrated modules in the text production and translation process. Automatic authoring support is monolingual; checking rules can only be applied to either the source language text or the target language text, without taking the translation into account. Therefore, multilingual terminology extraction on SMT training data is a first step towards multilingual checking.

In order to further expand the integration, it is necessary to involve more languages in the evaluation tasks. We plan to include Chinese in our inspections. As for the process itself, we will automate the pre- and post-editing process as much as possible and evaluate whether the machine translation results can be optimized with minimal or without any human intervention.

Acknowledgments

Most of the work described in this article was carried out when I was part of the company Acrolinx GmbH. We participated in a research project called taraXÜ, financed by TSB Technologiestiftung Berlin – Zukunftsfonds Berlin, co-financed by the European Union – European fund for regional development.

References

Aikawa, Takako, Lee Schwartz, Ronit King, Mo Corston-Oliver & Carmen Lozano. 2007. Impact of controlled language on translation quality and post-editing in a statistical machine translation environment. In *Proceedings of the MT Summit XI*, 10–14. Copenhagen, Denmark.

Allen, James F. 2001. Postediting: An integrated part of a translation software program. *Language International* 13(April 2001). 26–29.

Banerjee, Pratyush, Sudip Kumar Naskar, Johann Roturier, Andy Way & Josef van Genabith. 2012. Domain adaptation in SMT of user-generated forum content guided by OOV Word Reduction: Normalization and/or supplementary data? In *Proceedings of EAMT 2012*.

Eisele, Andreas. 2009. Hybrid architectures for better machine translation. In *GSCL Workshop "Kosten und Nutzen von MT", September 2009*. Potsdam.

Genzel, Dmitriy. 2010. Automatically learning source-side reordering rules for large scale machine translation. In *Proceedings of the 23rd International Conference on Computational Linguistics (COLING '10)*, 376–384. Stroudsburg, PA: Association for Computational Linguistics.

Hutchins, John W. 2005. Current commercial machine translation systems and computer-based translation tools: System types and their uses. *International Journal of Translation* 17(1-2). 5–38.

Klausner, Katharina. 2011. *Einsatzmöglichkeiten kontrollierter Sprache zur Verbesserung Maschineller Übersetzung*. Bachelorarbeit, Januar 2011.

Koehn, Philipp, Hieu Hoang, Alexandra Birch, Chris Callison-Burch, Marcello Federico, Nicola Bertoldi, Brooke Cowan, Wade Shen, Christine Moran, Richard Zens, Chris Dyer, Ondřej Bojar, Alexandra Constantin & Evan Herbst. 2007. Moses: Open source toolkit for statistical machine translation. In *ACL 2007, Proceedings of the Interactive Poster and Demonstration Sessions*, 177–180. Prague, Czech Republic.

Kohl, John R. 2008. *The global English style guide: Writing clear, translatable documentation for a global market*. Cary, N.C.: SAS Institute.

O'Brien, Sharon & Johann Roturier. 2007. How portable are controlled language rules? A comparison of two empirical MT studies. In *Proceedings of MT Summit XI*, 345–352.

Plitt, Mirko & François Masselot. 2010. A productivity test of statistical machine translation. Post-Editing in a typical localisation context. *The Prague Bulletin of Mathematical Linguistics* 93(93). 7–16.

Reuther, Ursula. 2003. Two in one – can it work? Readability and translatability by means of controlled language. In *Proceedings of EAMT-CLAW*.

Roturier, Johann. 2006. *An investigation into the impact of controlled English rules on the comprehensibility, usefulness and acceptability of machine-translated technical documentation for French and German users*. Dublin City University dissertation. Unpublished PhD dissertation.

Roturier, Johann, Linda Mitchell, Robert Grabowski & Melanie Siegel. 2012. Using automatic machine translation metrics to analyze the impact of source reformulations. In *Proceedings of AMTA 2012*.

Siegel, Melanie & Andrew Bredenkamp. 2011. Localization and writing for the international market. In *TC World, March 2011*.

Simard, Michel, Nicola Ueffing, Pierre Isabelle & Roland Kuhn. 2007. Rule-based translation with statistical phrase-based post-editing. In *ACL 2007 Second Workshop on Statistical Machine Translation*. Prague.

Somers, Harold & Gabriela Fernandez Diaz. 2004. Translation memory vs. example-based MT: What is the difference. *International Journal of Translation* 16(2). 5–33.

Thicke, Lori. 2011. Improving MT results: A study. *Multilingual* 22(1). 37–40.

Thurmair, Gregor. 2009. Comparing different architectures of hybrid machine translation systems. In *MT Summit XII: Proceedings of the twelfth Machine Translation Summit*, 340–347. Ottawa, Ontario, Canada. August 26-30, 2009.

Wahlster, Wolfgang. 2000. *Verbmobil: Foundations of speech-to-speech translation.* Berlin: Springer Verlag.

Chapter 7

Integration of machine translation in on-line multilingual applications: Domain adaptation

Mirela-Ştefania Duma

Cristina Vertan
University of Hamburg, Germany

Large amounts of bilingual corpora are used in the training process of statistical machine translation systems. Usually a general domain is used as the training corpus. When the system is tested using data from the same domain, the obtained results are satisfactory, but if the test set belongs to a different domain, the translation quality decreases. This is due to insufficient lexical coverage, wrong choice in case of polysemous words, and differences in discourse style between the two domains. Thus, the need to adapt the system is an ongoing research task in machine translation. Some challenges in performing domain adaptation are to decide which part of the system requires adaptation and to choose what method needs to be applied. In this paper, we used language model interpolation as a domain adaptation method and proved that it is a fast state of the art method that can be used in building adapted translation systems even when sparse domain specific material is available (i.e. especially in the case of low-resourced language pairs). The best improvement was of 15 BLEU points over the baseline system.

1 Introduction

As a response to the increased need of managing data available on-line, traditional content management systems extended their functionality by offering a web front-end facility, and more recently by including cloud services. In this article we will refer to this type of system as Web Content Management System (WCMS).

Mirela-Ştefania Duma & Cristina Vertan. Integration of machine translation in on-line multilingual applications: Domain adaptation. In Georg Rehm, Felix Sasaki, Daniel Stein & Andreas Witt (eds.), *Language technologies for a multilingual Europe: TC3 III*, 103–121. Berlin: Language Science Press. DOI:10.5281/zenodo.1291936

Existent WCMSs focus on storage of documents in databases and provide mostly full-text search functionality. These types of systems have limited applicability, due to two reasons:

- data available online is often multilingual and

- documents within a CMS are semantically related (share some common knowledge, or belong to similar topics).

In short, in production environments, currently available CMSs do not exploit modern techniques from information technology like text mining, the semantic web or machine translation. Current initiatives, such as the "Multilingual Web-LT" (http://www.multilingualweb.eu/), are now developing standards and best practices for dealing with multilingual content on the Web, but this has not yet been systematically applied to CMSs.

The ICT PSP EU project ATLAS – Applied Technology for Language-Aided CMS (http://www.atlasproject.eu) – aims to fill this gap by providing three innovative Web services within a WCMS. These three Web services, i-Librarian, EUDocLib and i-Publisher, are not only thematically differentiated, but also offer different levels of intelligent information processing.

The ATLAS WCMS makes use of state-of-the-art text-technological methods in order to extract information and cluster documents according to a given hierarchy. A text summarization module and a machine translation engine as well as a cross-lingual semantic search engine are embedded.

Currently the system is able to handle six languages (Bulgarian, English, German, Greek, Polish and Romanian) from four language families. However, the chosen framework allows other languages to be added at a later point.

The focus of this paper is on the machine translation engine within the ATLAS project and on performing domain adaptation which gives significant improvements over the baseline system when evaluated. It should also be stated that the aim of the ATLAS project is to adapt state-of-the-art methods in language technology with the purpose of being integrated into a content management system, thus the project is not only a research project, but also a product-oriented one. Our attention focused on selecting the most adequate state-of-the-art method in domain adaptation for machine translation.

In natural language processing, the notion of "domain" could refer to the genre, the text type or the style of a document (Lee 2001). In this paper, we use the definition from Plank (2011: Chapter 3) where a domain is defined by a corpus. The problem of domain adaptation could be formulated as follows: given a large amount of bilingual source data (training data) and a small amount of target data, the purpose of the domain adaptation task is to build a system that has a good performance when evaluated on test sets that belong to the target domain. We use the terms source domain and out-of-domain interchangeably. Also, the terms target domain and in-domain are used interchangeably.

The remainder of this paper is organized as follows. In Section 2, the ATLAS Content Management System is described with details on the integration of machine translation into the ATLAS system. Section 3 presents the state of the art in domain adaptation for statistical machine translation (SMT) with insight on the limitations of the current methods. The next section introduces the baseline translation system we used and the resources needed in order to build it. The experiments we performed in domain adaptation are presented in Section 5. We conducted two types of experiments: firstly, we identified a state of the art domain adaptation method that is easy to use and gives significant improvements over the baseline. Then, after deciding on the method, we performed various experiments on different domains from the ATLAS project and on different language pairs. The results are also presented in this section. The conclusions are presented in the last section.

2 The ATLAS content management system

The core online service of the ATLAS platform is i-Publisher, a powerful web-based instrument for creating, running and managing content-driven Web sites. It integrates language-based technologies to improve content navigation, e.g. interlinking documents based on extracted phrases, words and names, providing short summaries and suggesting categorization concepts. Currently two different thematic content-driven websites, i-Librarian and EUDocLib, are being built on top of the ATLAS platform, using i-Publisher as the content management layer. i-Librarian is intended to be a user-oriented website which allows visitors to maintain a personal workspace for storing, sharing and publishing various types of documents and to have them automatically categorized into appropriate subject categories, summarized and annotated with important words, phrases and names. EUDocLib is planned as a publicly accessible repository of EU legal documents from the EUR-LEX collection with enhanced navigation and multilingual access.

The i-Publisher service:

- is mainly targeted at small enterprises and non-profit organizations,

- gives the ability to use a point-and-click interface to build content-driven websites which provide a wide set of pre-defined functionalities and whose textual content is automatically processed, i.e. categorized, summarized, annotated, etc.,

- enables publishers, information designers and graphic designers to easily collaborate,

- aims at saving authors, editors and other contributors valuable time by automatically processing textual data and allowing them to work together to produce high quality content. The last evaluation round of the service indicates that users indeed see the benefit of LT-Technologies embedded into the system.

The i-Librarian service:

- addresses the needs of authors, students, young researchers and readers,

- gives the ability to easily create, organize and publish various types of documents,

- allows users to find similar documents in different languages, to share their own work with other people, and to locate the most relevant texts from large collections of unfamiliar documents.

The EUDocLib service is a particular refinement of i-Librarian targeted at the management of documents from the European Commission.

The services described above are supported through intelligent language technology components like automatic classification, named entity recognition and information extraction, automatic text summarization, machine translation and cross-lingual information retrieval. These components are integrated into the system in a brick-like architecture, which means that each component is building on top of the preceding one. The baseline brick is the language processing pipeline component which ensures homogeneous linguistic processing of all documents independent of their language (Belogay et al. 2011). A processing pipeline for a given language includes a number of existing tools, adjusted and/or fine-tuned to ensure their interoperability. In most respects, a language processing pipeline does not require development of new software modules, but rather a combination of existing tools. The core ATLAS software package is distributed under the GPL license. LT-plug-ins like the language processing chains or the MT-engine follow a commercial licensing. iLibrarian is available as a web service and it has unrestricted access.

2.1 Machine translation in the ATLAS system

Machine Translation is a key component of the ATLAS system. The development of the engine is particularly challenging as the translation should be applicable to different domains. Additionally, the considered language pairs belong to the low resourced group,[1] for which bilingual training and test material is available in limited amount.

The machine translation engine is integrated in two distinct ways into the ATLAS platform:

- for the i-Publisher Service (a generic platform for generating websites), the MT serves as a translation aid tool for publishing multilingual content. Text is submitted to the translation engine and the result is subject to human post-processing

- for i-Librarian and EUDocLib (dedicated Web services for collecting documents), the MT-engine provides a translation for evaluation, which means that the user retrieving documents in different languages will use the engine in order to get a clue about the documents, and decide if he will store them. If the translation is considered acceptable it will be stored in the database

The integration of a machine translation engine into a web-based content management system in general, and into the ATLAS system in particular, presents several challenges from the user's point of view, among which we mention two challenges that were dealt with within the ATLAS system:

1. The user may retrieve documents from different domains. Domain adaptation is a major issue in machine translation, and in particular in corpus-based methods. Poor lexical coverage and false disambiguation are the main issues when translating documents out of the training domain;

2. The user may retrieve documents from various time periods. As language changes over time, language technology tools developed for modern languages do not work equally well on diachronic documents.

With the currently available technology, it is not possible to provide a translation system which is domain and language variation independent and works for multiple heterogeneous language pairs. Therefore, our approach envisages a

---

[1]See http://www.meta-net.eu/whitepapers.

system of user guidance, so that the availability and the foreseen system performance are transparent at any time.

For the MT-engine of the ATLAS system we decided on a hybrid architecture
combining Example-Based Machine Translation (EBMT) (Gavrila 2011) and statistical machine translation (SMT) (Koehn et al. 2007) at the phrase-based level (no
syntactic trees will be used). An original approach of our system is the interaction of the MT-engine with other modules of the system:

- The document categorization module assigns to each document one or
  more domains. For each domain the system administrator has the possibility to store information regarding the availability of a corresponding
  specific training corpus. If no specific trained model for the respective domain exists, the user is provided with a warning that the translation may
  be inadequate with respect to the lexical coverage.

- The output of the summarization module is processed in such a way that
  ellipses and anaphoras are omitted, and lexical material is adapted to the
  training corpus.

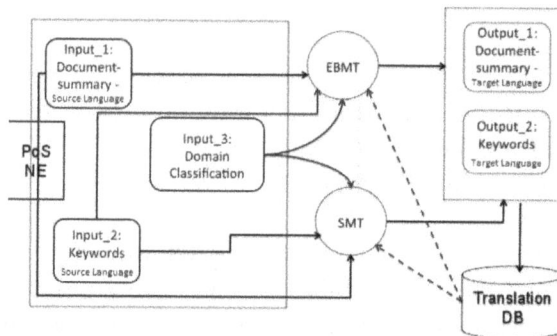

Figure 1: System architecture for the ATLAS-engine

The information extraction module provides information about document metadata including publication age. For documents previous to 1900 we will not
provide a translation, explaining to the user that in absence of a training corpus
the translation may be misleading.

The domain and dating restrictions can be changed at any time by the system administrator when an adequate training model is provided. The described
architecture is presented in Figure 1.

In order to perform domain adaptation we collected domain specific corpora for 13 upper domains in the categorization tree embedded in the ATLAS system and performed various experiments to choose a fast and easy to use domain adaptation method that can significantly improve the translation.

3 State of the art in domain adaptation for Statistical Machine Translation

Domain adaptation (DA) can be classified by taking into consideration the models that are adapted, the resources that are used or the type of supervision used.

In the following table, multiple types of approaches are presented. The numbers of the papers that appear after the table are given in the column "Reference" according to the approach the paper uses in adaptation.

Table 1: Classification of Domain Adaptation approaches for SMT

Approach	Type	Reference
Model	Word alignment model	2
	Language model	1, 3, 4, 6, 8
	Translation model	3, 4, 5, 7, 8
	Reordering model	4, 7, 9
Resources	Monolingual corpora	5, 6, 7
	Parallel corpora	1, 2, 3, 4, 6, 9
	Comparable corpora	5
	Web-crawled data	8
Supervision	Supervised	1, 2, 3, 4, 8, 9
	Unsupervised	5, 7
	Semi-supervised	6

In the following, the state of the art in domain adaptation for statistical machine translation (SMT) is presented with papers sorted chronologically by year of publication. All papers evaluated their methods using one or more evaluation metrics and the most common metric used was BLEU (Papineni et al. 2002).

1. An UNSUPERVISED LANGUAGE MODEL ADAPTATION method is explored in Zhao et al. (2004) where structured query models are used. Translations are

obtained using a baseline translation system that uses a general language model. Then the hypotheses from the output are converted into queries with the aim of retrieving similar sentences from very large news documents collections. Using these retrieved sentences, a language model (LM) is built and linearly interpolated with the baseline language model. The final step consists in using the interpolated language model to produce new translations.

2. Experiments in ALIGNMENT ADAPTATION were described in Wu et al. (2005) where out-of-domain data is used in order to get better results when performing in-domain word alignment. In their work, an alignment model is trained using the out-of-domain corpus and another alignment model is trained using the in-domain corpus (size of out-of-domain >> size of in-domain). A new alignment model results by interpolating the two models.

3. Multiple experiments in domain adaptation for SMT were explored by Koehn & Schroeder (2007). The baseline systems were trained using different methods: using only out-of-domain data, using only in-domain data and using concatenated out-of-domain and in-domain data. Among these three baselines the best BLEU score was obtained using the concatenated data. The adaptation methods used were: only use the in-domain data to build the language model, interpolate the LM estimated from out-of-domain data with the LM estimated from in-domain data, use both language models as separate features with weights set using MERT, and the last method made use of FACTORED TRANSLATION MODELS where two decoding paths corresponding to each translation table are used.

4. In Chen et al. (2008) n-best hypotheses are used for LANGUAGE, TRANSLATION AND REORDERING MODEL ADAPTATION. Each hypothesis holds phrase alignment information that is useful in the word reordering for the source text. The best word reordering for a source text is the one with the highest posterior probability. The source sentences are reordered taking into consideration the best word reordering. The weights of the decoder are optimized using the reordered source sentences.

5. One approach to TRANSLATION MODEL ADAPTION relies on using COMPARABLE CORPORA.[2] In Snover et al. (2008), monolingual target data is used in the improvement of an SMT system. The method consists in using multiple texts in the target language that have a similar topic as the source

---

[2]Texts that have the same topic and similar content.

language document that will be translated. The documents are used to increase the probability of generating texts that are similar to the comparable document.

6. The use of a DOMAIN DICTIONARY and MONOLINGUAL CORPORA is explored in Wu et al. (2008). The out-of-domain data is used in estimating a language model and constructing a phrase table, probabilities are assigned to entries in the in-domain translation dictionary, an in-domain phrase table is constructed, and the two phrase tables are combined. If in-domain target data is available, a language model is estimated and *combined* with the out-of-domain one. If in-domain source data is available, the already built model is used in translating the data, thus obtaining a synthetic corpus that is added to the training data.

7. MONOLINGUAL RESOURCES are also explored in Bertoldi & Federico (2009). The approaches pursued are: use the baseline translation system to generate synthetic bilingual data, use the generated data for translation and reordering model adaptation, and use the synthetic texts or given target texts for language model adaptation.

8. Recent work in DA forSMA focuses on using web-crawled data for building language models, improving translation models, tuning and testing. In Pecina et al. (2011) and Pecina et al. (2012), domain-specific data is obtained by web-crawling. The basic workflow of their work is: use focused web-crawling, text normalization, language identification, document clean-up and near-duplicate detection.

9. Ling et al. (2011) use WEIGHTED ALIGNMENT MATRICES FOR REORDERING MODELING. These matrices encode all possible alignments and generate better phrase-tables. The alignment matrix is used to create the translation model and the 1-best alignment to generate the reordering model. In their paper, two algorithms to generate the reordering model are presented: one uses the alignments for the phrase pairs, and the other algorithm makes use of the contextual information of the phrase pairs.

In Figure 2, a domain adaptation setup for statistical machine translation is presented.

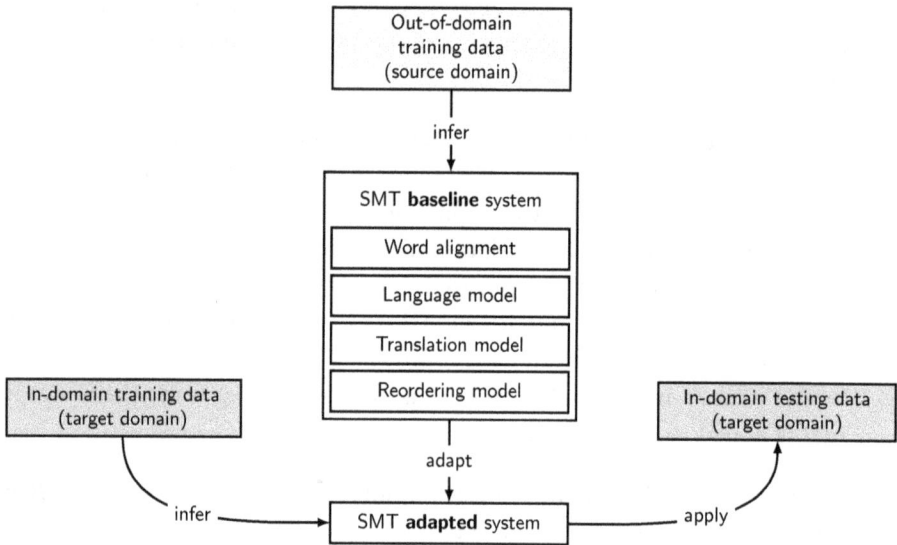

Figure 2: Domain adaptation setup. Figure adapted from Plank (2011: Chapter 3) where a DA setup is presented in the task of parser adaptation. The adapted system is made up of the same type of models as the baseline system, but these models were omitted in the drawing due to the fact that one or more models can be adapted.

4 The baseline translation system

The experiments were run using the widely-used open-source toolkit Moses.[3] Moses is a statistical machine translation toolkit which utilizes large parallel corpora in order to train the translation system. In our experiments, we used the phrase-based translation model provided by the Moses system. The training pipeline[4] consists of the following steps: pre-processing the data by tokenizing, true casing and cleaning using tools from the Moses toolkit, followed by language model training and translation training where a word-alignment is performed, phrases are extracted and multiple scores are computed. For the language model training, we chose the SRILM toolkit,[5] which is also open-source. It builds statistical language models and it also offers the possibility of interpolating language models. As for the word-alignments, they were performed using GIZA++,[6] a com-

---

[3]http://www.statmt.org/moses/index.php?n=Main.HomePage
[4]http://www.statmt.org/moses/?n=Moses.Baseline
[5]http://www.speech.sri.com/projects/srilm/download.html
[6]http://code.google.com/p/giza-pp/

monly used tool for word alignments. Because of the fact that this tool runs slowly on long sentences or fails to align them, we chose to work with a maximum sentence length of 50 words.

In order to train a statistical machine translation system, parallel corpora were needed. The JRC-Acquis[7] corpus is a multilingual parallel corpus for 22 European languages consisting of paragraph alignments for 231 pairs[8] of languages. The data is made up of a selection of European Union documents referred to as Acquis. This term identifies the body of common rights and obligations that bind all the member states of the European Union. The choice of using this corpus is motivated by the fact that it is freely available, it is sufficiently large and it contains aligned corpora for all the language pairs within the ATLAS project.

The experiments were evaluated using the common BLEU evaluation metric which uses n-grams counts.

5 Experiments in domain adaptation

In order to investigate current methods of domain adaptation, experiments were performed that were inspired by the work presented in Koehn & Schroeder (2007). In their work, the language pair French–English was used, with the Europarl corpus used as out-of-domain date. The in-domain data was made up of the News Commentary corpus. The BLEU scores for each of the adaptation methods proposed are presented in Table 2.

Table 2: BLEU scores for the experiments from Koehn & Schroeder (2007)

Method	BLEU
Large out-of-domain training data	25.11
Small in-domain training data	25.88
Combined training data	26.69
Language model interpolation	27.12
Two language models	27.30
In-domain language model	27.46
Two translation models	27.64

---

[7]http://ipsc.jrc.ec.europa.eu/index.php?id=1989
[8]http://langtech.jrc.ec.europa.eu/Documents/070622_Poster_JRC-Acquis.pdf

From the seven experiments conducted by Koehn & Schroeder (2007), we selected three experiments that can be easily reproduced (combined training data,
in-domain language model and interpolated language model). Then we identified
the best one according to the BLEU scores, which was the in-domain language
model method.

We performed three experiments using the out-of-domain JRC-Acquis, the in-
domain Politics from the ATLAS parallel corpora and the language pair Bulgarian–
English. Even though the out-of-domain and the in-domain data both belong to
the same topic, they differ in text style. The aim of these experiments was to
verify if using the in-domain language model method is also the best adaptation
method for our setting. But, as results show in Table 4, the best method actually
is language model interpolation (even though using only the in-domain language
model gives results close to language model interpolation).

In Table 3 and Table 4, the statistics for the corpora used and the BLEU results
are presented.

Table 3: Statistics for the corpora used in the experiments for BG–EN

#sentences in-domain Politics	#sentences out-of-domain JRC-Aquis	#sentences test-set (Politics domain)
56796	306767	3000

Table 4: BLEU results for the adaptation methods tested on BG–EN with
in-domain Politics

Method	BLEU
Combined training data	24.98
In-domain language model	39.07
Language model interpolation	39.36

In order to estimate language models and to perform language model interpolation, we used the SRILM toolkit. Two language models were built: one for the
target language estimated from the out-of-domain corpus and one for the target
language estimated from the in-domain corpus. Then, we used the *compute-best-
mix* script from SRILM to compute the best interpolation weight. This weight and
the two language models were used in order to build the interpolated language
model.

Table 5: Results of experiments on Business in-domain data

Lang. Pair	BLEU Adapted System	BLEU Baseline System	#sent. In-domain Corpus	#sent. Out-of-domain Corpus	#sent. Test Set	improvement
DE−EN	13.18	9.84	93160	1199447	4500	3.34
EN−DE	11.3	7.96	93160	1199447	4500	3.34
EN−RO	14.97	6.98	10109	336455	500	7.99
RO−BG	19.58	7.22	10410	241670	500	12.36
RO−EN	23.82	9.69	10109	336455	500	14.13

After deciding what the best adaptation method was in our current setting (LM interpolation), we conducted experiments on other ATLAS in-domain corpora: Sociology and Business. We wanted to check the correlation between the size of the out-of-domain data, the in-domain data and the improvement[9] on different language pairs: English−German, German−English, Romanian−English, English−Romanian and Romanian−Bulgarian. As can be seen in Table 5 and Table 6, there is a big difference between the sizes of the Business and the Sociology in-domain data. Another goal of our work was to evaluate the chosen DA method by comparing the BLEU scores of the baseline systems to the scores of the adapted systems.

The test sets belonged to the same domain as the in-domain corpus and the size of the test sets was set to approximately 5% of the size of the in-domain corpora.

Table 6: Results of experiments on Sociology in-domain data

Lang. Pair	BLEU Adapted System	BLEU Baseline System	#sent. In-domain Corpus	#sent. Out-of-domain Corpus	#sent. Test Set	improvement
DE−EN	30.05	22.3	1808	1199447	100	7.75
EN−DE	35.21	27.3	1808	1199447	100	7.91
EN−RO	30.46	21.92	2010	336455	100	8.54
RO−BG	17.68	7.31	2176	241670	100	10.37
RO−EN	36.82	21.71	2010	336455	100	15.11

---

[9]We use the term "improvement" to define the difference between the BLEU score of the adapted system and the BLEU score of the baseline system.

We observed from our experiments that there is a correlation between the size of the in-domain corpus, the out-of-domain corpus, the number of test sentences and the BLEU score. In the Sociology experiments, the size of test sets was set to 100 sentences and the size of the in-domain data was between 1800 and 2200 sentences. Even though the size of the in-domain data for RO–BG is similar to the size of the in-domain data for RO–EN, the size of the out-of-domain data for the two language pairs differs by almost 100000 sentences. This is the reason why there is a large difference in BLEU score improvements for the two systems (10.37 for RO–BG and 15.11 for RO–EN). The same correlations can be observed in the Business domain (12.36 for RO–BG and 14.13 for RO–EN).

While the most significant improvement among all ten experiments was on the on the RO–EN language pair in the Sociology domain (BLEU difference of 15.11), the least significant improvement of 3.34 BLEU points was made on the Business domain for the language pairs EN–DE and DE–EN. The reason for this small improvement lies in the large amounts of both in-domain and out-of-domain data. Sentence alignment problems appear in large corpora leading to word-alignment problems and, in the end, problems in the translation, which result in low BLEU scores.

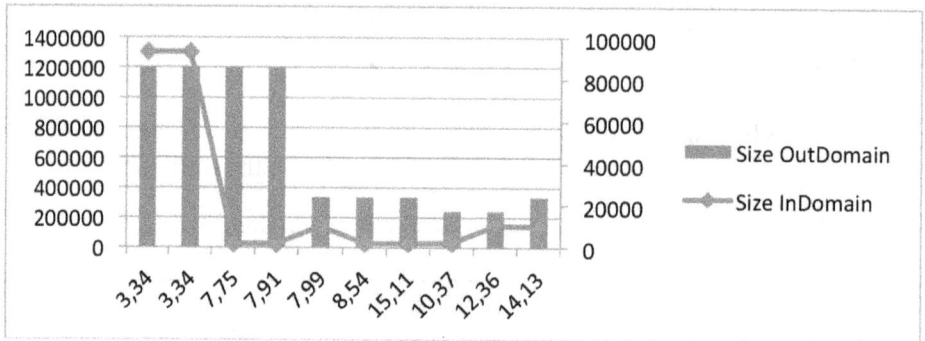

Figure 3: Improvement for the experiments in the Business domain

In Figure 3 we plotted on the X axis the improvement, on the left Y axis the size of the out-of-domain data and on the second Y axis the size of the in-domain data. It can be observed that for the experiments that used large amounts of both out-of-domain and in-domain data, the improvement was the lowest. When the out-of-domain corpus and the in-domain corpus had smaller dimensions, the improvement was significantly better. Hybrid cases, with a large out-of-domain corpus and small in-domain corpus, can be observed in Figure 4, where all ten experiments are illustrated. In this case, the improvement is also significant.

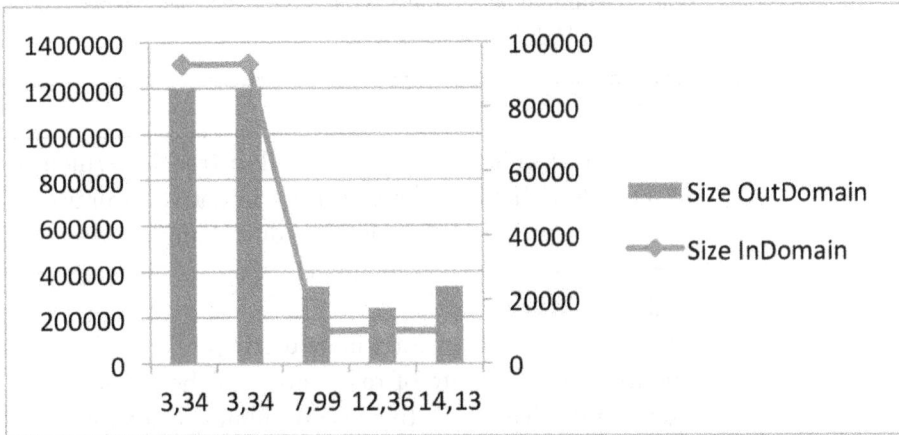

Figure 4: Improvement for all experiments

By looking at the improvements, we came to the conclusion that having more in-domain data does not necessarily lead to better results and that the chosen adaptation method is more important than the amount of in-domain data.

In Table 7, an example of translations in the domain of Sociology and the language pair Romanian–English is presented. This is the experiment that gave the best improvement among all experiments (15.11). In the sentence translated using the baseline system, unknown words are underlined. The adapted system was able to translate all the words in this case and the sense of the sentence is similar to the sense of the reference sentence.

Table 8 presents an example taken from the Business domain German–English language pair test set. This is the experiment that gave the lowest improvement among all experiments (3.34). Even though in the sentence translated by the adapted system there are no unknown words, the sense of the sentence is not very close to the sense of the reference sentence.

6 Conclusions

In this paper we presented the ATLAS Content Management System, focusing on the integration of machine translation into the system. A current problem of machine translation is domain adaptation, as many statistical systems are trained on a general domain and used on divergent domains. We have investigated three methods presented in Koehn & Schroeder (2007) in order to choose a domain

Table 7: Translation example using a test set sentence that belongs to the Sociology domain, RO–EN

Type	Sentence
Source	toate declarațiile de susținere vor fi distruseîn termen de 18 luni de la data de înregistrare a inițiativei propuse de cetățeni, sau, în cazul unor proceduri administrative sau juridice, cel târziu la o săptămână după data încheierii procedurilor în cauză.
Reference	all statements of support will be destroyed at the latest 18 months after the date of registration of the proposed citizens' initiative, or, in the case of administrative or legal proceedings, at the latest one week after the date of conclusion of the said proceedings.
Adapted System	all statements of support will be destroyed 18 months after the registration of initiative proposed by citizens, or, in the case of administrative procedures or legal, at the latest one week after the date of the procedures in question.
Baseline System	all declarațiile of susținere shall be destroyed within 18 months from the date of registration of inițiativei proposed by cetățeni, or, in the case of administrative or legal, not later than one week from the date of conclusion of the procedures in question.

adaptation method that can be easily and quickly integrated into the system. According to the original article, the best adaption method among these three was the usage of an in-domain language model. However, our experiments show that in our current setting, the best method is language model interpolation.

Subsequently, we wanted to evaluate the chosen DA method. For this reason, we performed experiments using baseline systems trained on JRC-Acquis and evaluated them using BLEU. In order to perform domain adaptation, we used the Business and Sociology in-domain data and the following language pairs: German–English, English–German, Romanian–Bulgarian, English–Romanian, and Romanian–English. The BLEU scores for all the adapted systems outperformed the BLEU scores of the baseline systems. It is important to emphasize the high BLEU differences between the baseline systems and the adapted systems (the best improvement was of 15.11 BLEU points).

Table 8: Translation example using a test set sentence that belongs to the Business domain, DE–EN

Type	Sentence
Source	eine solche anbindung birgt das risiko, dass aufwärts-gerichtete inflationsschocks zu einer lohn-preis-spirale führen, was sich in den betroffenen ländern nachteilig auf beschäftigung und wettbewerbsfähigkeit auswirken würde.
Reference	such schemes involve the risk of upward shocks in inflation leading to a wage-price spiral, which would be detrimental to employment and competitiveness in the countries concerned.
Adapted System	such carries the risk that monetary policy discussion of an early, in the countries concerned detrimental to employment and competitiveness.
Baseline System	such a link between carries the risk that aufwärtsgerichtete inflationsschocks lead to a lohn-preis-spirale, in the countries concerned on employment and competitiveness.

Two important ideas are highlighted by the results of our experiments. When performing domain adaptation, it is not necessary to have a large in-domain corpus in order to attain good adaptation results (a size of 2000 sentences is sufficient). The other conclusion is that in our current setting, choosing the right method of adaptation is more important than having a large in-domain corpus.

We conclude that having in-domain data is important for domain adaptation, but it is more important to choose a good adaptation method that gives significant improvements when applied to different in-domains and different language pairs.

Acknowledgements

ATLAS is a project funded by the European Commission under the CIP ICT Policy Support Program.

We want to thank the anonymous reviewers for their comments and constructive suggestions.

References

Belogay, Anelia, Dan Cristea, Eugen Ignat, Diman Karagiozov, Svetla Koeva, Maciej Ogrodniczuk, Adam Przepiórkowski, Raxis Przepiórkowski & Cristina Vertan. 2011. Language processing chains in ATLAS. In *Proceedings of the 5th Language and Technology Conference: Human Language Technologies as a Challenge for Computer Science and Linguistics*. Poznań, Poland.

Bertoldi, Nicola & Marcello Federico. 2009. Domain adaptation for statistical machine translation with monolingual resources. In *Proceedings of the 4th Workshop on Statistical Machine Translation*, 182–189.

Chen, Boxing, Min Zhang, Aiti Aw & Haizhou Li. 2008. Exploiting n-best hypotheses for SMT self-enhancement. In *Proceedings of ACL-08: HLT, ShortPapers (Companion Volume)*, 157–160.

Gavrila, Monica. 2011. Constrained recombination in an example-based machine translation system. In *Proceedings of the EAMT-2011: The 15th Annual Conference of the European Association for Machine Translation*. Leuven, Belgium.

Koehn, Philipp, Hieu Hoang, Alexandra Birch, Chris Callison-Burch, Marcello Federico, Nicola Bertoldi, Brooke Cowan, Wade Shen, Christine Moran, Richard Zens, Chris Dyer, Ondřej Bojar, Alexandra Constantin & Evan Herbst. 2007. Moses: Open source toolkit for statistical machine translation. In *ACL 2007, Proceedings of the Interactive Poster and Demonstration Sessions*, 177–180. Prague, Czech Republic.

Koehn, Philipp & Josh Schroeder. 2007. Experiments in domain adaptation for statistical machine translation. In *Proceedings of the Second Workshop on Statistical Machine Translation*, 224–227. Prague, Czech Republic.

Lee, David YW. 2001. Genres, registers, text types, domains, and styles: Clarifying the concepts and navigating a path through the BNC jungle. *Language, Learning and Technology* 5(3). 37–72.

Ling, Wang, Tiago Luis, Joao Graca, Luisa Coheur & Isabel Trancoso. 2011. Reordering modeling using weighted alignment matrices. In *Proceedings of the 49th Annual Meeting of the Association for Computational Linguistics*, vol. 2, 450–454. Portland, OR.

Papineni, Kishore, Salim Roukos, Todd Ward & Wei-Jing Zhu. 2002. BLEU: A method for automatic evaluation of machine translation. In *Proceedings of the 40th Annual Meeting of the Association for Computational Linguistics*, 311–318. Philadelphia, PA.

Pecina, Pavel, Antonio Toral, Vassilis Papavassiliou, Prokopis Prokopidis & Josef van Genabith. 2012. Domain adaptation of statistical machine translation using web-crawled resources: A case study. In *Proceedings of the 16th EAMT Conference.* Cincinnati, OH.

Pecina, Pavel, Antonio Toral, Andy Way, Vassilis Papavassiliou, Prokopis Prokopidis & Maria Giagkou. 2011. Towards using web-crawled data for domain adaptation in statistical machine translation. In *Proceedings of the 15th Conference of the European Association for Machine Translation.* Leuven, Belgium.

Plank, Barbara. 2011. *Domain adaptation for parsing.* University of Groningen dissertation. http://www.let.rug.nl/~bplank/proefschrift/thesis-bplank.pdf.

Snover, Matthew, Bonnie Dorr & Richard Schwartz. 2008. Language and translation model adaptation using comparable corpora. In *Proceedings of the 2008 Conference on Empirical Methods in Natural Language Processing,* 901–904. Honolulu, HI.

Wu, Hua, Haifeng Wang & Zhanyi Liu. 2005. Alignment model adaptation for domain-specific word alignment. In *Proceedings of the 43rd Annual Meeting of the Association for Computational Linguistics,* 467–474. Detroit, MI.

Wu, Hua, Haifeng Wang & Chengquing Zong. 2008. Domain adaptation for statistical machine translation with domain dictionary and monolingual resources. In *Proceedings of the 22nd International Conference on Computational Linguistics,* 993–1000. Manchester, UK.

Zhao, Bing, Matthias Eck & Stephan Vogel. 2004. Language model adaptation for statistical machine translation with structured query models. In *Proceedings of the 20th international conference on Computational Linguistics,* 411–417. Geneva, Switzerland.

Chapter 8

Disambiguate yourself: Supporting users in searching documents with query disambiguation suggestions

Ernesto William De Luca
University of Applied Sciences Potsdam, Germany

Christian Scheel
Technische Universität Berlin, DAI-Labor, Berlin, Germany

In this paper we present a query-oriented semantic approach and the respective architecture for supporting users in searching and browsing documents in a retrieval framework. While users are typing their queries a "meaning-oriented" analysis of each keystroke can provide different disambiguation suggestions (spelling correction, Named-Entity Recognition, WordNet- and Wikipedia-based suggestions) that can help users in formulating their queries for filtering relevant results. On the other hand systems can better interpret the query, because users implicitly tag the queries with the related meaning choosing the desired concept they had in mind. After the presentation of our architecture we show the results of two user studies, where users were asked to judge the support while typing their query and browsing documents. These results confirm that a semantic support is important in both cases.

1 Introduction

Keyword-based retrieval typically relies on keyword indexing and Boolean logic queries. These are sometimes provided with statistical methods like word frequency, where keyword lists are used to describe the content of information objects (e.g. also for finding synonyms of the query without taking into account the meaning of them). SEMANTIC INFORMATION RETRIEVAL is based on the cognitive

Ernesto William De Luca & Christian Scheel. Disambiguate yourself: Supporting users in searching documents with query disambiguation suggestions. In Georg Rehm, Felix Sasaki, Daniel Stein & Andreas Witt (eds.), *Language technologies for a multilingual Europe: TC3 III*, 123–138. Berlin: Language Science Press. DOI:10.5281/zenodo.1291938

view of the world, i.e. the meaning of a text (or word) depends on the conceptual relationships to objects in the world rather than to linguistic or contextual relations contained in texts or dictionaries. Sets of words, terms, etc. are mapped (in a conceptual structure) to concepts they encode. The concepts have to be identified inside the text and then classified (categorization) according to the given conceptual structure. The main types of conceptual structure are taxonomies, lexical resources (e.g. WordNet), general or domain ontologies or networks of concepts. These kind of resources have been already used for automatic disambiguation of concepts Haav & Lubi (2001).

Analyzing the current retrieval systems, we can state that query words are not considered in their different meanings, but only as keywords. Furthermore, they cannot deliver concept-based result lists. Because it is still difficult to understand the correlation of the search terms in a given context and documents, we believe that a semantic-based support can help in filling this gap while query typing and browsing.

Since the 1950s different researchers have tried to disambiguate words for different purposes such as machine translation, information retrieval and hypertext navigation, content and thematic analysis, grammatical analysis (Part-Of-Speech Tagging), speech or text processing Ide & Véronis (1998). A word is called AM-BIGUOUS if it can be interpreted in more than one way, thus having multiple senses. Disambiguation methods try to determine a specific sense of an ambiguous word. In general terms a word sense disambiguation process can be described as two steps, given a word w that should be disambiguated: For disambiguating word senses a variety of association methods (knowledge-driven, data-driven or corpus-based WSD) can be used Ide & Véronis (1998). Knowledge-based word sense disambiguation methods can be combined within semantic (or concept-based) information retrieval systems and represent one of the high-impact technologies for the next generation of IR systems. The search in this type of retrieval systems is based on the meaning of the searched information objects and not only on keywords in the object Haav & Lubi (2001).

In this paper we present a query-oriented semantic approach and the respective architecture for supporting users in searching and browsing documents in a retrieval framework. While users are typing their queries a "meaning-oriented" analysis of each keystroke can provide different disambiguation suggestions (spelling correction, Named-Entity Recognition, WordNet- and Wikipedia-based suggestions) that can help users in formulating their queries for filtering relevant results. On the other hand systems can interpret the query better, because users implicitly tag the queries with the related meaning choosing the desired concept they had in mind. After the presentation of our architecture we show the results of two user studies, where users were asked to judge the support while typing their query and browsing documents. These results confirm that a semantic support is important in both cases.

2 Supporting users with query disambiguation suggestions

In common information retrieval there is a distinction between term-based and phrase-based queries Singhal (2001). Some IR systems use single terms stored in the index, others also use multi-word phrases (e.g. "Information Retrieval") as index terms. In a similar way, in this work, users can query the index using SINGLE WORD SENSE QUERIES and MULTI WORD SENSE QUERIES. Single word sense queries are queries consisting of only one word that could have different meanings depending on the context they are related with. Multi word sense queries consist of the sum of different single word sense queries. Potentially, they provide more information about the context than a single word sense query.

Auto completion of query terms is a helpful and well known feature used by many search engines. It is used to suggest word and query completions or spelling corrections. To extend this approach for suggesting word senses, there is a need for detecting possible senses in written text. If users can define their query in a meaning-oriented way, the retrieved results can be navigated easily, because they are directly related to the meaning of the search.

In the following, we describe four support approaches for query disambiguation and query typing support. These approaches are based on different resources and help to disambiguate the sense of a query from different points of view. Specifically, the goal is to improve the semantic search process; therefore several problems have to be addressed. When users mistype when writing the query, the system has to be able to give correction alternatives which is described in the following section. After this section, it is shown how to recognize named entities and suggest context-aware disambiguating concepts to retrieve only query-related documents that are semantically related.

2.1 Spelling correction

An important task for retrieving relevant documents related to the query is to identify the misspelled words and correct them for a correct interpretation.

Figure 1: Spelling and auto completion suggestions

Auto completion and a list of term suggestions is the standard approach to support users in avoiding spelling mistakes as shown in Figure 1. For retrieving such suggestions, static dictionaries can be used, but for more query driven support, the selected suggestions should be related to the indexed documents. Therefore the dictionary of the index including all found senses should be used.

2.2 Named-entity recognition (NER, Stanford)

Because query words used for searching documents are not only common words, but may also represent locations, organizations, time expressions, and proper nouns, a named entity recognizer (NER) has been added to the system, in order to support the user, if the search engine cannot disambiguate this kind of information. The Stanford NER Finkel et al. (2005) can be used as a support for recognizing named entities, directing the user to the semantic search. If the user types, for example, only the name "Java", the NER should recognize the meaning of this instance and suggest more than one disambiguation possibilities (e.g. whether "Java" is related to the concept "island" or to the concept "programming language").

2.3 Lexical resources (WordNet)

In our work, we also use lexical and collaborative knowledge resources to support users in query disambiguation and semantic browsing.

LEXICAL RESOURCES provide linguistic information about words. This information can be represented in very diverse data structures, from simple lists to complex repositories with many types of linguistic information and relations attached to each entry, resulting in network-like structures. Lexical resources are used in Natural Language Processing (NLP), for example, to obtain descriptions and usage examples of different word senses. Different word senses refer to different concepts, and concepts can be distinguished from each other not only by their definitions or "glosses", but also by their specific relations to other concepts.

Such disambiguating relations are intuitively used by humans. However, if we want to automate the process of distinguishing between word senses, we have to use resources that provide appropriate knowledge, i.e. sufficient information about the usage context of a word. One of the most important resources available for this purpose is WordNet Fellbaum (1998) and its multilingual variants, including MultiWordNet Pianta et al. (2002) and EuroWordNet Vossen (1999).

WordNet Fellbaum (1998) is an electronic lexical database with its theoretical design based on psycholinguistic and computational theories of human lexical memory. It provides a list of word senses for each word, organized into synonym sets (synsets), each representing one constitutional lexicalized concept. Every synset is uniquely identified by an identifier (synsetId). It is unambiguous and carrier of exactly one meaning. Furthermore, different relations link these elements of synonym sets to semantically related terms (e.g. hypernyms, hyponyms, etc.). All related terms are also represented as synset entries. These synsets also contain descriptions of nouns, verbs, adjectives, and adverbs. With this information we can describe the usage context of a word.

2.4 Collaborative knowledge resources (Wikipedia)

The most well-known COLLABORATIVE KNOWLEDGE RESOURCE is Wikipedia[1]. It contains 16 million articles that have been written collaboratively by volunteers and can be edited by anyone with access to the site. It is the largest online encyclopedia which provides linked and partially annotated data and descriptive information. Based on the evaluation of articles types (e.g. disambiguation pages, category articles) and the analysis of templates (e.g. info boxes) even semantic knowledge can be extracted. A popular project aiming to provide structured information from Wikipedia is DBpedia Lehmann et al. (2009).

3 Building sense folders for disambiguating query terms

As already discussed in the previous section, users can be supported with semantic information for disambiguating search terms. The semantic-based approach we presented in De Luca & Nürnberger (2006) is used to simplify the search process by providing users with explicit information about ambiguities enabling them to easily retrieve the subset of documents they are looking for. In the following, we shortly describe the purpose of the *sense folder approach*, defining the

---

[1]http://en.wikipedia.org/wiki/Wikipedia

concept of a *sense folder*, and providing an overview of the system architecture. A detailed overview of the approach is given De Luca (2008).

3.1 Sense folder definition

The Sense Folder is an abstract concept that models the contextual information describing one meaning of a query word. More formally: Given a query term q, a sense folder is a container (prototype vector) that includes all selected linguistic information (linguistic context) of one sense of the query term retrieved from the different resources described above.

In this work, we dynamically create Sense Folders based on every single query term (single word sense) selected by the users. It means that every word sense of a given term chosen is retrieved by the Sense Folder Engine and information is obtained by retrieving the related meaning from the resources explained in §2.

3.2 System architecture

In order to support users in formulating queries, we decided to develop a system architecture that is able to handle two major use cases: on the one hand the system should help users in specifying an information need by using context-aware disambiguation suggestions (retrieved from different resources). On the other hand the system should support users in searching relevant information using context information implicitly retrieved by learned queries (e.g. queries that have already been typed by other users and being relevant for the given user context).

Figure 2 gives an overview of the system architecture (and the related disambiguation process). The process starts after the user submits different query words through a user interface. For instance, every time the user types a query word (e.g. the term "chair"), he/she will get some disambiguation suggestions (as shown in Figure 4) by the system. These can help him/her to better describe his/her information need. For every word contained in the query different pre-processing steps (e.g. spelling correction, named entity recognition) or semantic annotation steps (e.g. WordNet or Wikipedia annotation) can be applied and stored in Sense Folders (SF). All the terms are explicitly chosen by the user and describe this semantic vector SF that will be used to match and retrieve documents related to the query De Luca (2010).

During the query analysis, query annotation suggestions are given by the system and the user can decide to accept one of the suggested annotations in order

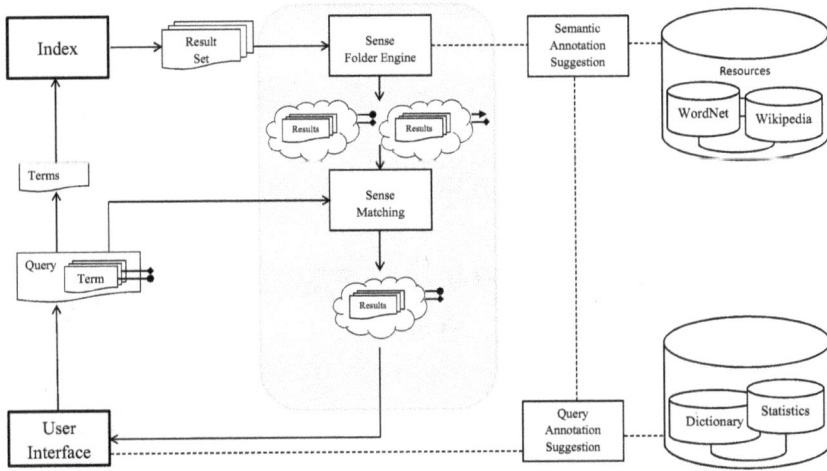

Figure 2: System architecture: Sense Folder approach view

to improve the context in which the query terms define the documents to be retrieved.

After the query has been processed, the users' keywords are simultaneously sent to the search engine and to the *sense folder engine*. While documents are retrieved, pre-processed and indexed, for every search term the different meanings of a term and the related linguistic relations are retrieved from the different available resource. For instance, Figure 3 presents an example of using linguistic relations retrieved from WordNet in order to semantically annotate every term. Every query term can be expanded with words defining the context for each of its meanings, thus forming the above defined. Based on all words included in the relations, semantic prototype vectors (Sense Folders) describing each semantic class are constructed. The use of Sense Folder can be helpful in order to classify or cluster similar documents and present only the relevant subset to the user De Luca (2008).

Figure 3 shows how the system helps the user to formulate a query. The user starts his/her interaction with the system by typing the term "chair" which is an ambiguous term (step 1). While typing, the system suggests different senses for this term that are included in the available resources (step 2). Using WordNet Fellbaum (1998), we can observe that the system retrieves five different senses (step 3). These senses are presented to the user, raising the user's awareness for the ambiguitiy of the given term and ask to choose the word sense he/she had in mind (step 4). In this example the user decides to search for the word sense of

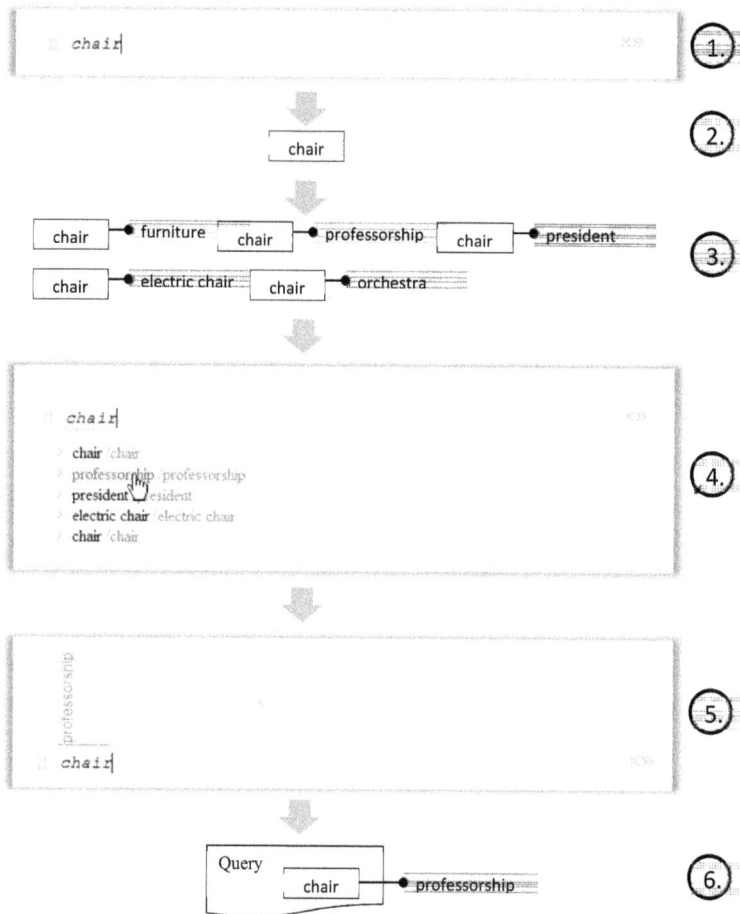

1. Event: User stops typing
2. Internal representation of query terms
3. Annotated candidates are created by the annotation suggestion module
4. Event: User selects the proper sense
5. Interface changes to visualize selection
6. Internal representation of annotated query term.

Figure 3: Interaction between user and the retrieval system. Semantic (WordNet) annotation example for the noun collocation of the term "chair".

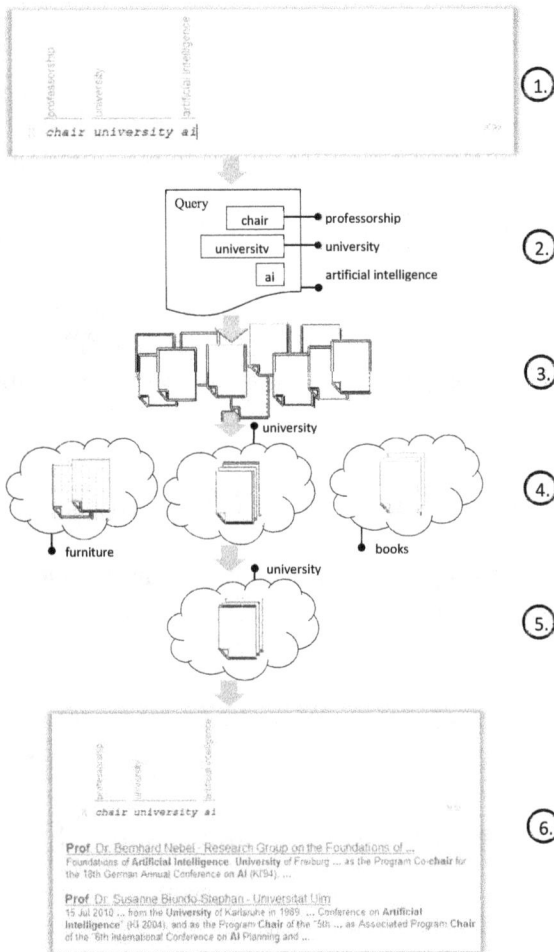

1. Event: User starts search, after annotating the query terms
2. Internal representation of query: each term is connected to a Wordnet sense ID
3. Based on the terms an index returns results
4. The sense folder architecture groups result by their meaning.
5. For given senses in the query, the best matching sense folder is chosen to be the result set.
6. Results are presented to the user.

Figure 4: Internal process of finding a result set matching user given senses

"chair" that is related to the professorship concept (step 5). After this step the system knows that the user submitting this query refers to the "chair professorship" concept, leading to filtering the results using only this concept and providing them in the correct context of this term (step 6).

Figure 4 presents the retrieval process after the selection of the single word sense query explained in Figure 3. In this example, the user annotates the three query terms (step 1) with the context information provided by WordNet (step 2) and the system merges them for filtering relevant documents (step 3). Potential results are collected by the combination of all given word senses (step 4). Then the Sense Folder system filters these results into sets of different meanings (step 5). These meanings are compared to the given senses from the query and the best matching set is selected to be presented to the user (step 6).

4 Evaluating the disambiguation support

In order to evaluate our approaches for semantic-based query disambiguation and browsing support we conducted a user study taking into account the functionalities mentioned in the previous sections. The query disambiguation support functionality was tested and examined by 12 subjects (see §4.1), while the browsing support was tested and examined by 16 subjects (see §4.2). In the following, we summarize the results of our findings.

4.1 User study on the query disambiguation support

In this user study we evaluated the query disambiguation support. A total of seven questions covering different aspects of typing and browsing were presented to participants. Twelve participants were presented with suggestion results retrieved from WordNet, Wikipedia, dictionaries (for spelling correction) and Named-Entity Recognition (from the Stanford NER). All questions had at least one negative and one positive answer, most allowed the participants to leave short comments and motivations to their answers. The user study showed that the query typing support received overall positive opinions from the participants. In the following we summarize the results achieved:

1. Users were asked to rate the relevance of the suggestions while typing a query. Ratings are based on a one to five scale. The rating scale was as follows: indispensable (5), important (4), nice to have (3), minor (2) or irrelevant (1). 38% said that spelling correction was 'indispensable'. WordNet

(53% of the participants) and Wikipedia disambiguation pages (46% of the participants) were seen as 'nice to have' features.

2. Similar to the first question, users were asked to rate the relevance of the suggestions while browsing the results. In this case spelling correction was a 'minor' issue (23%), while WordNet (66% of the participants) and Wikipedia disambiguation pages (50% of the participants) were seen as 'important' features.

3. We asked if the support was more important while typing, during the browsing or in both cases. 58% explained that both were relevant, while 17% preferred it while typing the query and 23% during the browsing.

4. Users were asked to prioritize the suggestions (spelling correction, NER, WordNet-based suggestions, Wikipedia-based suggestions) they would like to have while they are writing their query. On average participants wanted to have a first suggestion from a spell checker (75%), then from WordNet (58%), Wikipedia (50%) disambiguation pages and Named-Entity Recognizer (50%).

5. Participants were asked which kind of auto completion function they would like to have as a standard. 60% wanted to have the most frequent entities (e.g. persons, locations, and events), 23% the most frequent words (from a dictionary) and 17% the most frequent noun.

6. We asked if the auto completion function should complete the word when the cursor shows its correct form, and/or the respective concept is known. 75% would like to have this functionality, 25% would not.

7. Provided that the semantic-based query disambiguation functionality presented were to be integrated in the search engines of the future, we wanted to know if the users would use this possibility to narrow down the search results using the context suggestions presented. 41% would directly use it, 83% would use it, if they still could search in the normal way they are already comfortable with.

4.2 User study on the semantic-based browsing support

In this user study we evaluated the performance of the Sense Folder approach for browsing results. A total of 9 questions covering different aspects of the Sense Folder search results presentation were asked. Sixteen participants were

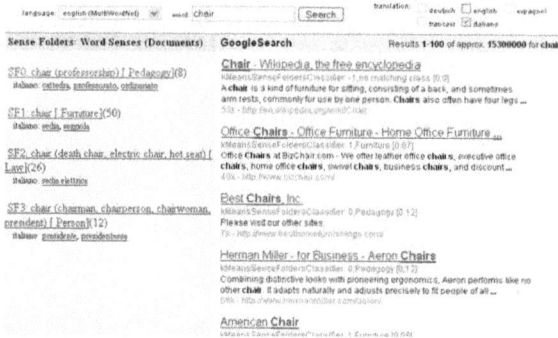

Figure 5: Using sense folders for browsing support

presented with results of the same queries from Google[2], Yippi[3] and a local deployment of the Sense Folder system (see Figure 5). Yippi was chosen because it groups similar results together into "clouds"[4]. All questions had at least one negative and one positive answer, most allowed the participants to leave short comments and motivations to their answers.

The user study showed that the Sense Folder Approach received overall positive opinions from the participants. In the following we summarize the results achieved:

1. Users were asked to recognize the different concepts of one given word related to the search results retrieved by the search systems. Most of them (93%) recognized between one and five concepts.

2. Users were asked whether or not they agreed with the concepts found by the Sense Folder approach (retrieved from WordNet). 80% said that all expected concepts were presented.

3. The participants had to estimate the difficulty of the interaction with the Sense Folder approach. 70% found it easy, while 17% difficult and the remaining 13% abstract.

4. Users were asked to describe the differences between Google, Yippi and the Sense Folder system. 76% were positive to the added value of the Sense Folder annotation. The system was intuitive and supported them in disambiguating the concepts related to the query (23.5%). The list of concepts

---

[2]http://www.google.com
[3]http://search.yippy.com/
[4]http://search.yippy.com/about-yippy-search

was seen as positive (52%). 23% recognized that the Sense Folder system clustered documents similarly to Yippi. They also noticed that Google and Yippi only covered one dominant concept. 6% of the participants observed that the Sense Folder system did not allow search for different media types.

5. We asked if the Sense Folder system had been helpful and why. 81% explained that the use of filtering by concept for the query was very positive (56%) and they could access information quickly and categorized by concepts. They saw an easy way of filtering results (25%). 18% claimed the coverage of topics was incomplete, while 6% said they preferred to use longer queries instead.

6. Participants were asked whether they would like to use features similar to the Sense Folder system in future search engines. 80% were positive. They also said that the feature reduced non-relevant information (33%), gives quick access to good results (40%). 6% said they preferred the Wikipedia disambiguation page due to its clustering. However, Wikipedia only presents concepts, without clustering.

7. We asked if the participants had suggestions for improving the Sense Folder system. The majority liked it as-is. They (66%) would however prefer a nicer user interface. This functionality is implicitly available as documents are already filtered by concepts, by clicking on a concept, others are automatically excluded.

8. Would they use the Sense Folder System instead of common search engine? 80% would. 20% of which due to the better support for finding relevant of documents, as well as the filtering of search results (60%). The 20%, who chose not to use the engine, said that old habits died hard (9%) and 11% questioned the usability.

9. We wanted to know which kind of search tasks users would use the Sense Folder system for. 49% would use it for all searches, 50% for specific searches and 6% for none of them.

4.3 Evaluation summary

Analyzing the results of our user studies we can say that semantic-based support can be very useful. This support during query typing and browsing is seen as positive and users would use it. However, it should not be intrusive. Different resources like WordNet and Wikipedia are seen as reasonable for semantic-based support services.

While typing a query, users like to have auto completion suggestions, but rather get suggestions that can be related to the concepts they are looking for. Context exploitation is an interesting issue, when users use multi word sense queries. While typing queries users want to have one context, where the concepts are related to one another. This is helpful and the best matching meanings (if there is more than one word) should be presented.

For browsing search results in a semantic way almost all participants explained that the use of filtering by concept for the query was very positive and that they could access information quickly and categorized by concepts. They would use the Sense Folder System instead of common search engines and appreciated the added value of the Sense Folder annotation. The system supported them in disambiguating the concepts related to the query. The list of concepts was seen as positive and was desired in both user studies.

It is interesting to observe that many users judge spelling correction as 'indispensable' while typing a query, but as 'minor' while browsing the results. WordNet and Wikipedia disambiguation pages are seen as 'nice to have' features while query typing, but as 'important' features for browsing.

5 Conclusion and future work

In this paper we presented a query-oriented semantic approach and the respective architecture for supporting users in searching and browsing. We have shown that a semantic-based support based on different types of suggestions (spelling correction, Named-Entity Recognition, WordNet- and Wikipedia-based suggestions) can help users in formulating their queries and systems in understanding the query-related meaning. We conducted two user studies, where users were asked to rate the support while typing their query and browsing the search results. At the moment we are working on an agent-based extension of the system architecture (based on the JIAC Agent Platform, see Hirsch et al. 2009), where every agent is responsible for a certain resource, provides services (e.g. spelling correction, WordNet-based suggestion, etc.) and can interact with other agents and the user. First tests have shown promising results regarding the flexible and reactive requirements of the proposed architecture. Together with automatic load balancing capabilities (based on concepts like agent cloning and mobility), we target an open dynamic environment for semantic user support.

References

De Luca, Ernesto William. 2008. Integrating Metaphor Information into RDF/OWL EuroWordNet. In European Language Resources Association (ELRA) (ed.), *Proceedings of the Sixth International Language Resources and Evaluation (LREC'08)*. Marrakech, Morocco: Shaker Publishers.

De Luca, Ernesto William. 2010. A Corpus for Evaluating Semantic Multilingual Web Retrieval Systems: The Sense Folder Corpus. In European Language Resources Association (ELRA) (ed.), *Proceedings of the Seventh International Language Resources and Evaluation (LREC'10)*. Malta, Valletta.

De Luca, Ernesto William & Andreas Nürnberger. 2006. Using Clustering Methods to Improve Ontology-Based Query Term Disambiguation. *International Journal of Intelligent Systems* 21. 693–709.

Fellbaum, Christiane (ed.). 1998. *WordNet: An electronic lexical database*. Cambridge, MA: MIT Press.

Finkel, Jenny Rose, Trond Grenager & Christopher Manning. 2005. Incorporating non-local information into information extraction systems by gibbs sampling. In *ACL '05: Proceedings of the 43rd annual meeting on association for computational linguistics*, 363–370. Ann Arbor, Michigan: Association for Computational Linguistics. DOI:http://dx.doi.org/10.3115/1219840.1219885

Haav, Hele-Mai & Tanel-Lauri Lubi. 2001. A survey of concept-based information retrieval tools on the web. In *Proceedings of 5th East-European Conference ADBIS*2001*, 29–41. Vilnius, Technika.

Hirsch, Benjamin, Thomas Konnerth & Axel Heßler. 2009. Merging Agents and Services: The JIAC Agent Platform. In Rafael H. Bordini, Mehdi Dastani, Jürgen Dix & Amal El Fallah Seghrouchni (eds.), *Multi-Agent programming: Languages, tools and applications*, 159–185. Heidelberg: Springer.

Ide, Nancy & Jean Véronis. 1998. Word sense disambiguation: The state of the art. *Computational Linguistics* 24:1. 1–40.

Lehmann, Jens, Chris Bizer, Georgi Kobilarov, Sören Auer, Christian Becker, Richard Cyganiak & Sebastian Hellmann. 2009. DBpedia: A crystallization point for the web of data. *Journal of Web Semantics* 7(3). 154–165.

Pianta, Emanuele, Luisa Bentivogli & Christian Girardi. 2002. MultiWordNet: Developing an aligned multilingual database. In *Proceedings of the First International WordNet Conference*, 293–302. Mysore, India.

Singhal, Amit. 2001. Modern information retrieval: A brief overview. *IEEE Data Eng. Bull.* 24(4). 35–43.

Ernesto William De Luca & Christian Scheel

Vossen, Piek. 1999. *EuroWordNet final report. Eurowordnet (lE-4003 and lE-8328) deliverable d041.* Tech. rep. University of Amsterdam.

Chapter 9

Multilingual knowledge in aligned Wiktionary and OmegaWiki for translation applications

Michael Matuschek

Ubiquitous Knowledge Processing Lab (UKP-TUDA)

Christian M. Meyer

Ubiquitous Knowledge Processing Lab (UKP-TUDA)

Iryna Gurevych

Ubiquitous Knowledge Processing Lab (UKP-TUDA, UKP-DIPF)

Multilingual lexical-semantic resources play an important role in translation applications. However, multilingual resources with sufficient quality and coverage are rare as the effort of manually constructing such a resource is substantial. In recent years, the emergence of Web 2.0 has opened new possibilities for constructing large-scale lexical-semantic resources. We identified Wiktionary and OmegaWiki as two important multilingual initiatives where a community of users ("crowd") collaboratively edits and refines the lexical information. They seem especially appropriate in the multilingual domain as users from all languages and cultures can easily contribute. However, despite their advantages such as open access and coverage of multiple languages, these resources have hardly been systematically investigated and utilized until now. Therefore, the goals of our contribution are three-fold: (1) We analyze how these resources emerged and characterize their content and structure; (2) We propose an alignment at the word sense level to exploit the complementary information contained in both resources for increased coverage; (3) We describe a mapping of the resources to a standardized, unified model (UBY-LMF) thus creating a large freely available multilingual resource designed for easy integration into applications such as machine translation or computer-aided translation environments.

Michael Matuschek, Christian M. Meyer & Iryna Gurevych. Multilingual knowledge in aligned Wiktionary and OmegaWiki for translation applications. In Georg Rehm, Felix Sasaki, Daniel Stein & Andreas Witt (eds.), *Language technologies for a multilingual Europe: TC3 III*, 139–180. Berlin: Language Science Press. DOI:10.5281/zenodo.1291940

Michael Matuschek, Christian M. Meyer & Iryna Gurevych

1 Introduction

In recent years, operating internationally has become increasingly important for governments, companies, researchers, and many other institutions and individuals. This raises a high demand for translation tools and resources. Statistical machine translation (SMT) systems are pervasive nowadays and their use has become very popular (especially among layman translators), but they are usually hard to adapt to specific needs as parallel texts for training are not available for many domains, and even if training data is available the error rate is considerable. Thus, they are mainly useful during the gisting or drafting phase of translating a text, or as a supplementary tool to provide additional translations for a word or phrase. However, high quality translations as they are needed for many real-life situations still require human effort and editing (Koehn 2009; Carl et al. 2010). SMT systems are not sufficient for this purpose, since there is usually no hint of what the translations actually mean and why one alternative is preferable when only a bare probability score is provided.

To produce translations of higher quality, additional tools and resources need to be considered. Translation Memory systems became very popular for this purpose in the 1990s (Somers 2003). They maintain a database of translations which are manually validated as correct and can be applied if the same or a similar translation is required. They can, to some extent, deal with unseen texts due to fuzzy matching, but while this approach yields a high precision, it cannot validate translations for entirely new content and is thus mostly useful in environments where the context does not change much over time. More recently, parallel corpora have been used to identify suitable translations in context; for example, through the *Linguee*[1] service. While this might help in identifying the correct translation, pinpointing the exact meaning can be hard because no sense definitions or any other lexicographic information is provided. Moreover, the lack of sufficiently large parallel corpora is also an issue here.

We argue that to support translators directly and to improve SMT, multilingual lexical resources such as bilingual dictionaries or multilingual wordnets (in addition to the tools mentioned) are required. Using the information in those multilingual resources (such as sense definitions), it becomes possible to manually or (semi-)automatically assess if a translation is appropriate in context and to perform corrections using a better suited translation found in the resource. As has been shown earlier, this is especially true for unusual language combinations and specific tasks such as cultural heritage annotation (Declerck et al. 2012; Mörth et al. 2011).

---

[1]http://www.linguee.com

Consider, for example, the English noun *bass*. In Google Translate,[2] probably the most popular SMT system to date, only the music-related word sense of *bass* is considered for the example translation into German shown in Figure 1. None of the translation alternatives addresses the less frequent animal-related word sense, which would be correct in this context. Moreover, there are no sense definitions or validated usage examples for the proposed translations.

In contrast, a multilingual lexical resource such as Wiktionary allows to easily distinguish between the two word senses of *bass* and provides a vast amount of lexicographic information to help identify a good translation. Although in this case of homonymy it would be comparatively easy to pick the correct sense, it poses a much greater problem for closely related senses sharing the same etymology. Figure 2 shows an excerpt of the animal-related word sense of *bass* in Wiktionary that contains the suitable German translation *Barsch* for the example discussed above. OmegaWiki encodes another possible translation *Seebarsch* and provides additional lexicographic information. An excerpt is shown in Figure 3.

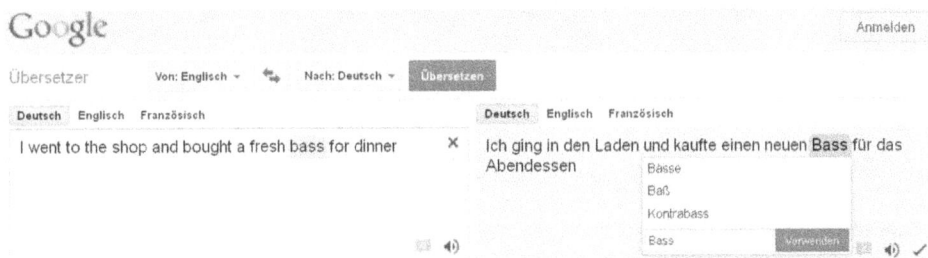

Figure 1: The translation alternatives for *bass* in Google Translate, accessed on May 20th, 2011

Among others, we identified the following three major requirements for such multilingual lexical resources to be useful for translation applications:

1. The resources should have a high coverage of languages and allow for continually adding or revising information. This is important to cater for neologisms or domain-specific terminology, and especially for correcting improper or adding missing translations. Terminology-rich resources are especially important for human translators, as SMT systems cannot cope well with domain-specific texts due to the lack of training data.

---

[2] http://translate.google.com

Etymology 2 [edit]

From Middle English *bas*, alteration of *bars*, from Old English *bærs* ("a fish, perch"), from Proto-Germanic **barsaz* ("perch", literally "prickly fish"), from Proto-Indo-European **bhars-*, **bharst-* ("prickle, thorn, scale"). Cognate with Dutch *baars* ("baars"), German *Barsch* ("perch"). More at barse.

a smallmouth bass (*Micropterus dolomieu*)

Pronunciation [edit]

- enPR: băs, IPA: /bæs/, X-SAMPA: /b{s/
- Audio (US) ▶(file)

Noun [edit]

bass (*plural* basses *or* bass)

1. The perch; any of various marine and freshwater fish resembling the perch, all within the order of Perciformes.

Usage notes [edit]

The plural **bass** refers to multiple fish of a single variety or species, whereas **basses** refers to multiple varieties or species.

Derived terms [edit]

- black bass
- black sea bass
- largemouth bass
- sea bass

- smallmouth bass
- spotted bass
- striped bass
- white bass

Translations [edit]

perch	[hide ▲]
Select targeted languages	
• Bulgarian: костур (bg)	• Hungarian: sügér (hu)
• Cherokee: ᎠᏣᏗ (chr)	• Italian: branzino (it) *m*, spigola (it) *m*
• Croatian: grgeč (hr) *m*	• Latvian: asaris (lv)
• Dutch: baars (nl) *m*	• Lithuanian: ešerys (lt)
• French: perche (fr) *m*	• Norwegian: bass (no)
• German: Barsch (de) *m*	• Russian: окунь (ru) (ókun') *m*
• Greek: πέρκα (el) (perka) *f*	• Spanish: róbalo *m*, lubina *f*, perca *f* (freshwater)
	• Add translation :
	Preview translation More

Figure 2: An excerpt of the Wiktionary entry on *bass*. http://en.wiktionary.org/wiki/bass

▼ Definition

Language ▼ Text

Castilian	Pez marino (Percicthyidae o Centrarchidae) popular para la pesca.
Dutch	Een zeevis (Percicthyidae of Centrarchidae) die populair is als sportvis.
English	A marine fish (Percicthyidae or Centrarchidae) that is popular as game.
French	Poisson d'eau de mer (Percicthyidae or Centrarchidae) populaire pour la pêche.
Slovak	Morská ryba (Percicthyidae alebo Centrarchidae) populárna ako lovná zver.

▼ Synonyms and translations

Expression

Language ▼ Spelling

Castilian	lubina
Castilian	róbalo
Castilian	robalo
Dutch	zeebaars
English	bass
French	basse
German	Seebarsch
Italian	spigola
Japanese	バス
Portuguese	robalo
Swedish	bass

▼ Annotation

Property ▼ Value

is part of theme fish

▼ Class membership

Class ▼

animal

Figure 3: An excerpt of OmegaWiki's Defined Meaning 5555 on *bass*.
http://www.omegawiki.org/DefinedMeaning:bass_(5555)

2. There should be a large variety of lexicographic information types, such as sense definitions, example sentences, collocations, etc. that illustrate the use of a translation without being redundant.

3. Ideally, the resources should be seamlessly integrable into the translation environment via established standards and interfaces.

Most popular expert-built resources such as WordNet (Fellbaum 1998) fail to fulfill some or all of these requirements. First of all, they need enormous building effort and are in turn rather inflexible with regard to corrections or addition of knowledge. This effort is also the reason why for many smaller languages such resources remain small or do not even exist. Second, expert-built resources usually have a narrow scope of information types. WordNet focuses, for example, on synsets and their taxonomy, but mostly disregards syntactic information. Finally, many expert-built resources utilize proprietary or non-machine-readable formats, which make the integration into a translation environment difficult.

In order to alleviate these problems, we study the collaboratively constructed resources Wiktionary[3] and OmegaWiki[4] and describe how multilingual lexical-semantic knowledge can be mined from and linked between these resources. This is meant as a first step to integrating them into SMT systems, computer-aided translation systems, or other applications in the future. For the sake of illustrating our methodology, we focus on the English and German versions of these resources, but our results and insights can for the most part be directly applied to other languages. Among others, Wiktionary and OmegaWiki have the following advantageous properties:

Easy contribution. Wiktionary and OmegaWiki are based on a wiki system, which allows any Web user to contribute. This crowd-based construction approach is very promising, since the large body of collaborators can quickly adapt to new language phenomena like neologisms while at the same time ensuring a remarkable quality – a phenomenon known as the "wisdom of crowds" (Surowiecki 2005).

Good coverage of languages. These resources are open to users from different cultures speaking any language, which is very beneficial to smaller languages. Meyer & Gurevych (2012) found, for instance, that the collaborative construction approach of Wiktionary yields language versions covering the majority of language families and regions of the world, and that it

---

[3]http://www.wiktionary.org
[4]http://www.omegawiki.org

covers a vast amount of domain-specific descriptions not found in word-nets.

Free availability. All the knowledge in these resources is available for free under permissive licenses. This is a major advantage of collaboratively constructed resources over efforts like EuroWordNet (Vossen 1998), where the aligned expert-built resources are subject to restrictive licenses.

To our knowledge, the collaboratively constructed lexical resources OmegaWiki and Wiktionary have not yet been discussed in the context of translation applications. There exists a significant amount of previous work using Wikipedia in the context of cross-lingual information retrieval for query expansion or query translation (Gaillard et al. 2010; Herbert et al. 2011; Potthast et al. 2008), but it is primarily an encyclopedic resource, which limits the amount of lexical knowledge available for the application we address here. In previous work, Müller & Gurevych (2009) discussed combining Wiktionary and Wikipedia for cross-lingual information retrieval, but also in this case Wiktionary is merely used for query expansion and most of the lexicographic knowledge encoded in it remains disregarded. However, this knowledge is essential for translation applications in order to make well-grounded decisions. To fill this gap, we present the following four contributions in this article:

1. We provide a comprehensive analysis of Wiktionary and OmegaWiki to characterize the information found therein, as well as their coverage and structure.

2. We automatically align Wiktionary and OmegaWiki at the level of word senses, that is we create a list of word senses in both resources which denote the same meaning so that we can benefit from the complementary lexicographic information types. For example, we aim at directly linking the animal-related word sense of *bass* in Wiktionary to its corresponding sense in OmegaWiki – but not to its music-related sense. As opposed to the mere linking at the lemma level, this is a non-trivial task because the resources differ greatly in the way they represent word senses (for example, different definition texts or varying granularity of senses). Solving this issue allows us to effectively use the variety of lexicographic information found in both resources without being redundant.

3. We standardize Wiktionary and OmegaWiki using the Lexical Markup Framework (Francopoulo et al. 2009). This is a necessary step for using

those resources in natural language processing systems and for integrating them with other resources.

4. We create a sense-aligned unified resource containing the English and German versions of Wiktionary and OmegaWiki, serving as an example of how the standardization process can be operationalized. We publish this aligned resource as integral part of UBY (Gurevych et al. 2012), our unified lexical-semantic resource which is freely available at http://www.ukp.tu-darmstadt.de/uby/. The alignment between Wiktionary and OmegaWiki, along with accompanying information, is available at http://www.ukp.tu-darmstadt.de/data/lexical-resources/wiktionary-omegawiki-alignment/ .

Since the data of Wiktionary and OmegaWiki is freely available with non-restrictive licenses, we are able to publish our sense alignment data and the standardized representation of the two resources.

Note that a task-based evaluation of our resulting resource is a crucial step to be taken. As this is still work in progress, we limit ourselves to presenting in detail the preparatory work that has been done with regard to analyzing, standardizing and combining Wiktionary and OmegaWiki.

The remaining article is structured as follows: in the first part, we carry out our analysis of Wiktionary and OmegaWiki in §2 and §3 to familiarize the reader with these resources. After this, in §4, we discuss previous work in the areas of multilingual resources, aligning them at the level of word senses, and using standardized models to represent them. Based on this, we introduce our work on aligning Wiktionary and OmegaWiki (§5) and discuss how to represent them in a standardized model (§6), before we conclude our article in §7.

2 Wiktionary

2.1 Overview

Wiktionary is a publicly available multilingual dictionary. It is based on the wiki principle that users are free to add, edit, and delete (only with admin right) entries collaboratively." entries collaboratively. Being a sister project of Wikipedia, gaining much attention, a rapid growth of dictionary articles ensued. Currently, Wiktionary is available in over 171 language editions providing more than 27.1 million articles (as of May 2018). The dictionary is organized in multiple *article pages*, each of them covering the lexicographic information about a certain word. This knowledge includes the lexical class, pronunciations, inflected forms, etymology, sense definition, example sentences, translations, and many other information types commonly found in dictionaries. Meyer & Gurevych (2012) give a more detailed introduction to the macro- and microstructure of Wiktionary.

Multilinguality is a key design feature of Wiktionary, which is implemented by two different notions:

1. For each language, there is a separate Wiktionary *language edition*, for instance, an English language edition available at http://en.wiktionary.org and a German language edition at http://de.wiktionary.org. The language of an edition determines the language of the user interface and of the encoded lexicographic information. The German Wiktionary edition hence uses the German language for its browsing and search tools as well as its sense definitions, usage examples, etc.

2. A language edition is not limited to words that are native to this language, but also allows the inclusion of *foreign language entries*. There is, for instance, an entry about the German verb *spazieren gehen* in the English Wiktionary. The rationale behind this is to become able to use one's native language for describing foreign words; for example, describing the German verb as *to take a stroll, to stroll, to take a paseo*. Defining foreign words in one's native language is important, as the actual native language definition *sich in gemütlichem Tempo zu Fuß fortbewegen, meist ohne Ziel* (English: *to wander on foot at comfortable speed, often without specific destination*) is often beyond the language proficiency of a non-native speaker or language learner.[5]

The different language editions are interlinked by *translation links* and *inter-wiki links*. The former are links between words with equivalent meanings in two languages. The German Wiktionary entry *spazieren gehen* has, for instance, an English translation *(to) walk*. The latter is a link to the same word form in another language edition, for example, from the German Wiktionary entry *spazieren gehen* to the English Wiktionary entry *spazieren gehen*. Using the inter wiki links, we are able to extract sense definitions of a word in multiple languages.

Table 1 shows the number of translations found within the English and German Wiktionary (in comparison with OmegaWiki). The table also shows the number of languages for which at least one translation is encoded and the number of translations for the most frequently used languages. Most translations are

---

[5]http://en.wiktionary.org/w/index.php?oldid=20466324 (12 May 2013), http://de.wiktionary. org/w/index.php?oldid=2706581 (19 October 2012).

found for languages spoken worldwide, such as English, French, Spanish, etc. Languages with only a few number of speakers also have only a small number of translation links. Besides a country's main languages, sometimes also dialects and ancient languages (like Egyptian) are included. An important difference between the language editions are the translations into the Wiktionary's native language: there are no translations to English within the English Wiktionary, while the German Wiktionary contains 69,135 translations into German. In the German edition, non-native entries are equipped with a translation into German. The entry for the English word *boat* encodes, for instance, a translation *Boot* into German. In the English edition, such translations are encoded as part of the definition texts. The number of languages seems to be extremely high, especially for the English Wiktionary. It should thus be noted that there are only a few translations for some of them.

2.2 Wiktionary as machine-readable resource

Wiktionary has been designed to be used by humans rather than machines. The entries are formatted for easy perception using appropriate font sizes and bold, italic, or colored text styles, while at the same time assuring that as much information as possible fits on a screen. For machines, data needs to be available in a structured manner in order to become able to obtain, for instance, a list of all translations or enumerating all English pronouns. This kind of structure is not explicitly encoded in Wiktionary, but needs to be inferred from the wiki markup of each article by means of an extraction software. The wiki markup is an annotation language consisting of a set of special characters and keywords that can be used to mark headlines, bold and italic text styles, tables, hyperlinks, etc. within the article. The four equality signs in "====Translations====" denote, for example, a small headline that usually precedes the list of a word's translations. Besides the mere formatting purpose, the wiki markup can be used by a software tool to identify the beginning of the translation section, which looks similar on each article page. The vast use of such markup structures allows us to extract each type of information in a structured way and use this kind of data in other contexts or process it automatically in natural language processing applications.

Although there are guidelines on how to properly structure a Wiktionary entry, it is permitted to choose from multiple variants or deviate from the standards if this can enhance the entry. This happens, for instance, for homonyms, which are distinguished by their differing etymology (as opposed to monosemous entries that do not require this distinction) and presents a major challenge for the automatic processing of Wiktionary data. Another hurdle is the openness of Wiktionary – that is, the opportunity to perform arbitrary changes at any time. While a key to Wiktionary's success and rapid growth, this might cause major structural changes, which raises the need for constant revision of the extraction software.

There are multiple software tools available for extracting lexicographic knowledge from Wiktionary, such as JWKTL (Zesch et al. 2008), Wikokit (Krizhanovsky & Lin 2009), or WISIGOTH (Navarro et al. 2009). We use JWKTL for our work. This is the only one capable of extracting information from both the English and the German Wiktionary editions, which are the ones we focus on in this work.

Table 1: Number of translations for selected languages and the sum of languages for which translations are available in Wiktionary and OmegaWiki

	Wiktionary		OmegaWiki	
Resource	En	De	En	De
Translations	190,055	449,517	335,173	304,590
into Chinese	5,067	10,194	4,377	4,248
into English	0	63,006	0	56,471
into Finnish	14,342	4,114	18,997	19,536
into French	5,388	53,364	54,068	46,931
into German	8,342	69,135	56,471	0
into Italian	3,243	26,759	27,499	25,288
into Japanese	11,905	7,883	10,879	11,088
into Spanish	5,852	41,114	67,622	47,554
Languages	597	234	279	265

3 OmegaWiki

3.1 Overview

OmegaWiki is a lexical-semantic resource which is freely editable via its Web frontend. To alleviate Wiktionary's problem of inconsistent entries caused by the free editing, OmegaWiki is based on a fixed database structure which users have to comply to. It was initiated in 2006 and explicitly designed with the goal of offering structured and consistent access to lexical information, or as the creators

Michael Matuschek, Christian M. Meyer & Iryna Gurevych

Table 2: Descriptive statistics about Wiktionary and OmegaWiki as of May 2011. Further statistics can be found on our website http://www.ukp.tu-darmstadt.de/uby/

	Wiktionary	OmegaWiki
Entries (Total)	14,021,155	442,723
Entries (English)	2,457,506	55,182
Entries (German)	177,124	34,559
Languages covered	>400	290
Languages with >10.000 entries	54	12
Information storing	Wiki Markup/XML	Relational DB

put it: "The idea of OmegaWiki was born out of frustration with Wiktionary."[6]

The central elements of OmegaWiki's organizational structure are language-independent concepts (so-called DEFINED MEANINGS) to which lexicalizations of the concepts are attached. These can be considered as multilingual synsets. This way, no language editions exist for OmegaWiki as they do for Wiktionary. Rather, all multilingual information is encoded in a single resource. As an example, Defined Meaning no. 5616 carries the lexicalizations *hand, main, mano,* etc. and also definitions in different languages which describe this concept, for example, *That part of the fore limb below the forearm or wrist.* This method of encoding the multilingual information in a synset-like structure directly yields correct translations as these are merely lexicalizations of the same concept in different languages.

Table 1 shows statistics about the translations between different languages that we derived from these multilingual synsets. As with Wiktionary, the number of languages into which translations are available should be taken with a grain of salt, as for many languages only very few translations exist. An important thing to note here is that the number of translations from English to German is the same as for the opposite direction. The reason is that translations only exist if a concept is lexicalized in both languages. The number of possible translations for a concept is then the product of the number of lexicalizations in either language, which is symmetric.

A useful consequence of this concept-centered design for multilingual applications such as cross-lingual semantic relatedness is that semantic relations are unambiguously defined between concepts regardless of existing lexicalizations. Consider for example the Spanish term *dedo*: it is marked as hypernym of *finger*

---

[6]http://www.omegawiki.org/Help:OmegaWiki, accessed on June 20th, 2012.

150

and *toe*, although there exists no corresponding term in English. This might also be immediately helpful for translation tasks, since concepts for which no lexicalization in the target language exists can be described or replaced by closely related concepts. Exploiting this kind of information is not as easy in resources like EuroWordNet where concepts are linked across languages, but the respective taxonomies are different (Jansen 2004).

3.2 OmegaWiki as machine-readable resource

OmegaWiki is based on a fixed structure, manifested in an sQL database. This fixed structure of OmegaWiki is proprietary in the sense that it does not conform to existing standards for encoding lexicographic information such as the Lexical Markup Framework. Plainly spoken, it was designed and over time extended in a "grass-roots approach" by the community to cater for the needs identified for such a multilingual resource.

While this approach to structuring the information is not easy to tackle in terms of interoperability, it still makes the use of this resource easier than for Wiktionary. The underlying database ensures straightforward structured extraction of the information and less error-prone results due to the consistency enforced by the definition of database tables and relations between them. This database structure is documented in the help pages. Most recently, we published a Java API for OmegaWiki (JOWKL[7]) which enables the easy usage of OmegaWiki in applications without resorting to using plain sQL.

However, the fixed structure also has the major drawback of limited expressiveness. As an example, the coding of grammatical properties is only possible to a small extent; complex properties such as verb argument structures can not be encoded at all. Moreover, an extension of this structure is not easy, as this would, in many cases, require a reorganization of the database structure by administrators to which present and future entries would have to conform. While it could be argued that such information is outside of the scope of the resource and thus does not need to be reflected, the possibility given in Wiktionary to (in theory) encode any kind of lexicographic information using the more expressive wiki markup makes it more attractive for future extension. In OmegaWiki, the users are not allowed to extend the structure and thus are tied to what has been already defined. Consequently, OmegaWiki's lack of flexibility and extensibility, in combination with the fact that Wiktionary was already quite popular at its creation, has caused it to grow less rapidly (see Table 2).

---

[7]http://code.google.com/p/jowkl/

Michael Matuschek, Christian M. Meyer & Iryna Gurevych

Despite the above-mentioned issues, we believe OmegaWiki is useful as a case study since it exemplifies how the process of collaboratively creating a large-scale lexical-semantic resource can be moderated by means of a structural "skeleton" in order to yield a machine-readable result for machine translation and related applications.

4 Related work

Previous work has been carried out in the areas of multilingual resources, sense alignment, and resource standardization. Table 3 summarizes the advantages and drawbacks of each type of resource which we discuss in greater detail below.

Table 3: Comparison of the advantages of different resource types (OIE = Open Information Extraction)

Resource type	Information types	Lexicon size	Computational usage	Update time	Quality
Dictionaries	many	considerable	hard	long	very high
Wordnets	limited	small	easy	long	very high
OIE-based	many	huge	easy	short	low
Wikipedia	encyclopedic	large	medium	short	high
Wiktionary	many	large	medium	short	high
OmegaWiki	many	medium	easy	short	high

4.1 Multilingual resources

Human translators traditionally utilize monolingual and bilingual dictionaries as a reference. Dictionaries provide many different kinds of lexicographic information, such as sense definitions, example sentences, collocations, idioms, etc. They are well-crafted for being used by humans, but pose a great challenge to using them computationally. Although machine-readable dictionaries allow processing their data automatically, computers are often overstrained to properly interpret the structure of an entry or resolve ambiguities that are intuitively clear to humans.

The Princeton WordNet (Fellbaum 1998) is a lexical knowledge base designed for computational purposes. The great success of the project motivated the creation of a large number of multilingual wordnets, such as EuroWordNet (Vossen 1998), BalkaNet (Stamou et al. 2002), or MultiWordNet (Pianta et al. 2002). While the nature of these resources seems to perfectly meet our requirements, none of these multilingual resources gained a significant size or provides as many different information types as dictionaries, such as etymology, pronunciation or derived terms.

A large problem of these expert-built resources (both dictionaries and word-nets) is their time-consuming and costly construction. The small number of experts, moreover, prevents timely updates featuring new or updated contents. Automatically induced resources based on the output of Open Information Extraction (OIE) systems such as KnowItAll (Banko et al. 2007) can be huge and kept up to date at any time. However, those resources are not sense-disambiguated *per se* and, due to the completely automatic creation process, limited in their quality.

Regarding collaboratively constructed resources, Wikipedia[8] has been found as a very promising resource for a multitude of natural language processing tasks (Zesch et al. 2007; Medelyan et al. 2009). Possibly the most well-known works are YAGO (Suchanek et al. 2008), DBpedia (Bizer et al. 2009), and WikiNet (Nastase et al. 2010) that provide the Wikipedia data in different machine-readable formats. The large size of Wikipedia and the overall high quality of the articles make Wikipedia a promising resource for translation tasks – for example, as a parallel corpus (Adafre & de Rijke 2006) and for mining bilingual terminology (Erdmann et al. 2009). However, the vast majority of information in Wikipedia is encyclopedic and almost entirely focusing on nouns. Translators also require lexicographic information types such as idioms, collocations, or usage examples as well as translations for word classes other than nouns – most importantly verbs, adjectives, and adverbs.

This is why we explore Wiktionary and OmegaWiki as two novel collaboratively constructed multilingual resources. Wiktionary and OmegaWiki combine the advantages of the other resources discussed above:

- They contain multiple different lexicographic information types.

- They are of considerable size and available in a large number of languages.

- Their data can be processed automatically.

- They are continually revised by the community and thus allow for timely updates.

- The information is provided by humans and therefore it is of higher quality than in resources that have been induced fully automatically.

---

[8]http://www.wikipedia.org

4.2 Word sense alignment

There have been many works on aligning resources at the level of word senses, as it is deemed more and more crucial for natural language processing to make use of complementary resources in an orchestrated manner; see for instance (Shi & Mihalcea 2005; Ponzetto & Navigli 2010). Most of them propose aligning the Princeton WordNet to other resources in order to improve its coverage and introduce novel types of information. It has been aligned to Roget's thesaurus and the Longman Dictionary of Contemporary English (Kwong 1998), the HECTOR corpus (Litkowski 1999), the Unified Medical Language System (Burgun & Bodenreider 2001), CYC (Reed & Lenat 2002), VerbNet and FrameNet (Shi & Mihalcea 2005), as well as the Oxford Dictionary of English (Navigli 2006).

A large body of work addresses the alignment of WordNet and Wikipedia. Automatic methods have been explored for aligning WordNet synsets with Wikipedia categories (Toral et al. 2009; Ponzetto & Navigli 2009) and WordNet synsets with Wikipedia articles (Ruiz-Casado et al. 2005; de Melo & Weikum 2010; Navigli & Ponzetto 2010; Niemann & Gurevych 2011).

In our own previous work, Wiktionary has been aligned to WordNet and FrameNet (Meyer & Gurevych 2011; Matuschek & Gurevych 2013; Hartmann & Gurevych 2013), OmegaWiki has been aligned to WordNet (Gurevych et al. 2012; Matuschek & Gurevych 2013), but they have not yet been aligned to each other. See §5 for details on our previously used alignment approach based on gloss similarity.

We go beyond this previous work by applying this approach to an alignment between two collaboratively-constructed resources which are inherently more error-prone. This has not been addressed so far in the literature. It is a very challenging task, as word sense representations (such as glosses), granularities, etc. vary greatly between different resources and the similarity between them has to be assessed appropriately. This is also part of the reason why using WordNet as a pivot resource, although tempting, did not give satisfactory results in preliminary experiments. Another reason is the small number of word senses in the intersection of the three resources, which would render the resulting aligned resource very small.

4.3 Standardized resources

Previous work on the standardization of resources includes models for representing lexical information relative to ontologies (Buitelaar et al. 2009; McCrae et al. 2011) and standardized single wordnets in English (Soria et al. 2009), German

(Henrich & Hinrichs 2010) and Italian (Toral et al. 2010) using the КYОТО standard Lexical Markup Framework (LMF) (Francopoulo et al. 2009). Wiktionary has also been modeled in LMF (Sérasset 2012) and other formats (Declerck et al. 2012) recently. LMF defines a meta-model for lexical resources and has proven to be the most flexible and powerful approach for modeling such resources.

Soria et al. (2009) define WordNet-LMF, an LMF model for representing wordnets used in the КYОТО project, and Henrich & Hinrichs (2010) do this for the German wordnet. These models are similar, but they still present different implementations of the LMF meta-model, which hampers interoperability between the resources. With UBY-LMF (Eckle-Kohler et al. 2012), we proposed a model for a broad variety of wordnets and dictionaries.

Sérasset (2012) proposes a transformation of Wiktionary to LMF. However, this approach does not include all information encoded in Wiktionary – translations, for instance, are modeled at the level of words rather than at the level of word senses. However, this is crucial for translators since words can have different translations with different meanings. The same holds for the approach proposed by McCrae et al. (2012), who focus on linking lexical information to ontologies and hence model only a small part of Wiktionary's lexicographic information in their LMF model. In contrast, we aim to cover all information contained in Wiktionary. Declerck et al. (2012) represent Wiktionary data using the Text Encoding Initiative (TEI) standard, an alternative to LMF. Although their model is able to represent translations and many other lexicographic information types found in Wiktionary, the model does, for example, not contain pronunciations. In addition to that, only a few major lexical resources have been encoded using the TEI standard, which limits the interoperability with other resources. To our knowledge, OmegaWiki has not been modeled in a standardized format by anyone else so far.

In §6, we will discuss the UBY-LMF model (Eckle-Kohler et al. 2012) in detail as this is the model we base our unified model of Wiktionary and OmegaWiki on.

5 Word sense alignment of Wiktionary and OmegaWiki

As we have seen in §2 and §3, the structures of Wiktionary (loosely defined and changeable by users) and OmegaWiki (fixed and well-defined) are quite different, and to some extent this is also true for their content. While Wiktionary offers a greater coverage and a richer variety of encoded information, OmegaWiki provides the advantage of unambiguous translations and relations which are potentially useful in translation applications. Thus, a crucial next step for exploiting both resources is combining them, or, more specifically, aligning them at the word sense level. This offers various advantages:

- Better coverage as the information from both resources can be considered.

- Exploitation of complementary information such as additional example sentences for a sense which help choosing the correct translation or additional translations contained in the additional resource.

- Better structuring of translation results, for example, by clustering the translations into the same language for aligned senses instead of simply considering all of them in parallel.

- Identical translations in both resources yield combined evidence and thus higher translation confidence; the redundancy in the displayed results can be avoided by collapsing these translations.

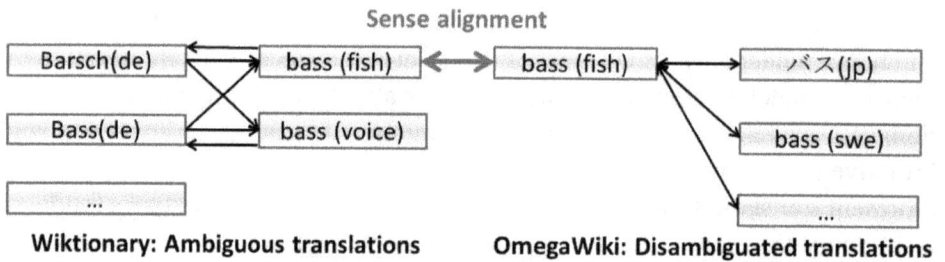

Figure 4: Illustration of the sense alignment between Wiktionary and OmegaWiki. As the translations in OmegaWiki are unambiguous, they directly apply to the aligned Wiktionary sense. Although this is not the case for the translations in Wiktionary, they still offer additional translation options. The ambiguity in Wiktionary is exemplified by the arrows pointing from German "Barsch" and "Bass" to both English senses of "bass" – there is no explicit link to the correct sense, only to the lexeme.

In this paper we align the English Wiktionary with OmegaWiki. As English is the language with the most entries in both resources, such an alignment yields the largest resulting resource and thus the greatest benefit. Moreover, there are no errors introduced into the alignment process by using machine translation, which would be a prerequisite for automatic cross-lingual alignment. As OmegaWiki is a multilingual resource by design, if Wiktionary (or any other resource) is aligned to OmegaWiki, we obtain an alignment to multilingual synsets – this means that the (disambiguated) translations encoded here apply to the aligned Wiktionary senses. This entails that the correct translation is immediately known once the word sense in the source document can be correctly identified, either by the user or by automatic word sense disambiguation. A similar argument also holds for Wiktionary – all aligned senses from OmegaWiki benefit from the additional translations available in Wiktionary. The only disadvantage in this case is that these are not disambiguated. This alignment is illustrated in Figure 4.

In the remaining section, we will present the alignment algorithm, evaluate the results and present examples where the combination of resources is beneficial.

5.1 The alignment procedure

Creating sense alignments between multilingual lexical resources automatically is a challenging task because of word ambiguities and different granularities of senses (Navigli 2006). For aligning Wiktionary and OmegaWiki, we used the flexible alignment framework described in Niemann & Gurevych (2011). The framework supports this task for a large number of resources across languages and allows alignments between different representations of senses as found in different resources, for example WordNet synsets, FrameNet frames or even Wikipedia articles. The only requirement is that the individual sense representations are distinguishable by a unique identifier in each resource.

The basic idea of the algorithm is, in a nutshell:

1. For each sense in one resource, all possible candidates in the other resource are retrieved, and a similarity score between the glosses is calculated. For instance, for the *programming* sense of *Java* in Wiktionary, the *programming, island* and *coffee* senses in OmegaWiki are considered.

2. For a subset of these (the gold standard), the alignment decision is manually annotated, and based on this, we can learn an optimal (in terms of F-measure) similarity threshold, that is the minimum similarity that is necessary for an alignment to be considered correct.

3. Using this threshold learned from the gold standard, the alignment decision is made for all candidates to produce a complete alignment of the resources.

In this case, we first extract OmegaWiki Defined Meaning candidates for each entry in the English Wiktionary. This is solely based on the combination of lemma and part-of-speech, that is, in the first step all senses for a word are considered potential candidates. Second, we create a gold standard by manually annotating a subset of candidate pairs as "valid" or "non-valid". Note that due to different granularities in these resources, it is well possible that $m : n$ alignments occur when, for example, one Wiktionary sense corresponds to several OmegaWiki senses. Then, we extract the sense descriptions to compute the similarity of word senses with two similarity measures:

(i) The COSINE SIMILARITY (COS) calculates the cosine of the angle between a vector representation of the two senses s_1 and s_2:

$$\text{COS}(s_1, s_2) = \frac{\text{BoW}(s_1) \cdot \text{BoW}(s_2)}{\| \text{BoW}(s_1) \| \, \| \text{BoW}(s_2) \|}$$

To represent a sense as a vector, we use a bag-of-words approach – that is, a vector BoW(s) containing the term frequencies of all words in the description of s. Note that there are different options for choosing the description of sense s. For Wiktionary, we selected the gloss, usage examples, and related words of the word sense. For OmegaWiki, we chose the gloss, usage examples, and synonyms in the same language.

(ii) The PERSONALIZED PAGERANK BASED MEASURE (PPR) (Agirre & Soroa 2009) estimates the semantic relatedness between two word senses s_1 and s_2 by representing them in a semantic graph and comparing the semantic vectors $\mathbf{Pr}_{s_1}$ and $\mathbf{Pr}_{s_2}$ by computing

$$\text{PPR}(s_1, s_2) = 1 - \sum_i \frac{(\mathbf{Pr}_{s_1,i} - \mathbf{Pr}_{s_2,i})^2}{\mathbf{Pr}_{s_1,i} + \mathbf{Pr}_{s_2,i}}$$

which is a χ^2 variant introduced by Niemann & Gurevych (2011). The main idea of choosing $\mathbf{Pr}$ is to use the personalized PageRank algorithm for identifying those nodes in the graph that are central for describing a sense's meaning. These nodes should have a high centrality (that is, a high PageRank score), which is calculated as

$$\mathbf{Pr} = c \, M \, \mathbf{Pr} + (1 - c) \, \mathbf{v}$$

with the damping factor c controlling the random walk, the transition matrix M of the underlying semantic graph, and the probabilistic vector $\mathbf{v}$, whose ith component $\mathbf{v}_i$ denotes the probability of randomly jumping to node i in the next iteration step.[9] Unlike in the traditional PageRank algorithm, the components of the jump vector $\mathbf{v}$ are not uniformly distributed, but personalized to the sense s by choosing $\mathbf{v}_i = \frac{1}{m}$ if at least one lexicalization of node i occurs in the definition of sense s, and $\mathbf{v}_i = 0$ otherwise. The normalization factor m is set to the total number of nodes that share a word with the sense descriptions, which is required for obtaining a probabilistic vector.

5.2 Aligning Wiktionary and OmegaWiki

The candidate extraction process yielded 98,272 unique candidate sense pairs overall, covering 56,111 Wiktionary senses and 20,674 OmegaWiki Defined Meanings (that is, synsets containing one or more senses). When we consider the over 400,000 word senses in Wiktionary and the over 50,000 senses in OmegaWiki, this confirms that there is a considerable lexical overlap between the two resources, as well as a large number of entries which are only available in either one of the resources. This suggests that a combination of the resources indeed leads to a significantly increased coverage.

For creating the gold standard, we randomly selected 500 Wiktionary senses, yielding 586 candidate pairs. These were manually annotated by a computational linguistics expert as representing the same meaning (190 cases) or not (396 cases). This gold standard was used for training the threshold-based machine learning classifier and the subsequent evaluation with 10-fold cross-validation. Note that the threshold was optimized for F-measure; optimizing for precision would have led to higher thresholds and thus fewer alignments. Table 4 summarizes the results for the different similarity measures and their combinations in terms of precision P, recall R, and F_1 measure (the harmonic mean of precision and recall). The results of a random baseline are given for comparison. As there is no explicit sense frequency information encoded in either resource, the application of a most frequent sense baseline is not possible. We also considered using the existing alignments to WordNet to directly infer an alignment between Wiktionary and OmegaWiki using WordNet as pivot, but the different sense granularities in combination with small lexical intersection of all three resources rendered this approach very ineffective.

We observe that the more elaborate similarity measure PPR yields worse results than cosine similarity (cos), while the best result is achieved by a combination of

---

[9]We use the publicly available UKB software (Agirre & Soroa 2009) for calculating the PageRank scores and utilize the WordNet 3.0 graph augmented with the Princeton Annotated Gloss Corpus as M. The damping factor c is set to 0.85.

Table 4: Alignment results

Similarity measure	P	R	F_1
Random	0.542	0.473	0.489
COS	0.774	0.771	0.773
PPR	0.745	0.582	0.582
PPR + COS	0.782	0.783	0.783

both. However, this difference between COS and the combination of COS and PPR is not statistically relevant at the 1% level (McNemar test). These results differ from those reported in our earlier work which might be due to the fact that, by our observation, some sense definitions in OmegaWiki have been copied or adapted from Wiktionary, so that Cosine similarity alone already gives a very strong hint towards the correct sense. All measures outperform the random baseline by a huge margin.

The F-measure of 0.783 in the best configuration is above the results we reported in Meyer & Gurevych (2011) (0.66) and Niemann & Gurevych (2011) (0.78) for alignments between Wiktionary and WordNet and Wikipedia and WordNet, respectively. The application of the trained classifier to all candidate pairs leads to a final alignment of 25,742 senses between Wiktionary and OmegaWiki.

5.3 Error analysis

We carried out an error analysis to identify the main errors made by our alignment algorithm. Of the 586 sense pairs in the gold standard, the classifier yielded 71 false positives (that is, incorrectly aligned senses) and 69 false negatives (that is, senses which should have been aligned but were not).

For the false positives, the main error we identified is that different senses were aligned because of very similar sense descriptions expressing only a slight difference which is hard to grasp for our approach. An example for this are two senses of *(to) carry*: (1) *To lift (something) and take it to another place; to transport (something) by lifting* (2) *To transport with the flow.*

For the false negatives, we could basically identify two categories of errors:

1. Different sense descriptions for the same concept. These are not easy to tackle as a certain degree of understanding and world knowledge would be required. An example for this are two senses of the adjective *aware* which should have been aligned, but were not because of insufficient overlap: (1)

Conscious or having knowledge of something (2) *noticing something; aware of something.*

2. Short definitions making references to other, closely related or derived words. An example are these two definitions of *alluvial:* (1) *Pertaining to the soil deposited by a stream* (2) *Of or relating to alluvium.* Without resolving the definition of the derived word a disambiguation is nearly impossible. This is, however, another word sense disambiguation problem which cannot be easily solved.

5.4 Discussion of alignment results

As mentioned earlier, the alignment yields a significantly increased lexical coverage as many entries are only contained in either resource. The other benefit, which we want to discuss in more detail, is the availability of additional information, and especially translations, for aligned resources. While a task-based evaluation of the sense-aligned resource is beyond the scope of this article and subject to future work, we would like to illustrate the advantages of the derived alignment on the example introduced earlier.

Consider again the noun *bass.* The word sense *A male singer who sings in the deepest vocal range* from OmegaWiki is automatically aligned with the sense *A male singer who sings in the bass range* from Wiktionary. While these two different definitions might themselves be useful for pinpointing the exact meaning of the term, there are a number of further valuable information sources:

- Wiktionary offers translations into Spanish, Dutch, Bulgarian, Tatar, Finnish, German, Greek, Hungarian, Italian, Japanese, Russian and Slovene, while OmegaWiki additionally encodes translations into French, Georgian, Korean and Portuguese. Only the Spanish translation *bajo* and the Italian translation *basso* are included in both. Thus, the alignment directly yields a significantly broader range of translations than either resource alone.

- OmegaWiki offers sense definitions of this word sense in Spanish, and French which are useful for a translator fluent in one of these languages. Moreover, the Spanish sense definition from OmegaWiki can directly be used to identify the correct sense of the Spanish translation, which is not disambiguated in Wiktionary.

- Wiktionary also offers additional information not included in OmegaWiki, such as etymology, pronunciation, and derived terms.

Table 5 summarizes the information that becomes available through the sense alignment of Wiktionary and OmegaWiki for our example word *bass*.

Table 5: Information gain through the alignment for one sense of *bass*

Resource	Translation languages	Available definitions	Additional information types
Wiktionary	12	1	5
OmegaWiki	6	3	0
Combined	16	4	5

6 Modeling Wiktionary and OmegaWiki in LMF

Our analysis in §2 and §3 showed that Wiktionary and OmegaWiki differ largely in the way they represent the encoded lexicographic information. In order to make use of this data we need to harmonize their heterogeneous representations and thus make them interoperable. Interoperability is a prerequisite for a smooth integration of multilingual resources into applications and for making them accessible in a unified user interface.

Ide & Pustejovsky (2010) distinguish *syntactic interoperability* and *semantic interoperability* as the two types of interoperability of computer systems. The former addresses the degree of the heterogeneity of the formats used to store and retrieve the language data. The latter represents the reference model for interpreting the language data. In terms of lexical resources, we need a structural model for storing and retrieving the data and a set of standardized information types for encoding the lexicographic data. For this purpose, the ISO standard *Lexical Markup Framework* (LMF: ISO24613 2008), a standard with a particular focus on lexical resources for natural language processing (Francopoulo et al. 2009), is an obvious choice. LMF has proven very useful for modeling wordnets (Soria et al. 2009; Henrich & Hinrichs 2010), but has only rarely been used for representing collaboratively constructed resources. Previous works on Wiktionary (McCrae et al. 2012; Sérasset 2012) did not model all information available in the resource, such as translations or information at the level of word senses. We are not aware of any works other than UBY-LMF modeling OmegaWiki in a standardized model.

6.1 The Lexical Markup Framework and UBY-LMF

LMF defines a meta-model for lexical resources using the Unified Modeling Language (UML). That is to say, LMF introduces a number of *classes* and *relationships* between them. The classes are organized in multiple packages (called *extensions*) that may be chosen according to the type of resource that is to be modeled. Examples are the *Machine Readable Dictionary* extension or the *NLP syntax* extension. The *core* package represents the essence of the standard and is to be used for each instance of LMF. It includes, among others, the LexicalEntry class for modeling lexical entries in accordance to dictionaries, the Form class for representing different orthographic variants of a lexical entry, and the Sense class for modeling one of multiple possible meanings of a lexical entry.

Since LMF is conceived as a meta-model for representing different kinds of resources, the standard does neither state which classes are to be used nor which attributes should be chosen to encode the language data in the resources. This is defined by the actual *lexicon model* – that is, an *instantiation* of the LMF standard. Eckle-Kohler et al. (2012) mention that a single lexicon model for standardizing divergent and multilingual resources has to be *comprehensive* (that is, the model covers all the information present in the resource) and *extensible*. Thus, we had to choose a model that is standard-compliant, yet able to express the large variety of information types contained in both resources. For our work, we use UBY-LMF (Eckle-Kohler et al. 2012), which defines a lexicon model for a broad variety of resources, including wordnets and collaboratively constructed resources.

UBY-LMF consists of 39 LMF classes and a huge number of attributes for representing lexicographic information (for example, the lemma form, sense definitions, example sentences). Each attribute is registered in ISOcat,[10] where a large amount of linguistic vocabulary is standardized as individual *data categories* following the KYOTO standard for data category registries (ISO12620 2009). The selection of a set of LMF classes and the relationships between them allows for structural interoperability, while the selection of data categories ensures the semantic interoperability of the lexicon model and hence of our standardized representation of Wiktionary and OmegaWiki.

6.2 A common LMF model for Wiktionary and OmegaWiki based on UBY-LMF

In this section, we describe the subset of the UBY-LMF model which is used to represent Wiktionary and OmegaWiki, as well as an extension (which has been

---

[10] http://www.isocat.org

integrated into UBY-LMF in the meantime) we deemed necessary for properly representing translation information. Figure 5 shows an overview of all classes and data categories used in our derived lexicon model.

Lexicon. In our LMF model, one unique LexicalResource instance which represents the complete resource consists of one or more Lexicon instances. In UBY-LMF, each integrated resource is modeled as a separate Lexicon. Note further that LMF requires each Lexicon instance to belong to exactly one language (that is, having exactly one language identifier) – a requirement that reflects the diversity of different languages at the morphosyntactic and lexical-syntáctic level. Therefore, the multilingual resource OmegaWiki is split into separate Lexicon instances for each language while each language edition of Wiktionary constitutes one Lexicon.

Lexical Entry and Sense. The lexical information is modeled using the LexicalEntry class, which is characterized by a Lemma (that is, a written form) and a part-of-speech. Each entry in Wiktionary naturally corresponds to exactly one LexicalEntry. In OmegaWiki, the LexicalEntry corresponds to each lexicalization of a Defined Meaning. Each LexicalEntry may be connected to multiple instances of the Sense class modeling a certain meaning of the lexical entry. Word senses are explicitly encoded in Wiktionary and can therefore be straightforwardly used to populate the Sense instances. In OmegaWiki, word senses are represented by the Defined Meanings.

Lexicographic Information. An integral part of our LMF model is the representation of the variety of lexicographic information found in Wiktionary and OmegaWiki, which is represented by different classes attached to Sense: While Definition and SenseExample are self-explanatory, the Statement class contains further knowledge about a Sense, such as etymological information. The SemanticLabel class contains labels for many different dimensions of semantic classification (for example, domain, register, style, sentiment) for word senses. Such labels are very useful, as they contain valuable hints on the situations or contexts in which a word sense is usually used. Relationships between word senses can be represented by means of paradigmatic relations, such as synonymy, antonymy, hyponymy that are modeled in the SenseRelation class.

Translation. In addition to the elements of UBY-LMF described above, we introduce a new Equivalent class which is essential for any of the translation applications we have in mind. In this class, we store translation equivalents

SenseExample
- id
- exampleType

TextRepresentation
- writtenText
- languageIdentifier
- orthographyName
- geographicalVariant

Statement
- statementType

Definition
- definitionType

Context
- contextType
- source

Sense
- id
- synset: IDREF
- incorporatedSemArg: IDREF
- transparentMeaning
- index

Equivalent
- targetLanguage
- writtenForm
- geographicalVariant
- orthographyName
- transliteration

MonolingualExtRef
- externalSystem
- externalReference

SemanticLabel
- label
- type
- quantification

Synset
- id

SynsetRelation
- target: IDREF
- relType
- relName

SenseRelation
- target: IDREF
- relType
- relName

SenseAxis
- id
- sense1: IDREF
- sense2: IDREF
- synset1: IDREF
- synset2: IDREF
- senseAxisType

SenseAxisRelation
- target: IDREF
- relType
- relName

FormRepresentation
- writtenForm
- languageIdentifier
- hyphenation
- orthographyName
- geographicalVariant
- phoneticForm
- sound
- script

Lemma

LexicalEntry
- id
- separableParticle
- partOfSpeech

Lexicon
- languageIdentifier
- name
- id

LexicalResource
- name
- dtdVersion

GlobalInformation

WordForm
- grammaticalNumber
- grammaticalGender
- case
- person
- verbFormMood
- tense
- degree

RelatedForm
- targetLexicalEntry: IDREF
- relType
- targetSense: IDREF

SyntacticBehaviour
- id
- subcatFrame: IDREF
- subcatFrameSet: IDREF
- sense: IDREF

SubcategorizationFrame
- id
- parentSubcatFrame
- subcatLabel

LexemeProperty
- auxiliary
- syntacticProperty

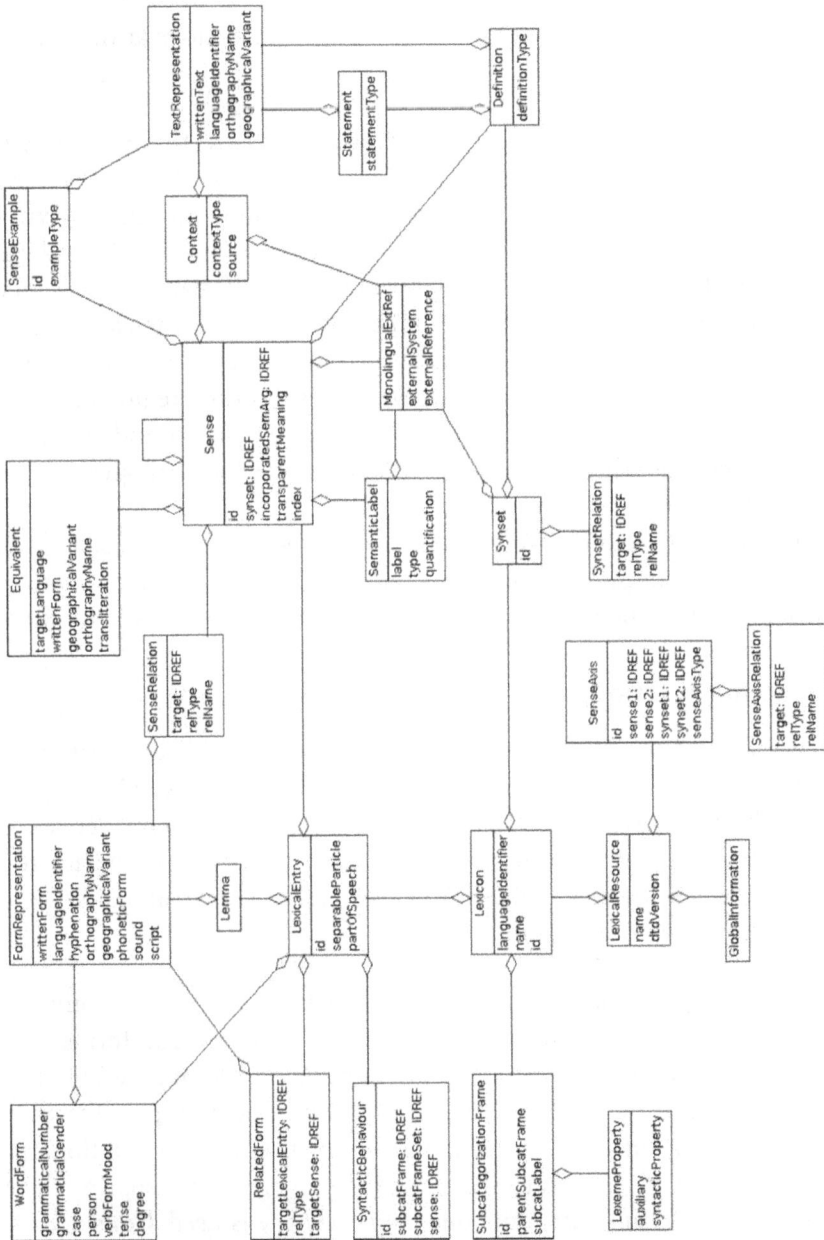

Figure 5: Overview of classes and data categories in our derived lexicon model

of a Sense, for example, the German translation *Barsch* of *bass*. Using the Equivalent class for this has been suggested before by Sérasset (2012), but – as opposed to our model – they represent translations at the word level rather than at the level of word senses.

For OmegaWiki, these translation equivalents are directly available via the lexicalizations in different languages attached to the same Defined Meaning. In Wiktionary, translation equivalents are encoded as links to other Wiktionary language editions. We create an instance of Equivalent for each of these translation links. The Equivalent class is designed to offer information that is vital for multilingual applications. Besides the written form of the translations and the target language, this includes: transliteration to encode different scripts (such as Cyrillic), geographicalVariant for representing a certain region in which the translated word is predominantly used (for example, Moscow), and orthography-Name for storing a certain orthographic variant, such as the German orthography reform of 1996.

In the following sections, we will discuss the special issues of standardizing Wiktionary and OmegaWiki. More precisely, we will discuss classes, data categories, and general modeling questions concerning only one of the resources.

6.3 Modeling Wiktionary in LMF

As discussed in §2, the guidelines for formatting entries in Wiktionary are not as strict as in OmegaWiki. This gap between the weakly structured Wiktionary articles and the rigidly structured LMF classes raises a number of challenges to our LMF representation of Wiktionary that we discuss below. Despite the heterogeneity of Wiktionary entries, we achieve a nearly lossless conversion of Wiktionary into the UBY-LMF representation.

Homonymy and Polysemy. Wiktionary distinguishes between homonymy and polysemy, as it is traditionally done in dictionaries. The former is used for words sharing the same form, but originating from different etymologies. Homonymy can be represented in our model by creating separate LexicalEntry instances for the homonymous entries in Wiktionary. The latter, polysemy, is used to encode different word senses sharing the same etymology. In this case, only one LexicalEntry is used. Consider the English noun *post* as an example: There are separate entries in Wiktionary that refer to the Latin *postis* (that is, the meaning of a *doorpost, pillar*) and the Latin *positum* (that is, the meaning of a place where one is stationed).

Hence, there are two instances of `LexicalEntry` representing the two different etymologies. Each of the lexical entries has multiple word senses modeling the polysemous meanings. For example, the distinction between a mail system (*sent via post*) and the assigned station (*leave one's post*).

Underspecified Relations. An important type of information are paradigmatic relations such as synonymy, hyponymy, antonymy, etc. which are modeled using the LMF `SenseRelation` class. The LMF standard, however, originally considers each `SenseRelation` to be defined between two instances of `Sense` – for example, between the message-system-related word senses of *post* and *mail*. In Wiktionary, only one of these word senses is explicitly defined: The first word sense of *mail* encodes, for example, a synonymy link to *post*, but does not give information about which word sense of *post* is to be used. This conforms to the layout of most printed dictionaries, which list synonyms for a certain word sense without explicitly specifying the word sense of the synonym. The rationale behind this is that humans can easily disambiguate the different meanings of *post* and do not require an explicit reference. To bridge the gap between this underspecification of Wiktionary's paradigmatic relations and our LMF representation, we introduce a new association relationship between the `SenseRelation` class and the `FormRepresentation` class. This way, we are able to store the word form of the relation targets without violating the model. In future work, we plan to automatically disambiguate the relations, so that we achieve a better structured representation of our resource.

In addition to those peculiarities of modeling Wiktionary in LMF, there is a number of information types found in Wiktionary, but not in OmegaWiki. We therefore use the following classes and data categories from the UBY-LMF model.

Phonetic Representation. Wiktionary contains a large number of phonetic representations explaining how a word is pronounced. For encoding this type of information, both IPA (International Phonetic Alphabet) and SAMPA (Speech Assessment Methods Phonetic Alphabet) notations are used; see Schlippe et al. (2010) for more details on Wiktionary's representation of phonetic information. For our LMF representation, we use the `phoneticForm` data category of the `FormRepresentation` class to represent the pronunciation information. While pronunciations are not very useful for translations of written text, they are very helpful for foreign language learners. Often, there are sound files attached to Wiktionary that allow for listening to native speakers pronouncing a certain word. Such sound files can be linked from the model and hence be exploited for translation-related applications.

Inflected Word Forms. A major problem when learning or translating to a foreign language is to use grammatically correct word forms. Although many inflected word forms are constructed using regular patterns, there are lots of exceptions that are difficult to remember or to manually encode into a translation system. The collaborative construction approach of Wiktionary can alleviate that, as a large number of people are involved and inflected word forms can quickly be encoded in a joint effort. In our model, we represent Wiktionary's inflected word forms using the WordForm class. For each word form, the grammatical number, gender, case, person, tense, etc. can be explicitly stored, such that an application using our resource can make use of this structured information.

Related Words. In addition to paradigmatic relations between word senses, there are relations between word forms encoded in Wiktionary; for example, the nominalization *driver* of the verb form *(to) drive*. This type of relation is stored using the RelatedForm class. Of particular interest for translation-based applications are relations between similar word forms that are often mixed up by language learners or layman translators. There are, for example, relations between *affect* and *effect* or between the German words *dediziert* (English: *dedicated*) and *dezidiert* (English: *determined*).

6.4 Modeling OmegaWiki in LMF

While the fixed database structure of OmegaWiki as discussed in §3 ensures that the information can be consistently mapped to our LMF model, there are still a number of issues which have to be addressed during the conversion process.

Splitting Defined Meanings. As mentioned before, OmegaWiki does not have separate editions for each language. Instead, OmegaWiki is based on the notion of multilingual synsets, that is, language-independent concepts to which lexicalizations of the concepts are attached. As the LMF standard requires that a Lexicon is monolingual, we have to split OmegaWiki's Defined Meanings to create artificial language editions. For example, when populating our LMF model with a Lexicon for the German OmegaWiki, we iterate over all Defined Meanings and only create those LexicalEntry, Sense, etc. instances for which German lexicalizations are present. In turn, this means that concepts which are not lexicalized in German are simply left out of this Lexicon. The lexicalizations in the other languages are, however, not lost, but stored as translations using the Equivalent class.

If more than one artificial language edition is created, there naturally exists a considerable overlap of concepts which are lexicalized in different languages. To express that the corresponding word senses in these languages refer to the same meaning, we utilize the SenseAxis class to link them. This is essentially the same mechanism as used to represent sense alignments between two resources (see §6.5 below). In other words, the information originally contained in OmegaWiki's Defined Meanings is preserved by modeling it as a cross-lingual sense alignment between the artificial language editions.

Synsets and Synset Relations. As we explained earlier, the word senses of a LexicalEntry are derived from OmegaWiki's Defined Meanings. In our model, these senses are subsequently grouped into Synsets. This reflects the fact that the different lexicalizations of the same Defined Meaning describe the same concept and are thus synonyms. Consequently, as all relations in OmegaWiki are encoded between Defined Meanings, the paradigmatic relations expressed by SenseRelation instances can also be trivially transferred to SynsetRelation instances. That is to say, the structure of OmegaWiki enforces that paradigmatic relations between synsets also hold for the contained senses and vice versa.

Another fact worth mentioning is that, other than Wiktionary, OmegaWiki also contains ontological (as opposed to linguistically motivated) relations – for instance, the *borders on* relation used to represent neighboring countries. This is very much in the spirit of OmegaWiki, being a collection of lexicalized concepts rather than a classic dictionary. This offers interesting ways of utilizing the multilingual information contained in our unified resource, such as using this ontological knowledge to enrich Wiktionary senses. Those relations are also modeled using the SenseRelation and SynsetRelation classes.

Syntactic Properties. To a small extent, OmegaWiki allows encoding syntactic properties such as verb valency. While this only affects a small fraction of the entries for now, we assume that the importance of this will increase as the resource is edited and extended by the crowd. Thus, we integrate this information to make the transformation as complete as possible or even lossless, and also to prepare the ground for integrating OmegaWiki with resources which specifically focus on syntactic properties. To cater for this, we are utilizing the classes SubcatFrame, LexemeProperty and SyntacticBehavior which enable us to model all of the syntactic information available in OmegaWiki. Providing information on the proper grammatical usage of a word is important for finding a good translation, in particular if the target language uses different structures than the source language.

6.5 Modeling sense alignments

The word sense alignments between Wiktionary and OmegaWiki (as discussed in §5) are modeled by means of SenseAxis instances. Note again that this is the same mechanism as for representing the multilingual information after splitting OmegaWiki into distinct language editions.

6.6 Populating the LMF model

As suggested by the LMF standard, we describe our model using a *Document Type Definition* (DTD) that describes each class and their data categories. Based on this DTD, we developed a software for converting Wiktionary and OmegaWiki to our LMF representation. The software is designed for easy adaptation in case the resources change in the future, so that transformation to the common LMF model is still possible. This has the advantage that applications using the standardized resources can be continually kept up to date without the need to adapt to changes of a certain resource, as all adaptation effort is concentrated on the conversion software.

Our resource consists of four Lexicon instances: one for each of the German and English Wiktionary, and one for each of the German and English parts of OmegaWiki. It should be noted at this point that we use English and German as a case study on how this can be done – the LMF converters allow to import other language editions with minor (Wiktionary) or no (OmegaWiki) modifications, and including more language editions into this resource is an important direction for future work.

Table 6 shows statistics about the most important LMF classes in our model regarding the single resources as well as the unified one. As can be seen, even with only two languages considered, we created a resource of an exceptional size with over 500,000 lexical entries and senses and well over 200,000 paradigmatic relations. Probably most important for translation applications, we also have almost 1,600,000 instances of the Equivalent class, which represent the translations (as discussed in §2 and §3; a breakdown into single languages can be found in Table 1). In Table 7, we can see that almost 90,000 SenseAxis instances have been created, over 25,000 of them stemming from our novel alignment of the two resources. Considering the around 58,000 senses in the English OmegaWiki, we have reached a fairly dense alignment of the two resources covering about half of OmegaWiki.

The final resource is published as an integral part of UBY and available from our homepage http://www.ukp.tu-darmstadt.de/uby/. We offer a downloadable database, along with the LMF model, an easy-to-use API, the converters and accompanying documentation.

Table 6: Statistics about the unified resource. The Equivalent class represents the translations found in each resource

Resource	LexicalEntry	Sense	SenseRelation	Equivalent
Wiktionary En	335,749	421,848	22,313	694,282
OmegaWiki En	51,715	57,921	7,157	335,173
Wiktionary De	85,575	72,752	183,684	250,674
OmegaWiki De	30,967	34,691	7,165	304,590
Total	504,006	587,212	220,319	1,584,719

Table 7: Sense alignment statistics

Resource Pair	SenseAxis	Comment/Information source
OmegaWiki En – OmegaWiki De	58,785	Orig. information by voluntary editors
OmegaWiki En – Wiktionary En	25,742	Automatically produced alignment
Total	84,527	

7 Conclusions and future work

In this article, we argued that collaboratively constructed multilingual lexical resources present a valuable source of knowledge for translation applications. They are maintained by a crowd of users, thus guaranteeing highly accurate and up to date information, while at the same time being available with almost no restrictions. We analyzed the two most prominent ones, Wiktionary and OmegaWiki in terms of (multilingual) content and structure and presented both their strengths and weaknesses: While the openness and flexibility of Wiktionary has attracted many users, leading to a resource of considerable size and richness, the non-standardized structure of entries also leads to difficulties in the integration into translation applications. OmegaWiki, on the other hand, does not suffer from this problem, but the self-imposed limitations to maintain integrity also constrain its expressiveness and, along with that, the range of information which can be represented in the resource.

As a consequence of the content-related differences, we proposed a method for automatically aligning the two resources at the level of word senses with good precision. This yields a substantial increase of coverage, especially concerning available translations. In this respect, the aligned resource outperfoms either single resource by far, justifying the few alignment errors which are introduced in the process. To cater for the differences at the structural and representational level, we describe a nearly lossless and robust conversion of these two resources to a common, standardized representation based on the UBY-LMF model (Eckle-Kohler et al. 2012), which we extended to also represent translation equivalents for word senses. As a result, we created a resource containing the English and German editions of OmegaWiki as well as Wiktionary, including translations into a multitude of additional languages, which is now an integral part of the unified resource UBY. In summary, our resource has the following properties:

Continuously updated lexical-semantic knowledge: The frequently updated and extended knowledge in both resources can at any time be integrated into the unified resource as the conversion routines into the common model need no or only minor modifications in the future. This also relieves the end user from the burden of adapting their application to changes in the underlying resources as the unified output model remains stable.

High coverage: The alignments at word sense level significantly improve upon the available information in the isolated resources, which is very valuable for translation purposes and other applications. The proposed generic alignment framework makes sure that alignments for future revisions of both resources can be performed with little effort.

A standardized structure: The LMF-based model, supported by a corresponding database or XML schema, ensures that the resource can be queried with consistent and reliable results.

Elaborate structure: The structure of the LMF model is elaborate and expressive enough to cater for a wide range of lexicographic information in different languages, so that an almost complete representation of the underlying resources is possible.

Interoperability: The resource is not only in a format which is machine readable, but it is also compliant to existing KYOTO standards to allow for easy reuse and integration into applications.

There are many directions to pursue for future work. First of all, we want to apply and extend our resource alignment approach to other pairs of lexico-graphic resources. A special focus will be on creating additional alignments between expert-built[11] and collaboratively constructed resources to actively exploit the complementary information in different types of resources, which have been constructed following different paradigms. The recently published alignment between Wiktionary and FrameNet based on the same approach (Hartmann & Gurevych 2013) is a first step in this direction.

Another goal is to apply the graph-based method for sense alignment we recently introduced (Matuschek & Gurevych 2013) to Wiktionary and OmegaWiki to validate its applicability in a setup with two collaboratively constructed resources. In this context, we will also explore how the combined evidence from already existing alignments could be used to infer new ones; here, graph-based methods operating on the graph of aligned senses seem to be a viable option. Also, the inclusion of more language editions of Wiktionary and OmegaWiki and, more generally, an improved treatment of cross-lingual alignments should be tackled in the future work.

A crucial point for further research is the actual usage of our unified resource in translation applications. The integration into a computer-aided translation environment or an SMT system as mentioned in the introductory section is particularly interesting. For this, we would be interested in collaborating with re-

---

[11]Note that "expert" in this context refers to linguists (language experts) and not professional translators.

searchers from the (machine) translation community in order to assess the use-fulness of aligned resources, and also to discover aspects in which further improvement is necessary, for example, regarding coverage or precision.

Lastly, further development of the API[12] and the accompanying Web interface[13] is necessary to make the resource more easily accessible to as many researchers and end users as possible. We especially deem the interface important as visually assessing and evaluating the generated sense alignments becomes increasingly difficult for larger lexical resources.

Acknowledgements

This work has been supported by the Volkswagen Foundation as part of the Licht-enberg Professorship Program under grant No. I/82806 and by the Hessian research excellence program "Landes-Offensive zur Entwicklung Wissenschaftlich-ökonomischer Exzellenz (LOEWE)" as part of the research center "Digital Humanities". We would like to thank Judith Eckle-Kohler, Silvana Hartmann, Tri-Duc Nghiem, Elisabeth Niemann, Yevgen Chebotar and Zijad Maksuti for their contributions to this work. We also thank the anonymous reviewers for their helpful remarks.

References

Adafre, Sisay Fissaha & Maarten de Rijke. 2006. Finding similar sentences across multiple languages in Wikipedia. In *Proceedings of the EACL '06 Workshop 'New Text: Wikis and Blogs and Other Dynamic Text Sources'*, 62–69. Trento, Italy.

Agirre, Eneko & Aitor Soroa. 2009. Personalizing PageRank for Word Sense Disambiguation. In *Proceedings of the 12th Conference of the European Chapter of the Association for Computational Linguistics (EACL'09)*, 33–41. Athens, Greece.

Banko, Michele, Michael J. Cafarella, Stephen Soderland, Matt Broadhead & Oren Etzioni. 2007. Open information extraction from the web. In *Proceedings of the 20th International Joint Conference on Artificial Intelligence (IJCAI-07)*, 2670–2676. Hyderabad, India.

---

[12]https://code.google.com/p/uby/
[13]https://uby.ukp.informatik.tu-darmstadt.de/webui

Bizer, Christian, Jens Lehmann, Georgi Kobilarov, Sören Auer, Christian Becker, Richard Cyganiak & Sebastian Hellmann. 2009. DBpedia: A Crystallization Point for the Web of Data. *Journal of Web Semantics: Science, Services and Agents on the World Wide Web* 7(3). 154–165.

Buitelaar, Paul, Philipp Cimiano, Peter Haase & Michael Sintek. 2009. Towards linguistically grounded ontologies. In Lora Aroyo, Paolo Traverso, Fabio Ciravegna, Philipp Cimiano, Tom Heath, Eero Hyvänen, Riichiro Mizoguchi, Eyal Oren, Marta Sabou & Elena Simperl (eds.), *The Semantic Web: Research and applications*, vol. 5554 (Lecture Notes in Computer Science), 111–125. Berlin/Heidelberg: Springer.

Burgun, Anita & Olivier Bodenreider. 2001. Comparing terms, concepts and semantic classes in WordNet and the unified medical language system. In *Proceedings of the NAACL '01 Workshop 'WordNet and Other Lexical Resources: Applications, Extensions and Customizations'*, 77–82. Pittsburgh, PA.

Carl, Michael, Martin Kay & Kristian Jensen. 2010. Long-distance revisions in drafting and post-editing. *Research in Computing Science – Special Issue: Natural Language Processing and its Applications* 46. 193–204.

de Melo, Gerard & Gerhard Weikum. 2010. Providing multilingual, multimodal answers to lexical database queries. In *Proceedings of the 7th International Conference on Language Resources and Evaluation (LREC'10)*, 348–355. Valletta, Malta.

Declerck, Thierry, Karlheinz Mörth & Piroska Lendvai. 2012. Accessing and standardizing wiktionary lexical entries for the translation of labels in cultural heritage taxonomies. In *Proceedings of the 8th International Conference on Language Resources and Evaluation (LREC'12)*, 2511–2514. Istanbul, Turkey.

Eckle-Kohler, Judith, Iryna Gurevych, Silvana Hartmann, Michael Matuschek & Christian M. Meyer. 2012. UBY-LMF: A uniform model for standardizing heterogeneous lexical-semantic resources in ISO-LMF. In *Proceedings of the 8th International Conference on Language Resources and Evaluation*, 275–282. Istanbul, Turkey.

Erdmann, Maike, Kotaro Nakayama, Takahiro Hara & Shojiro Nishio. 2009. An approach for extracting bilingual terminology from Wikipedia. In Jayant Haritsa, Ramamohanarao Kotagiri & Vikram Pudi (eds.), *Database systems for advanced applications*, vol. 4947 (Lecture Notes in Computer Science), 380–392. Berlin/Heidelberg: Springer.

Fellbaum, Christiane (ed.). 1998. *WordNet: An electronic lexical database (language, speech, and communication)*. Cambridge, MA: MIT Press.

Francopoulo, Gil, Nuria Bel, Monte George, Nicoletta Calzolari, Monica Mona-chini, Mandy Pet & Claudia Soria. 2009. Multilingual resources for NLP in the lexical markup framework (LMF). *Language Resources and Evaluation* 43(1). 57–70.

Gaillard, Benoît, Malek Boualem & Olivier Collin. 2010. Query translation using wikipedia-based resources for analysis and disambiguation. In *Proceedings of the 14th Annual Conference of the European Association for Machine Translation (EAMT2010)*. Saint-Raphaël, France.

Gurevych, Iryna, Judith Eckle-Kohler, Silvana Hartmann, Michael Matuschek, Christian M. Meyer & Christian Wirth. 2012. UBY: a large-scale unified lexical-semantic resource based on LMF. In *Proceedings of the 13th Conference of the European Chapter of the Association for Computational Linguistics*, 580–590. Avignon, France.

Hartmann, Silvana & Iryna Gurevych. 2013. FrameNet on the way to Babel: Creating a bilingual FrameNet using wiktionary as interlingual connection. In *Proceedings of the 51th Annual Meeting of the Association for Computational Linguistics (ACL 2013)*, to appear. Sofia, Bulgaria.

Henrich, Verena & Erhard Hinrichs. 2010. Standardizing Wordnets in the ISO Standard LMF: Wordnet-LMF for GermaNet. In *Proceedings of the 23rd International Conference on Computational Linguistics*, 456–464. Beijing, China.

Herbert, Benjamin, György Szarvas & Iryna Gurevych. 2011. Combining query translation techniques to improve cross-language information retrieval. In *Proceedings of the 33rd European Conference on Information Retrieval*, vol. 6611 (Lecture Notes in Computer Science), 712–715. Berlin/Heidelberg: Springer.

Ide, Nancy & James Pustejovsky. 2010. What does interoperability mean, anyway? Toward an operational definition of interoperability for language technology. In *Proceedings of the Second International Conference on Global Interoperability for Language Resources*. Hong Kong, China.

ISO12620. 2009. *Terminology and other language and content resources: Specification of data categories and management of a Data Category Registry for language resources*. Geneva: Geneva, International Organization for Standardization.

ISO24613. 2008. *Language resource management: Lexical markup framework (LMF)*. Geneva: Geneva, International Organization for Standardization.

Jansen, Peter. 2004. Lexicography in an interlingual ontology: An introduction to EuroWordNet. *Canadian Undergraduate Journal of Cognitive Science* [3]. 1–5.

Koehn, Philipp. 2009. A process study of computer aided translation. *Machine Translation* 23(4). 241–263.

Krizhanovsky, Andrew & Feiyu Lin. 2009. Related Terms Search Based on Word-Net / Wiktionary and its Application in Ontology Matching. In *Proceedings of the 11th Russian Conference on Digital Libraries*, 363–369. Petrozavodsk, Russia.

Kwong, Oi Yee. 1998. Aligning WordNet with Additional Lexical Resources. In *Proceedings of the COLING-ACL '98 Workshop 'Usage of WordNet in Natural Language Processing Systems'*, 73–79. Montreal, QC, Canada.

Litkowski, Kenneth C. 1999. Towards a Meaning-Full Comparison of Lexical Resources. In *Proceedings of the ACL Special Interest Group on the Lexicon Workshop on Standardizing Lexical Resources*, 30–37. College Park, MD.

Matuschek, Michael & Iryna Gurevych. 2013. Dijkstra-WSA: A graph-based approach to word sense alignment. *Transactions of the Association for Computational Linguistics (TACL)* 1. 151–164.

McCrae, John, Elena Montiel-Ponsoda & Philipp Cimiano. 2012. Integrating WordNet and wiktionary with lemon. In Christian Chiarcos, Sebastian Nordhoff & Sebastian Hellmann (eds.), *Linked data in linguistics*, 25–34. Berlin / Heidelberg: Springer.

McCrae, John, Dennis Spohr & Philipp Cimiano. 2011. Linking lexical resources and ontologies on the semantic web with lemon. In Grigoris Antoniou, Marko Grobelnik, Elena Simperl, Bijan Parsia, Dimitris Plexousakis, Pieter De Leenheer & Jeff Pan (eds.), *The Semantic Web: Research and applications*, vol. 6643 (Lecture Notes in Computer Science), 245–259. Berlin/Heidelberg: Springer.

Medelyan, Olena, Catherine Legg, David Milne & Ian H. Witten. 2009. Mining meaning from Wikipedia. *International Journal of Human-Computer Studies* 67(9). 716–754.

Meyer, Christian M. & Iryna Gurevych. 2011. What psycholinguists know about chemistry: Aligning wiktionary and WordNet for increased domain coverage. In *Proceedings of the 5th International Joint Conference on Natural Language Processing*, 883–892. Chiang Mai, Thailand.

Meyer, Christian M. & Iryna Gurevych. 2012. Wiktionary: A new rival for expert-built lexicons? Exploring the possibilities of collaborative lexicography. In Sylviane Granger & Magali Paquot (eds.), *Electronic lexicography*, chap. 13, 259–291. Oxford: Oxford University Press.

Mörth, Karlheinz, Thierry Declerck, Piroska Lendvai & Tamás Váradi. 2011. Accessing multilingual data on the web for the semantic annotation of cultural heritage texts. In *Proceedings of the 2nd International Workshop on the Multilingual Semantic Web*, 80–85. Bonn, Germany.

Müller, Christof & Iryna Gurevych. 2009. Using Wikipedia and Wiktionary in domain-specific information retrieval. In Carol Peters, Thomas Deselaers,

Nicola Ferro, Julio Gonzalo, Gareth Jones, Mikko Kurimo, Thomas Mandl, Anselmo Penas & Vivien Petras (eds.), *Evaluating systems for multilingual and multimodal information access – 9th Workshop of the Cross-Language Evaluation Forum, CLEF 2008, Aarhus, Denmark, September 17-19, 2008, Revised Selected Papers*, vol. 5706 (Lecture Notes in Computer Science), 219–226. Berlin/Heidelberg: Springer.

Nastase, Vivi, Michael Strube, Benjamin Boerschinger, Cäcilia Zirn & Anas Elghafari. 2010. WikiNet: A very large scale multi-lingual concept network. In *Proceedings of the 7th International Conference on Language Resources and Evaluation*, 1015–1022. Valetta, Malta.

Navarro, Emmanuel, Franck Sajous, Bruno Gaume, Laurent Prévot, Hsieh ShuKai, Kuo Tzu-Yi, Pierre Magistry & Huang Chu-Ren. 2009. Wiktionary and NLP: Improving synonymy networks. In *Proceedings of the ACL '09 Workshop 'The People's Web Meets NLP: Collaboratively Constructed Semantic Resources'*, 19–27. Singapore.

Navigli, Roberto. 2006. Meaningful clustering of senses helps boost word sense disambiguation performance. In *Proceedings of the 21st International Conference on Computational Linguistics and the 44th Annual Meeting of the Association for Computational Linguistics*, 105–112. Sydney, Australia.

Navigli, Roberto & Simone Paolo Ponzetto. 2010. BabelNet: Building a very large multilingual semantic network. In *Proceedings of the 48th Annual Meeting of the Association for Computational Linguistics*, 216–225. Uppsala, Sweden.

Niemann, Elisabeth & Iryna Gurevych. 2011. The people's web meets linguistic knowledge: Automatic sense alignment of wikipedia and WordNet. In *Proceedings of the Ninth International Conference on Computational Semantics*, 205–214. Oxford, UK.

Pianta, Emanuele, Luisa Bentivogli & Christian Girardi. 2002. MultiWordNet: Developing an aligned multilingual database. In *Proceedings of the First International WordNet Conference*, 293–302. Mysore, India.

Ponzetto, Simone Paolo & Roberto Navigli. 2009. Large-scale taxonomy mapping for restructuring and integrating Wikipedia. In *Proceedings of the 21st International Joint Conference on Artificial Intelligence*, 2083–2088. Pasadena, CA.

Ponzetto, Simone Paolo & Roberto Navigli. 2010. Knowledge-rich word sense disambiguation rivaling supervised systems. In *Proceedings of the 48th Annual Meeting of the Association for Computational Linguistics*, 1522–1531. Uppsala, Sweden.

Potthast, Martin, Benno Stein & Maik Anderka. 2008. A wikipedia-based multilingual retrieval model. In *Advances in information retrieval: 30th European*

Conference on IR Research, vol. 4956 (Lecture Notes in Computer Science), 522–530. Glasgow, UK: Springer.

Reed, Stephen L. & Douglas B. Lenat. 2002. Mapping ontologies into cyc. In *Proceedings of the AAAI '02 Workshop 'Ontologies and the Semantic Web'*, 1–6. Edmonton, AB, Canada.

Ruiz-Casado, Maria, Enrique Alfonseca & Pablo Castells. 2005. Automatic assignment of Wikipedia encyclopedic entries to WordNet synsets. *Advances in Web Intelligence: Proceedings of the Third International Atlantic Web Intelligence Conference* 3528. 380–386.

Schlippe, Tim, Sebastian Ochs & Tanja Schultz. 2010. Wiktionary as a source for automatic pronunciation extraction. In *Proceedings of the 11th Annual Conference of the International Speech Communication Association*, 2290–2293. Makuhari, Japan.

Sérasset, Gilles. 2012. Dbnary: Wiktionary as a LMF based multilingual rdf network. In *Proceedings of the 8th International Conference on Language Resources and Evaluation*, 2466–2472. Istanbul, Turkey.

Shi, Lei & Rada Mihalcea. 2005. Putting pieces together: Combining FrameNet, VerbNet and WordNet for robust semantic parsing. In Alexander Gelbukh (ed.), *Computational linguistics and intelligent text processing: 6th international Conference*, vol. 3406 (Lecture Notes in Computer Science), 100–111. Berlin/Heidelberg: Springer.

Somers, Harold. 2003. Translation memory systems. In Harold Somers (ed.), *Computers and translation: A translator's guide*, vol. 35 (Benjamins Translation Library), chap. 3, 31–47. Amsterdam: John Benjamins.

Soria, Claudia, Monica Monachini & Piek Vossen. 2009. Wordnet-LMF: Fleshing out a standardized format for wordnet interoperability. In *Proceedings of the 2009 International Workshop on Intercultural Collaboration*, 139–146. Palo Alto, CA.

Stamou, Sofia, Kemal Oflazer, Karel Pala, Dimitris Christoudoulakis, Dan Cristea, Dan Tufi, Svetla Koeva, Gheorghi Totkov, Dominique Dutoit & Maria Grigoriadou. 2002. BALKANET: A multilingual semantic network for the balkan languages. In *Proceedings of the First International WordNet Conference*, 12–14. Mysore, India.

Suchanek, Fabian, Gjergji Kasneci & Gerhard Weikum. 2008. YAGO: A large ontology from wikipedia and wordnet. *Web Semantics: Science, Services and Agents on the World Wide Web* 6(3). 203–217.

Surowiecki, James. 2005. *The wisdom of crowds*. New York, NY: Anchor Books.

Toral, Antonio, Stefania Bracale, Monica Monachini & Claudia Soria. 2010. Rejuvenating the italian WordNet: Upgrading, standarising, extending. In *Proceedings of the 5th Global WordNet Conference*. Mumbai, India.

Toral, Antonio, Oscar Ferrandez, Eneko Agirre & Rafael Munoz. 2009. A study on linking wikipedia categories to wordnet synsets using text similarity. In *Proceedings of the 7th International Conference on Recent Advances in Natural Language Processing*, 449–454. Borovets, Bulgaria.

Vossen, Piek (ed.). 1998. *EuroWordNet: A Multilingual Database with Lexical Semantic Networks*. Dordrecht: Dordrecht: Kluwer Academic Publishers.

Zesch, Torsten, Iryna Gurevych & Max Mühlhäuser. 2007. Analyzing and accessing wikipedia as a lexical semantic resource. In *Datenstrukturen für linguistische ressourcen und ihre anwendungen / data structures for linguistic resources and applications: Proceedings of the biennial GLDV Conference 2007*, 197–205. Tübingen: Gunter Narr.

Zesch, Torsten, Christof Müller & Iryna Gurevych. 2008. Extracting lexical semantic knowledge from Wikipedia and Wiktionary. In *Proceedings of the 6th International Conference on Language Resources and Evaluation*, 1646–1652. Marrakech, Morocco.

Chapter 10

The BerbaTek project for Basque: Promoting a less-resourced language via language technology for translation, content management and learning

Igor Leturia
Elhuyar Foundation

Kepa Sarasola

Xabier Arregi

Arantza Diaz de Ilarraza
IXA Group, University of the Basque Country

Eva Navas

Iñaki Sainz
Aholab Group, University of the Basque Country

Arantza del Pozo
Vicomtech-IK4

David Baranda

Urtza Iturraspe
Tecnalia

Igor Leturia, Kepa Sarasola, Xabier Arregi, Arantza Diaz de Ilarraza, Eva Navas, Iñaki Sainz, Arantza del Pozo, David Baranda & Urtza Iturraspe. The BerbaTek project for Basque: Promoting a less-resourced language via language technology for translation, content management and learning. In Georg Rehm, Felix Sasaki, Daniel Stein & Andreas Witt (eds.), *Language technologies for a multilingual Europe: TC3 III*, 181–204. Berlin: Language Science Press.
DOI:10.5281/zenodo.1291942

Basque is both a minority language (only a small proportion of the population of the Basque Country speaks it) and also a less-resourced language. Fortunately, the Basque regional government is committed to its recovery, and has adopted policies for funding, among other things, language technologies, a field which a language aiming to survive cannot dispense with. BerbaTek was a 3-year (2009–2011) strategic research project on language, speech and multimedia technologies for Basque carried out by a consortium of five members, all prominent local organizations dedicated to research in the above-mentioned areas, and partially funded by the Departments for Industry and Culture of the Basque Government. Collaboration in BerbaTek allowed to carry out a great amount of both basic and applied research. In addition, various prototypes were developed to show the potential of integrating the developed technologies to the language industry sector.

1 Introduction

The Basque language is one of the oldest alive in Europe, although it has suffered continuous regression over the last few centuries. However, many citizens and local or regional governments have been promoting its recovery since the 1970s. Now, Basque holds partial co-official language status in the Basque regions of Spain but it has no official standing in the Northern Basque Country in France, neither in the European institutions. Today, there are about 700,000 Basque speakers, around 25% of the total population of the Basque Country, but they are not evenly distributed, and the use of Basque in industry and especially in Information and Communication Technology is still not widespread. In September 2012, META-NET placed Basque as one of the 21 European languages that are in danger of digital extinction[1]. A language that seeks to survive in the modern information society has to be present also in such fields and this calls for language technology products. Basque, like other minority languages, has to make a great effort to address this challenge (Williams et al. 2001).

In this context, BerbaTek[2] was a strategic research project in language, speech and multimedia technologies developed over the years 2009–2011. Its consortium was made up of the Elhuyar Foundation, the IXA and Aholab research groups of the UPV/EHU (University of the Basque Country), the Vicomtech-IK4 Visual Interaction and Communication Technologies Centre and the Tecnalia Research & Innovation foundation. The project was partly funded by the Departments for Industry and Culture of the Government of the Basque Autonomous Community (region of Spain).

---

[1]http://www.meta-net.eu/whitepapers/press-release
[2]http://www.berbatek.com/en

The members of the consortium had been collaborating since 2002 in two similar previous projects, Hizking (Diaz de Ilarraza et al. 2003) and AnHitz (Arrieta et al. 2008), in which basic foundations, tools and applications were created for Basque.

We believe that research and development for less-resourced languages should be addressing following four points: (1) high standardization, (2) open-source, (3) reuse of language foundations, tools and applications, and (4) incremental design and development. Any HLT project relating to a less-privileged language should follow those guidelines, but from our previous experience we knew that in most cases they did not. We believe that if Basque is now in a fairly good position in HLT, it is because these guidelines have been applied, even though in some cases it was easier to create "toy" resources or easily obtainable tools (Alegria et al. 2011).

2 The consortium

Vicomtech-IK4[3] is an applied research center whose main lines of research are graphic computation, interaction and multimedia. Three of its groups participated in BerbaTek: (i) the Speech and HLT group, (ii) the 3D Animation group, and (iii) the Audiovisual Content Analysis group.

Tecnalia[4] is a private, applied research center specialized in information and telecommunication technologies.

The *Elhuyar Foundation*[5] is a not-for-profit organization, set up with the aim of bringing science and the Basque language together. Elhuyar is firmly established in the market for dictionaries, educational software, multimedia products, plugins and Machine Translation. In 2001, it set up a LT unit.[6]

IXA[7] is a group of the University of the Basque Country (UPV/EHU), consisting of 43 researchers, which works on NLP specialized in the processing of written texts at different levels. The main projects IXA is currently working on are the PATH, OpeNER and NewsReader European STREP projects.

The *Aholab Signal Processing Laboratory*[8] is a research group of the University of the Basque Country (UPV/EHU), with broad experience in voice technologies

---

[3]http://www.vicomtech.org
[4]http://www.tecnalia.com
[5]http://www.elhuyar.org
[6]http://www.elhuyar.org/hizkuntza-zerbitzuak/EN/R-D
[7]http://ixa.si.ehu.es
[8]http://aholab.ehu.e/

and digital signal processing. Aholab developed the first commercial TTS system for Basque, AhoTTS,[9] as well as most of the resources and voice processing tools publicly available for Basque.

3 Objectives

The main aim of BerbaTek was the research and development of language, speech or multimedia technologies, so that they could provide the technological basis to support the economic sector of the language industries in the Basque Country.

The key challenge was to prove that Basque processing technologies could be useful to improve the performance, social impact and competitiveness of some industrial products. This challenge required the partners to take a new significant step forward in the strengthening of the language industries by incorporating the results and devices into real market scenarios. This point was particularly relevant given that basic resources and tools must be robust enough to support industrial use.

As most companies do not want to take on this task as it is expensive and commercially not profitable, we considered this initiative a social investment. Tools for languages like Basque are usually developed at universities or research centres and adapting those linguistic tools to the real industrial scenario is crucial.

BerbaTek was geared towards applications. Without neglecting basic research, it was endeavouring to present experimental applications which could subsequently be developed further and turned into products by companies. The importance of generating knowledge in the area of language technologies for voice and multimedia lies in their potential for applications mainly in the language industry sector:

Translation: interpretation, dubbing, localization, human translation etc.

Content industry: Internet, audiovisual sector, the media, off- and on-line publishing, multimedia companies, etc.

Training: language learning, technical and professional education, ongoing training, etc.

---

[9]http://aholab.ehu.es/tts/tts_en.html

Table 1: Resources developed or improved during BerbaTek

Corpus resources	Basque Dependency Treebank (BDT), 300,000-word corpus.
	Basque Propbank and tools for its development (Aldezabal et al. 2010).
	AhoSyn, a large speech database (6 hours per speaker) (Sainz et al. 2012).
	AhoSpeakers, database designed for voice conversion (Sainz et al. 2012).
	AhoEmo3, created for emotional speech synthesis (Sainz et al. 2012).
	A large general corpus (+100M words) collected automatically from the web (Leturia 2012).
Ontology resources	Basque WordNet (Pociello et al. 2011), the Basque version of WordNet.
	WNTerm (Pociello et al. 2008), WordNet + 25,000 science and technology terms.
	Termide, automatic ontology building out of corpora.
	QAWS, question answering over Linked Data.
Dictionary resources	Various bilingual dictionaries created automatically using a pivot language (Saralegi et al. 2012).

4 Resources, tools and applications developed

The partners had been working in NLP and Language Engineering for Basque since 1990. The most basic tools and resources (lemmatizers, POS taggers, lexical databases, speech databases, electronic dictionaries, etc.) had been developed before, but most of them were further improved within the project, and many others were created in BerbaTek.

BerbaTek carried out basic research and built many resources and tools that are necessary for the development of applications. Tables 1, 2 and 3 show the resources, tools and applications developed or improved during the project. The key resources and tools in the development of applications on the aforementioned areas of translation, content management and learning were the following:

Table 2: Tools developed or improved during BerbaTek

Analysis tools	Dependency Parsing (Bengoetxea & Gojenola 2010; Agirre et al. 2011). UKB (Agirre & Soroa 2009) graph-based Word Sense Disambiguation ArikIturri (Aldabe & Maritxalar 2010), automatic creation of exercises out of corpora.
Web as corpus tools	Co3 (Leturia et al. 2009), building multilingual comparable corpora. PaCo2 (San Vicente & Manterola 2012), collecting parallel corpora.

- Tools for building corpora from the web (monolingual and multilingual, general and domain-based, comparable and parallel), and various corpora collected by using these.

- Syntactic dependency analysers, semantic analyzers and systems for identifying sentence and phrase boundaries.

- Terminology extraction from corpora and automatic building of dictionaries.

- General and domain-specific ontologies and semantic search engines.

- Cross-lingual search and question answering.

- Machine translation systems (rule-based, statistical and hybrid).

- Techniques for voice segment detection and text/image alignment in video.

- Engine for continuous speech recognition; text-to-speech conversion systems.

- Speaking avatars.

- Writing aids and automatic exercise creation.

Table 3: Applications developed or improved during BerbaTek

Automatic dictionary building	AzerHitz (Saralegi et al. 2008), extraction of equivalent terms from comparable corpora. PiboLex (Saralegi et al. 2012), building new dictionaries using a pivot language. Phraseology and idiomatic expressions extractor (Gurrutxaga & Alegria 2011).
Information retrieval	Ihardetsi (Ansa et al. 2008; Agirre, Ansa, et al. 2009), a Question-Answering system. Elezkari (Saralegi & Lacalle 2009), CLIR (Basque, Spanish and English).
Machine translation	Opentrad-Matxin (Alegria et al. 2007; Alegria et al. 2008; Mayor et al. 2011), open-source rule-based machine translation system for Spanish-Basque. EUsmt, statistical Machine Translation from Spanish to Basque. (Labaka 2010).
Speech synthesis	AhoT2P, a letter to allophone transcriber for standard Basque. AhoTTS_Mod1, a linguistic processor for speech synthesis. AhoTTS, modular Text-To-Speech conversion for Basque, Spanish and English. TTS system based on HTS (Erro et al. 2010), with own vocoder (Erro et al. 2011a). Hybrid AhoTTS combining advantages from statistical and unit selection speech synthesis (Erro et al. 2010).
Speech recognition	AhoSR (Odriozola et al. 2012), speech recognition engine (standard Basque).

5 Prototypes

Throughout the project, we created some demos to show the usefulness of the linguistic tools and the potential of the integration of language-, speech- and multimedia-technologies when it comes to creating applications for the areas of language industries, i.e., for translation, contents and teaching. These are the demos we built:

- Automatic dubbing of documentaries into Basque using subtitles in Spanish (with possible automatic creation of the Spanish subtitles from the Spanish audio, by means of ASR).

- Two multimedia and multilingual semantic web search engines on science and technology content, one of them including subsequent navigation through related content or similar images.

- Personal tutor in language learning through a speech-driven avatar, with automatically created grammar and comprehension exercises, writing aids (dictionaries, writing numbers, spelling…) and automatic evaluation of pronunciation.

5.1 Automatic dubbing of documentaries

The automatic dubbing of films is still a difficult challenge (different voices, speed and tones, colloquial language etc.), but for some types of documentaries (single speaker, voice-over, coordination of the lips not necessary or unimportant) we produced a demo that performs satisfactorily. The general structure of the application developed is shown in Figure 1. Given a documentary in Spanish and its transcription (the transcription can be obtained automatically by means of any of the available dictation programs for Spanish), Vicomtech-IK4's alignment technology creates a subtitles file (the transcription with time marks for the beginning and end of each sentence). Then, IXA group's Matxin MT system automatically translates the subtitles into Basque, and Aholab's text-to-speech technology produces the synchronized voice output. We successfully applied this demo to the single-speaker sections of the television programme Teknopolis produced by Elhuyar.

The automatic alignment of speech and text is based on speech recognition technology. In this case, it is forced to recognize the text of the transcription and provided timing information at phoneme and word levels. That way, the start and end time-codes of each word are obtained automatically and used to synchronize subtitles with the video image.

The translation of subtitles is done using Opentrad-Matxin (Mayor et al. 2011) adapting it to the domain of science and technology. Matxin is a rule-based deep syntactic transfer system for translation into Basque. It translates text from Spanish into Basque, but its architecture allows for an easy implementation of new systems for translating other languages into Basque (Mayor & Tyers 2009). Opentrad-Matxin is open source. The free code of the Spanish-Basque system with a reduced version of the bilingual lexicon can be downloaded from http://matxin.sourceforge.net. The system can be used at http://www.opentrad.org.

The average HTER evaluation result of Matxin was 0.42, meaning that 42 editing corrections are required for every 100 tokens. One of the key features of our

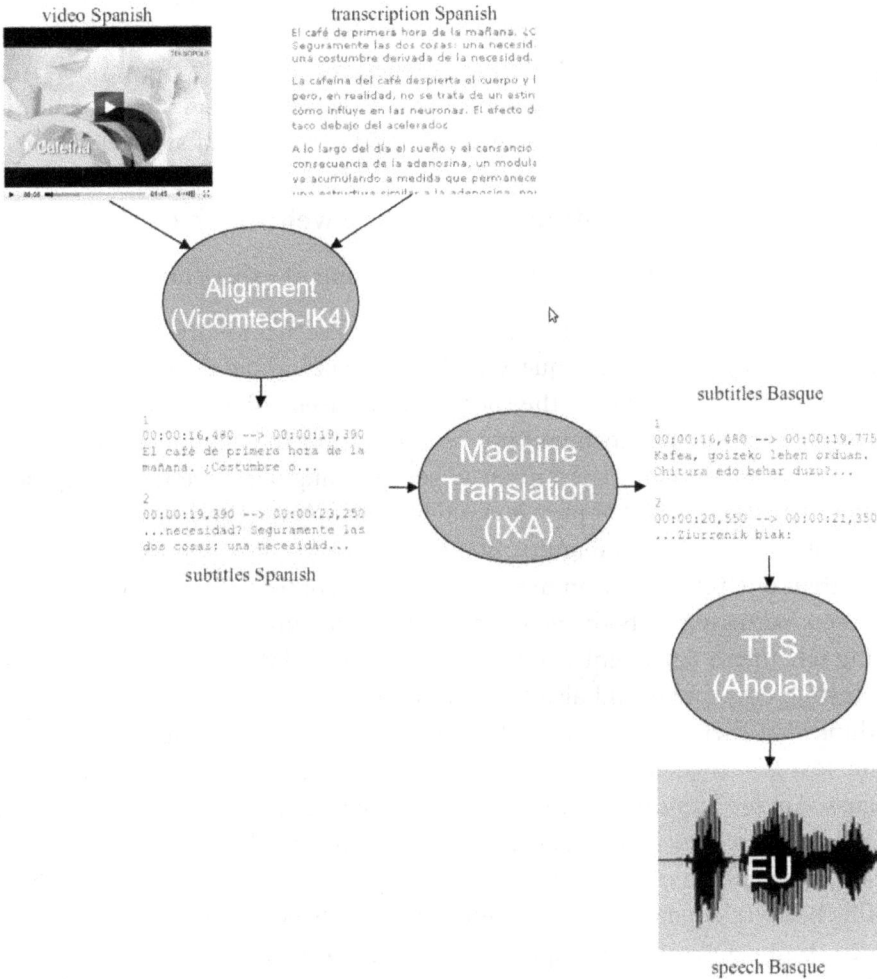

Figure 1: Scheme of the automatic dubbing of documentaries demo

work is the reuse of existing linguistic resources: we created the system's lexicon by automatically processing high-coverage dictionaries. Given that we reused previously created resources, the XML-based format guaranteed their interoperability. Now we are working on the construction of SMT systems and a hybrid system including three subsystems based on different approaches (España-Bonet et al. 2011).

Regarding speech production, we use the HMM-based synthesis engine. First, its Basque linguistic module extracts linguistic features from the input text. Then the acoustic engine uses them to select previously trained statistical models and generate a sequence of suitable acoustic parameters. Finally, the synthetic speech signal is constructed from the aforementioned parameters by AhoCoder. Alignment time stamps are used to synchronize the synthetic audio and the original video, by modifying either the speech rate or the duration of silences.

5.2 Multimedia and multilingual semantic web search engines

5.2.1 Semantic retrieval system based on document expansion

One of the main problems IR systems have to deal with is the vocabulary mismatch problem between the query and documents: some documents might be relevant for the query even if the specific terms used differ substantially. On the contrary, some documents might not be relevant for the query even if they have some terms in common. The former is because languages are rich in the sense that more than one word or phrase could be used for expressing one idea or thing. The latter is because of ambiguity, in other words, because one word could have more than one interpretation depending on the context. If a system only relies on terms occurring in both the query and the document when it comes to deciding whether a document is relevant, it might be difficult to find some of the interesting documents and also to reject non-relevant documents. It seems fair to think that there will be more chances of successful retrieval if the meaning of the text is also taken into account. Even though this problem has been widely discussed in the literature ever since the early days of IR, it remains unsolved and there is still a high degree of uncertainty about the possibility of overcoming the problem by making use of any NLP technique.

This BerbaTek demo explored whether NLP can benefit the effectiveness of the search engine (Otegi 2012): http://ixa2.si.ehu.es/BerbatekDemo/bilatu.

Although in principle synonymy, polysemy, hyponymy or anaphora should be taken into account in order to obtain high retrieval relevance, the lack of algorithmic models has prohibited any systematic study of the effect of these phenomena on retrieval. Instead, researchers have resorted to distributional semantic models to try to improve retrieval relevance, and overcome the brittleness of keyword matches. Most research has concentrated on Query Expansion (QE) methods, which typically analyze term co-occurrence statistics in the corpus and in the highest scored documents for the original query in order to select terms for expanding the query terms (Manning et al. 2009). Document expansion (DE) is a natural alternative to QE, but, surprisingly, it has not been explored until very recently. Several researchers have used distributional methods from similar documents in the collection to expand the documents with related terms that do not actually occur in the document. The work carried out in BerbaTek was complementary in that we also explored DE, but used WordNet instead of distributional methods (Agirre et al. 2010).

Our key insight was to expand the document with related words according to the background information in WordNet (Fellbaum 1998), which provided generic information about general vocabulary terms. WordNet groups nouns, verbs, adjectives and adverbs into sets of synonyms (synsets), each expressing a distinct concept. Synsets are interlinked with conceptual-semantic and lexical relations, including hyperonymy, meronymy, causality, etc.

In contrast to previous work, we selected those concepts that are most closely related to the document as a whole. For that, we used a technique based on random walks over the graph representation of WordNet concepts and relations. We represented WordNet as a graph as follows: nodes represent concepts (synsets) and dictionary words; relations among synsets are represented by undirected edges, and dictionary words were linked to the synsets associated to them by directed edges. We used version 3.0, with all relations provided, including the gloss relations. This was the setting that achieved the best results in a word similarity dataset (Agirre, Soroa, et al. 2009).

Given a document and the graph-based representation of WordNet, we obtained a ranked list of WordNet concepts as follows:

- We first pre-processed the document to obtain the lemmas and parts of speech of the open category words.

- We then assigned a uniform probability distribution to the terms found in the document. The remaining nodes were initialized to zero.

- We computed personalized PageRank (Haveliwala 2002) over the graph, using the previous distribution as the reset distribution, and producing a probability distribution over WordNet concepts. The higher the probability for a concept, the more related it was to the given document.

This method revealed important concepts, even if they were not explicitly mentioned in the document. Once we had the list of words for document expansion, we created one index for the words in the original documents and another index with the expansion terms. This way, we were able to use the original words only, or to include the expansion words during the retrieval as well.

The retrieval system was implemented using MG4J (Boldi & Vigna 2005), as it provided state-of-the-art results and allowed several indices over the same document collection to be combined. BM25 was the scoring function of choice. It was one of the most relevant and robust scoring functions available (Robertson & Zaragoza 2009).

5.2.2 Multilingual semantic search engine for science and technology based on a specialized ontology, with similar image search

As proof of what language technologies could bring to the field of content, we also created a semantic multimedia search engine for science and technology. This search engine is based on the WNTerm ontology (Pociello et al. 2008) specialized in science and technology and created by Elhuyar and IXA (a network in which scientific and technological terms were semantically related to each other, with subclasses, synonyms, etc.), and works on content from Elhuyar (text and images from the Elhuyar magazine, videos from the *Teknopolis* TV show and audio files from the radio programme *Norteko Ferrokarrilla*). Using Tecnalia's technology, the search for a term also shows results containing synonyms, subclasses or superclasses, via the ontology. The resulting search engine is available in two versions, simple and advanced; the advanced version allows to choose an intelligence level (a higher level exploits more the relationships between the concepts in the ontology) and a type of document (image, video, audio and text) and enables filtering by subject. Furthermore, when the result is an image, it shows similar images by means of technology developed at Vicomtech-IK4. A demo is available online at http://bilatzailesemantikoa.berbatek.com/.

One of the first tasks launched was the analysis of the aggregated collection of digital resources made available by the Zientzia.net web site on our semantic search engine site. It was deduced that the Science and Technology domain covered the following subjects: general subjects, computer science, earth science, environment, health, life science, physics, mathematics and chemical science, space and technology in general.

Constructing the BerbaTek ontology included the following steps:

- The manual creation of a skeleton ontology that specified what the root concepts of the ontology were, e.g., Life Science, Technology, Earth science and Computer science. This skeleton should be modified if new knowledge sources were added for the annotation process.

- An ontology with 25,000+ concepts of science and technology was built by hierarchically organizing the terms of the Basque Encyclopaedic Dictionary of Science and Technology produced by Elhuyar. Every term from this ontology, called WNTERM, was mapped to one of the root concepts or areas.

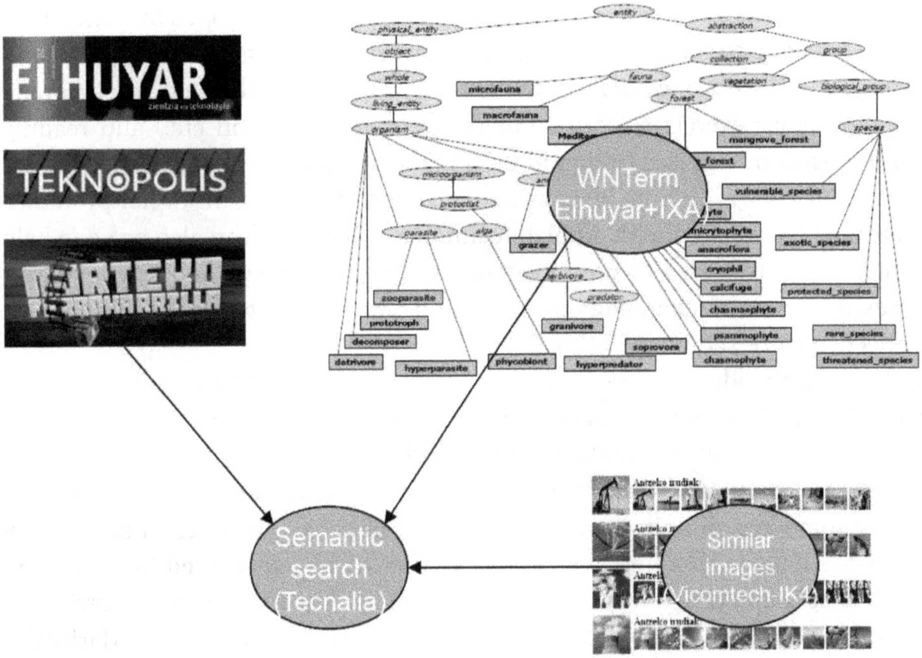

Figure 2: Scheme of the semantic search engine demo

For describing the resources, we decided to adopt an existing and standard metadata model to describe resources, in order to ensure interoperability with other organizations showing interest in sharing resources or contents with our semantic web search engine. Dublin Core was the metadata model selected.

The annotators were provided with a metadata editor where resources could be manually annotated, thus allowing the user to choose the topic or topics for the annotation by selecting from the different predefined concepts in our ontology.

The semantic search engine service was built onto the semantic layer, and we developed in the service layer the semantic search engine service.

If the search term entered was detected as a concept in the ontology, searches for related concepts were proposed (synonyms, hyponyms, hyperonyms etc.).

If the type of result obtained was an image, the search engine allowed the user to display a list of up to 10 similar pictures. This was because each recorded image had been pre-processed, generating a resemblance relationship.

5.3 Personal tutor for language learning

For the field of education, we created a demo consisting of a tutor for language learning. This tutor is a 3D avatar that showed emotions, developed by Vicomtech-IK4; it speaks Basque and understands what is said in Basque, using Aholab's technology. The tutor assists the student in various tasks: the student can orally solve grammar exercises (verb conjugation, word inflection etc.) and reading comprehension exercises (filling in gaps in a text, multiple choice tests) that are created automatically from texts using technology from IXA; his or her pronunciation can be evaluated with Aholab technology; The tutor can also provide help for writing texts, such as word inflection, writing of numbers or querying dictionaries, by means of technology from IXA and Elhuyar. The technologies included in this demo are shown in Figure 2.

The avatar module includes all the necessary functionalities to show and animate the 3D character that acts as the front-end of the demo. Its lip animation is synchronized with the audio synthesized by the TTS module, and it can also show facial emotions when required. In addition, the module generates blinking and head movement animations through a set of behaviour rules in order to increase the illusion that the 3D character is alive. It was developed in C++, using OpenSceneGraph (http://www.openscenegraph.org) as its graphic library.

For the automatic creation of exercises, we use ArikIturri (Aldabe & Maritxalar 2010). This is a system for generating different types of questions. It uses as input a set of morphologically and syntactically analyzed sentences represented in XML, and it transforms them into the generated questions, also represented in XML.

There are some differences between the architecture of our and previous systems (Kraift et al. 2004; Schwartz et al. 2004). We separate an *Answer focus identificator* module and an *Ill-formed questions rejecter* module. Sumita et al. (2005) also included a module to reject questions, which was based on the web. Depending on the parameters' specifications, the *Sentence retriever* selects candidate sentences from the tagged source corpus. In a first step, it selects the sentences where the specified linguistic phenomena appear. Then the *Candidates selector* studies the percentages of the candidates in order to make a random selection of sentences depending on the number of questions specified in the input parameters. Once the sentences are selected, the *Answer focuses identifier* marks out some of the chunked phrases as answer focuses, depending on the morphosyn-

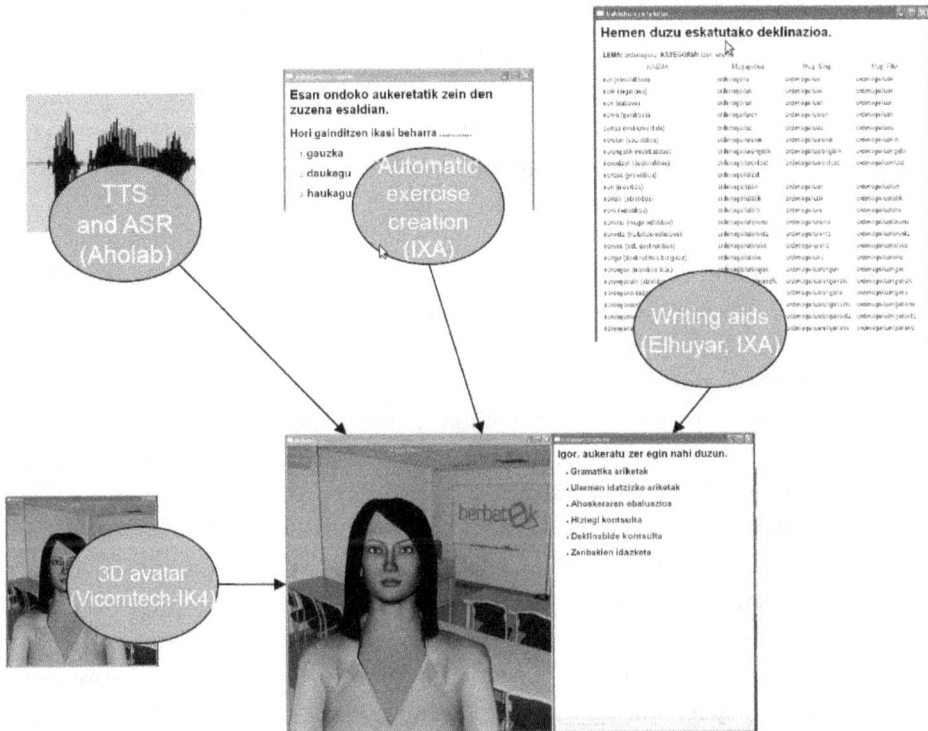

Figure 3: Personal tutor in language learning demo

tactic information of the phrases. Then the *Item generator* creates the questions depending on the specified exercise type. This is why this module contains the *Distractor generator* submodule. By this time, the system has already constructed the question instances. However, as the whole process is automatic, some questions might be ill-formed. That is why we include the *Ill-formed questions rejecter* in the architecture.

With regard to writing aids, the system offers three possible types of help: inflection of words, writing of numbers and querying dictionaries.

The module for helping with inflections asks for a word, then for the case (absolutive, dative, etc.) and then for definiteness and number (singular, plural, indefinite). For the latter two, it can be told to come up with the inflections for all of them. The system calls a web service developed by Elhuyar that generates inflections of words based on a two-level morphology transducer, and returns a table with the inflections of the chosen word.

The writing of numbers module asks for a 1 to 10 suite of one-figure numbers (for example "*hiru zazpi lau lau bost bat*", which means "*three seven four four five one*") and it tells the user how to write and pronounce the number produced (in the example "*hirurehun eta hirurogeita hamalau mila, laurehun eta berrogeita hamaika*", which means "*three hundred and seventy four thousand, four hundred and fifty one*), using a system developed by Elhuyar.

Finally, the dictionary-querying module asks for a Basque word and looks it up in various online dictionaries produced by Elhuyar (a Basque-Spanish dictionary, a Basque-French dictionary, a Basque-English dictionary and a synonyms dictionary), showing all the results found.

Speech technologies are extensively used in this demo. AhoSR, the ASR engine for Basque, is used to recognize the choices and answers of the students, and AhoTTS to generate the responses of the avatar. There is also a module to automatically evaluate the correctness of the segmental pronunciation.

The AhoTTS version based on HMM is used in this demo. As HTS does not perform any kind of linguistic analysis, the output of the first module of AhoTTS has to be translated into proper labels containing phonetic and linguistic information. See Erro et al. (2010) for a detailed list of the kinds of features encoded into context labels. In order to extract the frame-wise parametric representation of both the spectrum and the excitation, an HNM (Harmonics plus Noise Model)-based vocoder, AhoCoder, is used (Erro et al. 2011b). This vocoder allows speech to be reconstructed, too. The voice built is a female voice created using a speech database with the same characteristics as the AhoSyn database (Sainz et al. 2012). A female and a male synthetic voice are used in the demo. The female voice is built following the standard procedure, and the male one is obtained by applying voice transformation techniques (Erro et al. 2013). This AhoTTS version is bilingual, works for Spanish and Basque and is available online: http://sourceforge.net/projects/ahotts/.

Regarding the system that evaluates the correctness of the pronunciation, normally specific databases designed for CAPT (Computer-Assisted Pronunciation Training) purposes are used. But there is currently no available CAPT database for Basque. Although there are some speech recognition databases for Basque, the only one which is publicly available (Hernáez et al. 2003) was recorded over the fixed telephone network, so it is not suitable for CAPT purposes, where speech is usually recorded over a microphone. This is why pronunciation teaching systems for Basque have to be developed with other available data.

The database we use was designed for the training and development of speech recognition for Basque. It is a Speecon-like database (Siemund et al. 2000) and contains recordings from native and non-native speakers, as well as dialectal and standard Basque data for the former. It contains data from a total of 230 speakers, collected in different places of the Basque Country, where Basque has a different official status, health and phonetic influence of neighbouring languages (mainly French and Spanish). During the recording, speakers were asked about their level of language knowledge, so the database could be divided into different subcorpora according to this information. The native speakers' subcorpus was composed of 149 speakers. Non-native speakers spoke Basque as a second language at two different levels: the high level non-natives' subcorpus included 56 speakers and the low level non-natives' subcorpus 25. Due to dialectal variation and also to the different level of fluency, there were some irregularities in the pronunciation of several phonemes, which were not labeled in the transcription. However, they could be partially deduced from the information provided about the speaker. For example, we could obtain information about the region of origin of the speakers and their Basque level through the labels that indicated their city of birth, city of youth and language level. The audio files had their corresponding orthographic transcription file, and the rule-based AhoT2Ptranscriber was used to obtain phonetic transcriptions.

Due to the lack of a suitable speech database with recordings of Basque non-native speakers, the pronunciation evaluation module was developed using a general purpose ASR speech database (Odriozola et al. 2012). More precisely, the method applied consisted of automatically determining the threshold of GOP (Goodness Of Pronunciation) scores, which were used as pronunciation scores at phone-level. Two score distributions were obtained for each phoneme: one corresponding to its correct pronunciation and the other one to its incorrect pronunciation. The distribution of the scores for erroneous pronunciations was calculated artificially by inserting controlled errors in the dictionary, so that each changed phoneme was randomly replaced by a phoneme from the same group. These phoneme groups were obtained by means of phonetic clustering performed by using regression trees. After obtaining both distributions, the EER (Equal Error Rate) of each distribution pair was calculated and used as a decision threshold for each phoneme. The results of the experiments showed that this method was useful even when there was no database specifically designed for CAPT systems, although it was not as accurate as those specifically designed for this purpose. For the speech recognition module and also for the verification of the correctness of responses, the same database was used.

6 Conclusions

Being present in ICTs, in general, and in language, speech and multimedia technologies, in particular, is, in our opinion, absolutely necessary for any language that intends to go on living in a world that is becoming more and more mobile, digital and interconnected.

As Alegria et al. (2011) stated there is a need of incremental design and development of language resources, tools, and applications in a parallel and coordinated way in order to get the best benefit from them. Our experience in BerbaTek proved that collaboration between research agents working in the aforementioned fields is the right way to go. Apart from doing basic research and developing and putting into the hands of the users a considerable number of basic tools and resources, the integration of the different technologies made it possible to create prototypes of advanced applications for the language industry, i.e., translation, content management and learning.

The results of the cross-language comparison[10] provided by the META-NET White Paper Series showed that Basque now stands in a better position than some European official languages such as Croatian, Icelandic, Irish, Latvian or Lithuanian; and that Basque is in the 4th among 5 possible levels of support through language technology on Speech, Text Analytics and Languages Resources. The particular White Paper on Basque (Hernáez et al. 2012) concluded that there were application tools for speech synthesis, speech recognition, spelling correction, and grammar checking, and that there are also some applications for automatic translation, mainly between Spanish and Basque.

Figure 4 shows graphically the classification of the languages in the world proposed by Alegria et al. (2011) according to their degree of development in language technology. As of 2012 Basque is located on an intermediate position in the set of the around 60 languages with some language technology application. It was the 35th language in number of Wikipedia articles. There were 6 products for Basque in the ELRA catalogue[11], 15 products in the ACL wiki[12], and more than 40 on-line dictionaries in the local site hiztegiak.com (although only 5 of them were reflected in yourdictionary.com).

The correlation between Basque speakers and the number of available language products for this language is unusually high. This is due to the coordinated efforts of a few ambitious and productive groups working in successive projects

---

[10]http://www.meta-net.eu/whitepapers/key-results-and-cross-language-comparison
[11]http://www.elra.info/
[12]http://aclweb.org/aclwiki/index.php?title=List_of_resources_by_language

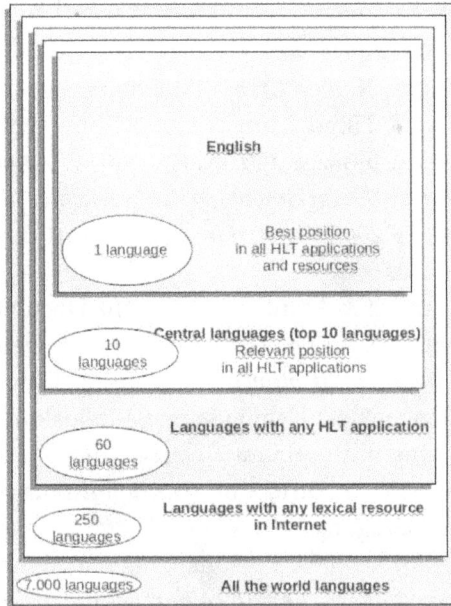

Figure 4: Six different levels for less resourced languages

such as BerbaTek. The collaboration of the five main players in Language Technology for Basque in BerbaTek allowed to make a step further in this direction: this cooperation enabled the creation of many new tools and resources and of three new prototypes in the fields of translation, content management and learning.

In the future, we intend to continue our collaboration and move forward with both the basic research and the development of applications and prototypes, for the language industry and also for other fields. But we also intend to go beyond prototypes and, in collaboration with companies devoted to translation, content management and learning, develop and put onto the market real applications for users, which is the next logical step. It will be a challenge that the members of the BerbaTek consortium are willing and prepared to face.

Acknowledgements

This research was partially funded by the Regional Government of the Basque Autonomous Community (BerbaTek project, IE09-262) and by the Spanish Ministry of Education and Science (OpenMT2, TIN2009-14675-C03-01; Know2, TIN2009-14715-C04-01; HibridoSint;TIN2010-20218).

References

Agirre, Eneko, Olatz Ansa, Xabier Arregi, Maddalen Lopez de Lacalle, Arantxa Otegi, Xabier Saralegi & Hugo Zaragoza. 2009. Elhuyar-IXA: Semantic relatedness and crosslingual passage retrieval. In *Multilingual information access evaluation i: Text retrieval experiments, 10th Workshop of the Cross-Language Evaluation Forum, CLEF 2009, Corfu, Greece*, vol. 6241 (Lecture Notes in Computer Science), 273–280.

Agirre, Eneko, Xabier Arregi & Arantxa Otegi. 2010. Document expansion based on WordNet for Robust IR. In *Proceedings of the 23rd International Conference on Computational Linguistics (Coling)*, 9–17. Beijing, China.

Agirre, Eneko, Kepa Bengoetxea, Koldo Gojenola & Joakim Nivre. 2011. Improving dependency parsing with semantic classes. In *Proceedings of the 49th Annual Meeting of the Association of Computational Linguistics, ACL-HLT 2011 Short Paper*. Portland, Oregon.

Agirre, Eneko & Aitor Soroa. 2009. Personalizing PageRank for word sense disambiguation. In *Proceedings of the 12th conference of the European chapter of the Association for Computational Linguistics (EACL-2009)*, 33–41. Athens, Greece.

Agirre, Eneko, Aitor Soroa, Enrique Alfonseca, Keith Hall, Jana Kravalova & Marius Pasca. 2009. A study on similarity and relatedness using distributional and WordNet-based approaches. In *NAACL'09 Proceedings of Human Language Technologies: The 2009 Annual Conference of the North American Chapter of the Association for Computational Linguistics*, 19–27. Boulder, CO.

Aldabe, Itziar & Montse Maritxalar. 2010. Automatic distractor generation for domain specific texts. In *Proceedings of the 7th International Conference on NLP, IceTAL 2010*, 27–38. Reykjavik, Iceland.

Aldezabal, Izaskun, Maria Jesus Aranzabe, Arantza Diaz de Ilarraza, Ainara Estarrona & Larraitz Uria. 2010. EusPropBank: Integrating semantic information in the Basque dependency treebank. *Lecture Notes in Computer Science* 6008. 60–73.

Alegria, Iñaki, Xabier Artola, Arantza Diaz de Ilarraza & Kepa Sarasola. 2011. Strategies to develop language technologies for less-resourced languages based on the case of Basque. In *Proceedings of the 5th Language and Technology Conference: Human language technologies as a challenge for computer science and linguistics*, 42–46. Poznań, Poland.

Alegria, Iñaki, Arantza Casillas, Arantza Diaz de Ilarraza, Jon Igartua, Gorka Labaka, Mikel Lersundi, Aingeru Mayor & Kepa Sarasola. 2008. Spanish-to-Basque MultiEngine machine translation for a restricted domain. In *Proceed-*

ings of the 8th Conference of the Association for Machine Translation in the Americas (AMTA-2008), 57–69. Honolulu, HI.

Alegria, Iñaki, Arantza Diaz de Ilarraza, Gorka Labaka, Mikel Lersundi, Aingeru Mayor & Kepa Sarasola. 2007. Transfer-based MT from Spanish into Basque: Reusability, standardization and open source. *Lecture Notes in Computer Science* 4394. 374–384.

Ansa, Olatz, Xabier Arregi, Arantxa Otegi & Ander Soraluze. 2008. Ihardetsi question answering system at QA@CLEF 2008. In *Working notes of the Cross-Lingual evaluation forum*. Aarhus, Denmark.

Arrieta, Kutz, Arantza Diaz de Ilarraza, Inma Hernáez, Urtza Iturraspe, Igor Leturia, Eva Navas & Kepa Sarasola. 2008. AnHitz, development and integration of language, speech and visual technologies for Basque. In *Proceedings of the second international symposium on universal communication*, 338–344. Osaka.

Bengoetxea, Kepa & Koldo Gojenola. 2010. Application of different techniques to dependency parsing of Basque. In *Proceedings of the First Workshop on Statistical Parsing of Morphologically Rich Languages SPMRL 2010*. Los Angeles, CA. NAACL Workshop.

Boldi, Paolo & Sebastiano Vigna. 2005. MG4J at TREC 2005. In *Proceedings of the annual meeting for the Text REtrieval Conference (TREC)*. Gaithersburg, MD.

Diaz de Ilarraza, Arantza, Antton Gurrutxaga, Kepa Sarasola, Inma Hernáez & Nuria Lopez de Gereñu. 2003. HIZKING21: Integrating language engineering resources and tools into systems with linguistic capabilities. In *Proceedings of the Workshop on NLP of Minority Languages and Small Languages. TALN 2003. Nantes.*

Erro, Daniel, Eva Navas & Inma Hernáez. 2013. Parametric voice conversion based on bilinear frequency warping plus amplitude scaling. *IEEE Transactions on Audio, Speech and Language Processing* 21(3). 556–566.

Erro, Daniel, Iñaki Sainz, Iker Luengo, Igor Odriozola, Jon Sánchez, Ibon Saratxaga, Eva Navas & Inma Hernáez. 2010. HMM-based speech synthesis in Basque language using HTS. In *Proceedings of the Jornadas en Tecnología del Habla (JTH)*. Vigo, Spain.

Erro, Daniel, Iñaki Sainz, Eva Navas & Inma Hernáez. 2011a. HNM-based MFCC+F0 extractor applied to statistical speech synthesis. In *Proceedings of the International Conference on Acoustics, Speech, and Signal Processing (ICASSP)*. Prague, Czec Republic.

Erro, Daniel, Iñaki Sainz, Eva Navas & Inma Hernáez. 2011b. Improved HNM-based vocoder for statistical synthesizers. In *Proceedings of the Interspeech Conference*. Florence, Italy.

España-Bonet, Cristina, Gorka Labaka, Arantza Diaz de Ilarraza, Lluís Màrquez & Kepa Sarasola. 2011. Hybrid machine translation guided by a rule-based system. In *Proceedings of the Machine Translation Summit (MT Summit)*. Xiamen, China.

Fellbaum, Christiane (ed.). 1998. *WordNet an electronic lexical database*. Cambridge, MA ; London: The MIT Press. http://mitpress.mit.edu/catalog/item/default.asp?ttype=2&tid=8106.

Gurrutxaga, Antton & Iñaki Alegria. 2011. Automatic extraction of NV expressions in Basque: Basic issues on cooccurrence techniques. In *Proceedings of the Workshop on Multiword Expressions: From Parsing and Generation to the Real World (MWE 2011)*. Portland, OR. ACL/HLT conference.

Haveliwala, Taher H. 2002. Topic-sensitive PageRank. In *Proceedings of the World Wide Web conference (WWW)*. Honolulu, HI.

Hernáez, Inmaculada, Iker Luengo, Eva Navas, Maren Zubizarreta, Iñaki Gaminde & Jon Sánchez. 2003. The Basque speech_dat (II) database: A description and first test recognition results. In *Proceedings of the Eurospeech conference*. Geneva, Switzerland.

Hernáez, Inmaculada, Eva Navas, Igor Odriozola, Kepa Sarasola, Arantza Diaz de Ilarraza, Igor Leturia, Araceli Diaz de Lezana, Beñat Oihartzabal & Jasone Salaberria. 2012. Euskara aro digitalean: the Basque language in the digital age. In Georg Rehm & Hans Uszkoreit (eds.), *The Basque language in the digital age/Euskara aro digitalean* (METANET White Paper Series), 35–62. Berlin Heidelberg: Springer.

Kraift, Olivier, Georges Antoniadis, Sandra Echinard, Mathieu Loiseau, Thomas Lebarbé & Claude Ponton. 2004. NLP tools for CALL: The simpler, the better. In *Proceedings of the Workshop on NLP and Speech Technologies in Advanced Language Learning Systems*. Venice, Italy.

Labaka, Gorka. 2010. *EUSMT: Incorporating linguistic information into SMT for a morphologically rich language. Its use in SMT-RBMT-EBMT hybridation*. UPV/EHU-University of the Basque Country dissertation.

Leturia, Igor. 2012. Evaluating different methods for automatically collecting large general corpora for Basque from the web. In *Proceedings of the 24th International Conference on Computational Linguistics (COLING 2012)*. Mumbai, India.

Leturia, Igor, Iñaki San Vicente & Xabier Saralegi. 2009. Search engine based approaches for collecting domain-specific Basque-English comparable corpora from the Internet. In *Proceedings of the Workshop on Web as Corpus (WAC)*. Donostia, Spain.

Manning, Christopher D., Prabhakar Raghavan & Hinrich Schütze. 2009. *An introduction to information retrieval*. Cambridge: Cambridge University Press.

Mayor, Aingeru, Iñaki Alegria, Arantza Diaz de Ilarraza, Gorka Labaka, Mikel Lersundi & Kepa Sarasola. 2011. Matxin, an open-source rule-based machine translation system for Basque. *Machine Translation Journal* 25(1). 53–82.

Mayor, Aingeru & Francis Tyers. 2009. Matxin: Moving towards language independence. In *Proceedings of the Workshop on Free/Open-Source Rule-Based Machine Translation (FreeRBMT)*. Alacant, Spain.

Odriozola, Igor, Eva Navas, Inma Hernáez, Iñaki Sainz, Ibon Saratxaga, Jon Sánchez & Daniel Erro. 2012. Using an ASR database to design a pronunciation evaluation system in Basque. In *Proceedings of the Language Resources and Evaluation Conference (LREC)*. Istanbul, Turkey.

Otegi, Arantxa. 2012. *Hedapena informazioaren berreskurapenean: Hitzen adieradesanbiguazioaren eta antzekotasun semantikoaren ekarpenak*. UPV/EHU-University of the Basque Country dissertation.

Pociello, Elisabete, Agirre Eneko & Izaskun Aldezabal. 2011. Methodology and construction of the Basque Wordnet. *Language Resources and Evaluation* 45(2). 121–142.

Pociello, Elisabete, Antton Gurrutxaga, Eneko Agirre, Izaskun Aldezabal & German Rigau. 2008. WNTERM: Combining the Basque wordnet and a terminological dictionary. In *Proceedings of the Language Resources and Evaluation Conference (LREC)*. Marrakesh, Morocco.

Robertson, Stephen & Hugo Zaragoza. 2009. The probabilistic relevance framework: BM25 and beyond. *Foundations and Trends in Information Retrieval* 3(4). 333–389.

Sainz, Iñaki, Daniel Erro, Eva Navas, Inma Hernáez, Jon Sanchez, Ibon Saratxaga & Igor Odriozola. 2012. Versatile speech databases for high quality synthesis for Basque. In *Proceedings of the Language Resources and Evaluation Conference (LREC)*. Istanbul, Turkey.

San Vicente, Iñaki & Iker Manterola. 2012. PaCo2: A fully automated tool for gathering parallel corpora from the web. In *Proceedings of the Language Resources and Evaluation Conference (LREC)*. Istanbul, Turkey.

Saralegi, Xabier & Maddalen Lopez de Lacalle. 2009. Comparing different approaches to treat translation ambiguity in CLIR: Structured queries vs. target co-occurrence-based selection. In *Proceedings of the Workshop on Text-Based Information Retrieval (TIR)*. Linz, Austria.

Saralegi, Xabier, Iker Manterola & Iñaki San Vicente. 2012. Building a Basque-Chinese dictionary by using English as a pivot. In *Proceedings of the Language Resources and Evaluation Conference (LREC)*.

Saralegi, Xabier, Iñaki San Vicente & Maddalen López de Lacalle. 2008. Mining term translations from domain restricted comparable corpora. *Procesamiento del Lenguaje Natural* 41. 273–280.

Schwartz, Lee, Takako Aikawa & Michel Pahud. 2004. Dynamic language learning tools. In *Proceedings of the Workshop on NLP and Speech Technologies in Advanced Language Learning Systems*. Venice, Italy.

Siemund, Rainer, Harald Höge, Siegfried Kunzmann & Krzysztof Marasek. 2000. SPEECON-speech data for consumer devices. In *Proceedings of the International Conference on Language Resources and Evaluation (LREC)*. Athens, Greece.

Sumita, Eiichiro, Fumiaki Sugaya & Seiichi Yamamoto. 2005. Measuring non-native speakers' proficiency of English by using a test with automatically-generated fill-in-the blank questions. In *Proceedings of the Workshop on Building Educational Applications Using NLP*. Ann Arbor, MI.

Williams, Briony, Kepa Sarasola, Donncha Ó'Cróinin, Climent Nadeu & Bojan Petek. 2001. Speech and language technology for minority languages. In *Proceedings of the Eurospeech conference*. Aalborg, Denmark.

Name index

www.ingramcontent.com/pod-product-compliance
Lightning Source LLC
Chambersburg PA
CBHW080915100426
42812CB00007B/2276